COMMUNITY
&
SOCIETY

COMMUNITY
&
SOCIETY

by

FERDINAND TÖNNIES

TRANSLATED FROM THE GERMAN BY C.P. LOOMIS

MOCKINGBIRD
PRESS

Cover Art, "La Place de la Bastille," Gustave Loiseau 1922
Cover Design by Nami Kurita, Copyright © 2020 Mockingbird Press
Interior Design by Maria Johnson

Publisher's Cataloging-In-Publication Data

Tönnies, Ferdinand, author; with Loomis, C.P., editor
Community and Society / Ferdinand Tönnies; with C.P. Loomis.

Paperback	ISBN-13:	978-1-953450-18-0
Hardback	ISBN-13:	978-1-953450-19-7
Ebook	ISBN-13:	978-1-953450-20-3

1. Social Science—Sociology—Social Theory. 2. Society and Social Sciences—Sociology and Anthropology. I. Ferdinand Tönnies. II. C.P. Loomis. III. Title.

SOC026040 / JH

Type Set in SchoolBook / **Franklin Gothic Demi**

Mockingbird Press, Augusta, GA

Contents

TÖNNIES

COMMUNITY
& SOCIETY

(Gemeinschaft und Gesellschaft)

Translated and Edited By
CHARLES P. LOOMIS

Acknowledgments

As translator, I wish to acknowledge the assistance of Professor and Mrs. Rudolf Heberle, who have compared the English manuscript with the original and who have made substantial contributions to the rendition of difficult passages. Likewise, I wish to thank Professors Pitirim A. Sorokin, Talcott Parsons, and Kimball Young for suggestions and advice; also, Dr. Berta Asch, Mr. Gerhard Dittmann, Dr. B. Landheer, and Kathryn Van Hyning for technical assistance. For reading and rereading manuscript and proof, and for many improvements in final rendition, I am very much indebted to Dr. Nellie Loomis. Special acknowledgment is also due to the Social Science Research Council for a grant-in-aid which enabled me to complete the work. In addition, William V. D'Antonio prepared the index and Carle P. Graffunder assisted in proofreading.

CHARLES P. LOOMIS

FOREWORD

LIKE MANY an eminent thinker, Tönnies was a man of one central idea, which he developed in its various ramifications in practically all his theoretical works. This central idea is, of course, his theory of *Gemeinschaft* and *Gesellschaft* as two different modes of mentality and behavior, and as two different types of society. In its essentials the theory did not originate with Tönnies. Like many fundamental categories of social thought, it is in a sense eternal, appearing long before Tönnies and reiterated after him. The Gemeinschaft type of mentality and society was extolled by Confucius: Confucius' theory of the five fundamental social relationships of father and son, elder brother and younger, husband and wife, ruler and subject, friend and friend closely resembles Tönnies' main Gemeinschaft ties between mother and child, father and children, sisters and brothers, friends and friends, and rulers and subjects. Confucius not only unfolded the Gemeinschaft type of society but also set it off against the Gesellschaft type. In his theory of the main stages of human society he differentiated the Gesellschaft type by the term "Small Tranquillity" in contradistinction to that of the "Great Similarity," or Gemeinschaft stage.

Plato in his *Republic* and *Laws* likewise gave a full portrait of both types of society, as well as of human personality. His ideal republic, especially the personality and social regime of the Guardians, is clearly and definitely of the Gemeinschaft type, while his detailed picture of the oligarchic or capitalistic society and man is a conspicuous example of the Gesellschaft type. Aristotle and, after him, Cicero, in their analyses of the true and false friendship, gave us in clearcut form the classical outlines of the two types. The same types are found running through the works of the Church fathers, especially those of St. Augustine. Here the theory of the Church and the "City of God" as the *corpus mysticum* of Gemeinschaft type is contrasted to the "society of man" depicted along the lines of the Gesellschaft type. Throughout the writings of the great medieval thinkers like

Joachim de Fiore, Albertus Magnus, St. Thomas Aquinas, Nicolaus Cusanus, and others the dichotomy persists. On the other hand it is also the central idea of the great Arabian thinker, Ibn Khaldun, in his *History of Berbers* and in his *Prolegomenes to the Universal History.* His analysis of both types is one of the most penetrating, detailed, and enlightening.

In varied forms the categories continued to function in the writings of the social thinkers of the later centuries. In Germany particularly, as Gierke has clearly shown, the Gemeinschaft type was deeply rooted in the very soil of the Teutonic culture since its emergence on the historic scene. In the time immediately preceding the appearance of Tönnies' work both types of society and personality were well depicted by many a German thinker, beginning with the leaders of the Historical School, Savigny and Puchta, and ending with Hegel, whose "Family-Society" and "Civic Society" are almost twins of Tönnies' Gemeinschaft and Gesellschaft.

The two types continued to be reiterated after Tönnies by many: Durkheim, Makarewitz, Kistiakowsky, up to the writer of this preface. The above "genealogy" is mentioned not for the purpose of detracting from the value of the contribution made by Tönnies but for establishing a proper historical perspective in regard to it. After all, among the fundamental categories and concepts of the social science there is hardly one that was not mentioned, developed, and used by the social thinkers of antiquity and past centuries. If a modern social scientist makes an artful use of them in his individual manner, showing their value and painting his own picture with their help, his contribution is made, and its greatness will depend upon the artistry used. That is exactly what Tönnies did, giving us his "variation on the eternal theme of the Gemeinschaft and Gesellschaft." We should accord Tönnies even greater acknowledgment in view of the fact that he published his work when the Gesellschaft type of society was at its climax, full of vigor and life, showing no signs of weakness, and triumphantly driving out of existence the Gemeinschaft type. At that time few thinkers could see its inherent and well-hidden weaknesses, and still fewer were able to go to their roots as Tönnies did. No wonder that his book in its first edition produced little response, and even that was largely negative. Subsequent decades have shown, however, the validity of most of the conclusions of Tönnies. At the present time most intelligent men probably know that the hidden weaknesses of the Gesellschaft type of society and man have grown to such an extent that the type is in the deepest crisis and is crumbling before our very eyes. The contemporary crisis of what many call capitalistic or contractual society is but a different name for a crisis of the Gesellschaft type of society and man. From this standpoint Tönnies' work is in a sense prophetic and has theoretical as well as a deep, practical significance.

PITIRIM A. SOROKIN

Harvard University

PREFACE

When Tönnies published the first edition of his *Gemeinschaft und Gesellschaft* (1887), sociology was practically identical with Spencer's evolutionary theory of history or, in Germany, with Schaeffle's organi-zistic system. One was historically naïve and politically inconsistent, the other delighted in absurd and childish analogies between society and biological organisms. Neither could win the respect of serious philosophers and social scientists. Yet Germany had also produced the keenest critic of the contemporary social and economic order, Karl Marx, who predicted the emergence of a socialistic order out of the inherent contradictions of capitalism. He owed possibly more than he admitted to the early works of Lorenz Stein—a landsman of Tönnies, who taught at the University of Kiel some forty years before Tönnies. Stein, who was the first German expert on French socialism and communism, had realized that these ideas should be understood not as mere fancies of unbalanced minds but as the creeds of a forceful social movement, which if not intercepted and channelized by appropriate social reforms would lead to the destruction of civil society.

Tönnies intended to show that communism and socialism were indeed actual, empirical patterns of social life, and that their elements were contained in present-day predominantly individualistic society— one as survivals from the past, the other as the germs of a future social order. The purpose of *Gemeinschaft und Gesellschaft* was not to trace the evolution from primitive communism through individualism to socialism: that was reserved for a later work of which only fragments have been published (Geist der Neuzeit, 1935). The immediate purpose was to develop scientific concepts which could be used as tools to grasp the historical process.

This was done on three levels of analysis: first, by a phenomenological (as we would say today) consideration of the archetypes of social relationships (or "social entities," as Tönnies later said): kinship, neighborhood, friendship, barter, contract and so forth; second, by an inquiry into the nature of human will in its social implications; third, by a synthesis of the old controversy concerning the nature of society. The last point is especially important: Tönnies showed that Aristotle and Hobbes were both right. Each had focused on different aspects of social life: Man was indeed by his very nature a social being who would unfold his essence only by living in communities of kinship, space (neighborhood), and spirit, but who was also capable of forming and, at certain stages in history, compelled to form new kinds of associations by agreements—associations which could be understood as instruments for the attainment of certain ends—whereas those "older" communities were taken as ends in themselves and therefore could not be understood by a utilitarian approach.

This theorem required a psychological underpinning, which Tönnies undertook to supply by the conceptual distinction between two types of human will, individual as well as social and collective. For, social relationships were to him "willed" relationships, wanted and maintained by the more or less instinctive or purposive-rational volition of the related persons. Moreover, the old problem of group will or collective will also had to be solved; Tönnies showed by an intricate analysis that the "will" of a social relationship between, let us say, two friends or two business partners, is expressed in rules of conduct in essentially the same sense in which customs, ethics, laws, and public opinion can be perceived to express the will of larger collective groups.

Thus, the four fundamental concepts—*Wesenwille* and *Kürwille, Gemeinschaft* and *Gesellschaft*—constitute the basis of an elaborate and complex, but well-balanced, sociological theory that comprises social entities (or groups and relationships) as well as social norms (or codes of conduct). The meaning of these concepts, and their function in the system are not so easily understood, largely because their author developed them against a background of contemporary thought which has lost a good deal of its relevance to present-day sociology. No wonder, then, that a recent critic of Tönnies' theory claimed to have found seven different meanings of the two chief concepts that lent the work its title—the same critic who highly praised a later essay of Tönnies entitled *Die Sitte* ("On Mores"), which squarely rests on the two pairs of concepts. His conclusion that nothing remains of the major work but one great confusion (*"eine einzige grosse Unklarheit"*) can only be the result of a misapprehension of its true scope.

A "deep" book like *Gemeinschaft und Gesellschaft* is, of course, not free of apparent obscurities and real difficulties—and the present translation will not be able to achieve the impossible, that is, to improve on the original. Certainly, this is an intricate work which makes great demands on the reader. But a sympathetic and patient reader will find himself stimulated rather than confused as he follows the unfolding exposition of those concepts in what is one of the few classic treatises in sociology—a classic in both form and content.

RUDOLF HEBERLE

Louisiana State University

INTRODUCTION

Tönnies and His Relation to Sociology

ORIENTATION OF GEMEINSCHAFT UND GESELLSCHAFT

In 1887, Ferdinand Tönnies, at the early age of thirty-two, produced a small volume which was destined to wield great influence upon sociological thinking. For the next fifteen years this *Gemeinschaft und Gesellschaft,* with its unique, difficult,[1] old German diction, was read by only a small circle. Its second edition, however, gained much attention and ran through six more editions, one after another, achieving an international reputation for its author. The volume pointed back into the Middle Ages and ahead into the future in its attempt to answer the questions: What are we? Where are we? Whence did we come? Where are we going?

The romantic characteristics and ominous prophecy of *Gemeinschaft und Gesellschaft* might have attracted more attention had it appeared during a previous period, when a strong current of German tradition was being carried through the works of Stein, Mohl, Riehl, Herder, Kant, Moser, Arndt, Fichte, and Schleiermacher. Hans Freyer[2] has dramatized the role Tönnies played in preserving the German tradition in sociology from the positivism which prevailed in America, France, and England.

Gemeinschaft und Gesellschaft appeared as a synthesis of rationalism and romanticism, idealism and materialism, realism and nominalism.[3] It is the more remarkable because it did not branch off solely from German philosophical idealism but rather sank its roots into economic and legal history,[4] deriving what nourishment the mind of its creative author required, especially from Maine, Gierke, Marx, and Hobbes.

This, combined with his knowledge of the ethnology, psychology, philosophy, and sociology of the time, led to the great synthesis.

It would be a mistake to assume that the roots of *Gemeinschaft und Gesellschaft* had no foundation other than the literature with which the author was familiar. They ran deep into the subsoil of Tönnies' own experience and observation. As a son of a well-to-do peasant family, he saw the influence of rationalism as the old rural culture of his native province, Schleswig-Holstein, had to submit to the inroads of mechanization and commercialization. Furthermore, his oldest brother was engaged in trading with English merchants so that he had, while very young, firsthand contact with two worlds—the world of the peasant rooted to his soil and the world of the merchant whose soul is in the profits of his trade. After receiving his doctor's degree at the age of twenty-one at Tubingen, he returned to his native province and set himself to the task of writing *Gemeinschaft und Gesellschaft,* concerning which he said: "The work occupied my time day and night continuously for the following six or seven years, whether I was at home, at my writing desk, taking a walk, or traveling." Its first draft was presented to the faculty of the University of Kiel in 1881, at which time its author began his long period of lecturing there.

APPLIED SOCIOLOGY

It is altogether fitting that almost half a century after the publication of *Gemeinschaft und Gesellschaft,* which was the creative effort of a youthful mind, Tönnies' book on "The Spirit of Modern Times," *Geist der Neuzeit,*[5] was published in 1935, half a year before Tönnies' death. This work and *Gemeinschaft und Gesellschaft* will go down through history together, not as the beginning and end of one man's career, but as guideposts to past, present, and future. Some critics believe they have detected a note of pessimism[6] in Tönnies' descriptions of the village, town, and estate of the Middle Ages in his works. Following are a few observations from *Geist der Neuzeit*: In the Middle Ages there was unity, now there is atomization: then the hierarchy of authority was solicitous paternalism, now it is compulsory exploitation; then there was relative peace, now wars are wholesale slaughter; then there were sympathetic relationships among kinsfolk and old acquaintances, now there are strangers and aliens everywhere; then society was chiefly made up of home- and land-loving peasants, now the attitude of the businessman prevails; then man's simple needs were met by home production and barter, now we have world trade and capitalistic production; then there was permanency of abode, now great mobility; then there were folk arts, music, and handicrafts, now there is science—and the scientific method applied, as in the case of the cool calculations of the businessman, leads to the point of view which deprives one's fellow men and one's society of their personality, leaving only a framework of dead symbols and generalizations.

Tönnies continually reminded his readers that the process of change through which the individual who was controlled by natural or integral will in his Gemeinschaft was "freed" and became the subject of rational will, was "healthy" and "normal." (See note 1 on page 284.) Although critics accused him of recommending Gemeinschaft as good and condemning Gesellschaft as bad, he disclaimed any such intention. (See note 2 on page 284.) For him Gemeinschaft represented the youth, and Gesellschaft the adulthood, of society. Although societies, like individuals, could die from old age, no objective physician or student of medicine could condemn old age.[7] In his last work Tönnies hinted that the process of change from Gemeinschaft to Gesellschaft might be reversed by real causes if such existed, but not by speeches and sentimental romanticizing about the past.[8]

Notwithstanding the important role played by the ideological elements encompassed in natural will and rational will, Tönnies, like Marx, was addicted to the economic interpretation of history.[9] Tönnies believed that with the development of trade, the modern state, science, the natural will and Gemeinschaft-like characteristics of social entities, norms, and values gave way to rational will and Gesellschaft-like characteristics. Unlike Marx, who believed technical conditions and progress to be the prime mover in change, Tönnies ascribed this role to a large-scale trade involving the desire for the profitable use of money, which led to the development of capitalism. According to Tönnies the introduction of this type of trade into the integrated communities of agrarian and town societies liquidated the old ideologies and brought about the capitalistic age with its rationalistic intellectual attitude. In this interpretation, Tönnies was influenced by 17th- and 18th-century social science of England and France, as well as by Marx.[10]

In the small volume on "Progress and Evolution in Society" *(Fortschritt und Soziale Entwicklung)*,[11] appearing in 1926, which resulted from the compilation of several papers, Tönnies discussed the concept of progress and described in concrete terms the development of a universal culture in the world. *Progress and Evolution in Society* and *The Spirit of Modern Times,* with the more specialized volumes on the folkways and mores[12] and public opinion,[13] represent penetrating interpretations of reality through the application of the concepts Gemeinschaft and Gesellschaft, and are Tönnies' most important contributions to his applied *(angewandte)* sociology, which is one of the three disciplines of Tönnies' sociology proper *(spezielle Soziologie)*.

SPECIAL AND GENERAL SOCIOLOGY

Tönnies' sociology proper includes: (1) Pure or theoretical *(reine, theoretische)* sociology; (2) applied sociology; and (3) empirical *(empirische)* sociology, or sociography.

Sociology proper, social biology, social psychology, and demography constitute general sociology. This latter term was used by Tönnies to indicate all-inclusiveness as contrasted with the narrower field of sociology proper. Social biology, broadly considered, studies the interactions which result from the living together of plants and animals; however, general sociology concerns itself only with those of its aspects which relate to human living together. Social biology, as a part of general sociology, is social anthropology abstracted from all psychology and as such involves the biological study of race and genetics, as well as other biological considerations, and is studied in connection with ethnography, demography, and other disciplines which may be classified with sociology proper. Social psychology considers the inner psychical or subjective aspects of human living together.

PURE OR THEORETICAL SOCIOLOGY

Although Tönnies made important contributions in applied and empirical sociology, he is best known for his work in the pure or theoretical field. This latter is made up of a logical system of concepts of ideal types[14] and of social entities *(soziale Wesenheiten)* in a static condition. Such a system is required for the description and understanding of empirical social phenomena, just as in some other fields mathematics is required. By way of analogy, Tönnies described such concepts as nails on which the facts of experience could be hung, or clamps which would clasp bundles of reality, thus serving as efficient tools in the production of knowledge.[15] By use of his system of concepts he was able to demonstrate the possibility of combining formal sociology with historical sociology.[16] Tönnies' system finds its most adequate description in his *Introduction to Sociology*,[17] which appeared four years before his death; and, although it never attained the recognition of *Gemeinschaft und Gesellschaft*, is more readable and is a great help in the understanding of his sociology.

A. The First Sphere of Tönnies' Pure Sociology—Fundamental Concepts of Gemeinschaft and Gesellschaft

The keystones of Tönnies' system are the concepts or ideal types, Gemeinschaft and Gesellschaft, which are based primarily upon natural will and rational will. In his sociological system these four concepts hold the center of the stage and all of the other concepts are related to them.[18] Since the fundamental concepts of the system are adequately set forth by Tönnies himself in Part Five, "The Summing Up," on pages 237-59, no extended discussion of this aspect of his system will be required here.

Tönnies assumes that all social relationships are created by human will.[19] As social facts they exist only through the will of the individuals to associate. This will and the inner relationship of the associated individuals with one another may vary from one situation to another. For instance, a group or a relationship can be willed because those involved wish to attain through it a definite end and are willing to join hands for this purpose, even though indifference or even antipathy may exist on other levels. In this case rational will *(Kürwille)*, in which means and ends have been sharply differentiated, as in Max Weber's *"Zweckrationalem"* behavior, prevails. On the other hand, people may associate themselves together, as friends do, because they think the relation valuable as an end in and of itself. In this case natural or integral will predominates. Natural will is the conditioning and originating element in any process of willing which is derived from the temperament, character, and intellectual attitude of the individual, whether it has its origin in liking, inclination, habit, or memory.[20] It cannot be inferred, however, that natural will is always irrational. There are degrees of rationality of natural will and of the communities and groups which it forms. Thus, in order of the importance of rationality there are the Gemeinschaft groups based on friendship, on neighborliness, and on blood relationships. Groups in which natural will predominates may range from those held together by intellectual ties to those bound by the instinctive liking or sympathy of biologically related individuals.[21]

Thus, the businessman, scientist, person of authority, and the upper classes are relatively more conditioned by rational will[22] than the peasant, the artist, and the common people, who are more conditioned by natural will. In general, women and young people are conditioned predominantly by natural will, and men and older people by rational will.[23]

In making these distinctions, Tönnies is constantly thinking in terms of means and ends.[24] The work of the peasant, hunter, artisan, or artist is a way of life, not merely a means to an end. Even the tools and utensils which such people use as means are less sharply differentiated from the ends than the means used by merchants, business entrepreneurs, and army leaders. The fields, soil, and livestock of the peasant are in and of themselves ends, whereas the means to the profits of the trader are sharply differentiated from the ends.[25] The horseman may value his horse because of liking, sympathy, or even love, or he may value it solely as a work animal, as a means to an end. Ordinarily, language, as a means of expressing oneself, is at least partially an end in itself. For traders and designing, ambitious persons, even language becomes a tool used to attain ends—to deceive, to advertise, to exaggerate, to overcome sales resistance. A utensil, tool, or instrument may become so embodied in the activities of a man that it is almost a part of him, a third hand or, better, an extension of his own hand, through the use of which man's creative abilities are expressed. The introduction of the machine destroyed the previous unity or blending of the three elements—man, instrument, and work.

In all walks of life individuals live in the service of other individuals, and are in a sense tools or machines. When people are used as mere means to ends, even as "inanimate things," such usage is governed by rational will. The slave driver or industrial magnate is governed by rational will in his use of men; the peasant by natural will in the use of his family and servants. The more the actions of man are controlled by love, understanding, custom, religion,[26] folkways, and mores, the less people, animals, and things are thought of as mere means to ends and the less important the role of such socially sanctioned means as paper money, tricks of the trade, and the businessman's intellectual attitude. With the coming of the economic man who, characterized by Tönnies as the businessman, uses all means to attain wealth, and of the political man who, like the Machiavellian dictator, uses all available means to increase his power, and of the scientific man who, like the mathematician, uses logical concepts in descriptions which deprive things and man of life, means and ends come to be sharply differentiated and rational will prevails. It was Tönnies' belief that it remained for the scientific man to devise means of freeing the majority from the role of mere machines or puppets; but that the scientist must have different eyes than those of the so-called social engineer who constructs or copies Utopian plans and attempts to fit people into them; he must learn that society is a living, organic thing, unfolding naturally from within like a growing embryo or plant bud; and he must learn that this fact is just as real as the facts which make it possible to build bridges by following mathematical logic and constructed models. For Tönnies, the actions of people who are controlled by natural will resemble the organic functions of growing things. Those who are governed by rational will are more apt to follow models or plans with logical precision.[27]

Although there are some elements in common between the use of ideal types and the use of a classificatory system such as is employed in biology, Gemeinschaft and Gesellschaft are not to be thought of in this light. They are logical concepts which, like the concept of the electron in physics or the vitamin in dietetics, assist in description of relevant areas of consideration. However, the two logical concepts of Tönnies' system differ from such concepts as are used in natural science in that social life based entirely upon one type to the exclusion of the other would be inconceivable. Tönnies' types are not merely types but ideal types or mental constructs which do not actually exist empirically in pure form, and no society could exist if one form or type existed to the exclusion of the other. Man's behavior is never motivated solely by rationality and reason. Passions and emotions play a role in all actual human associations.[28]

Tönnies has been criticized for using the dichotomy Gemeinschaft and Gesellschaft on various occasions as antithetical conceptual categories in a static state as well as a means of representing stages in historical development. The categories, however, are ideal types and as such can be used to describe both change and the differences between groups at any one time. Thus, the Middle Ages are characterized as having more Gemeinschaft-like relationships than modern times. Also, the family is described as having more of the characteristics of Gemeinschaft than a joint-stock company. The essential point to be kept in mind is that neither the family nor the Middle Ages are really Gemeinschaft; but any group or definite period in history may be compared with such mental concepts or constructs as Gemeinschaft and Gesellschaft.

In fact, one of Tönnies' great contributions was his characterization of various groups in a given period, or in different periods of history, by the use of these two types. For instance, the families of peasants and city workers may be compared in time and space by the use of these conceptual tools.

B. Second Sphere—The Theory of Relationships or Social Entities[29]

The concepts Gemeinschaft and Gesellschaft are used to differentiate social entities *(soziale Wesenheiten)*. These are classified as (1) social relationships *(Verhältnisse)*,[30] (2) collectives *(Samtschaften)*, and (3) social organizations or corporations *(Körperschaften)*. Social relationships result from psychical relationships which are willed. Such relationships are conditioned by the wills of others not directly involved, inasmuch as society has established or institutionalized rights and duties of individuals. Between individuals in social relations with each other, there always exists a consciousness of something toward which the participants have rights and duties. Thus, I might think, "I must do this because you are my brother," or "I cannot do that because we are both friends of A." A people, a racial or a language group, a class or an estate is a collective which lacks the means of giving expression to the collective wills of the individuals composing it through a representative person or body. Social organizations or corporate bodies that do have this means of expression may be thought of as persons. Their members are conscious of the ability of their respective groups to make decisions and act in accordance. The most important social organizations are states.[31] The concepts, social relationships, collectives, and social organizations, and their relations to various types of authority in Gemeinschaft and Gesellschaft, are described in the first section of the translation.[32]

C. The Third Sphere—Social Norms[33]

Without regularity in the behavior of individuals there could be no group life. Tönnies described three types of norms: (1) order, (2) law, and (3) morality, which make for regularity in social relationships in collectives and social organizations. The norms classified under the category "order" are of the most universal nature. Just as the biologists might think of vegetative life as more universal and more fundamental than animal life, the norms of order may be conceived as more universal than law. Tönnies goes further with this analogy, indicating that the differentiation made between human life and other forms is comparable to the differentiation between the norms classified under the category morality and those classified under the categories law and order.[34] However, the categories, as Tönnies admits, are not mutually exclusive, and it is not always possible to classify norms under one of the three categories—order, law, or morality—any more than it is possible to classify all living beings as plant, animal, or human.

The social will which is characteristic of morality and law reacts more strongly and more perceptibly upon the thinking individual than does the social will governing the norms classified under order.[35] Among the norms classified under the category order are the succession of, times of, and behavior at, meals. The more complicated and difficult social life becomes, the more such order must be regulated by rationality and policed direction, as in traffic on a city street. When group life has the characteristics of Gemeinschaft, the norms of order are based upon concord *(Eintracht)*; when the life is essentially that of the Gesellschaft, they are based upon convention.[36]

Since one of Tönnies' original interests was the philosophy of law, he gives considerable attention to the various norms related to law.[37] He defines as norms of law those norms which are interpreted and enforced by judicial decision. Law is created either by custom or by legislation. For Tönnies, custom, which is rooted in common habits, is the will of social entities. His conception thus differs from custom as generally conceived in that it is not necessarily the common origin of all norms out of which the laws and morality of higher cultures evolve. In fact, in exceptional cases custom can result from law.[38]

His distinction between rational law, as characterized by Hobbes, and "original natural law," which is composed of norms valid under all conditions of human society, is essential for his distinction between Gesellschaft and Gemeinschaft. Since customary law may be codified and become embodied in legislation, the distinction between written and unwritten law is not the essential difference between the law characterizing Gemeinschaft as contrasted with Gesellschaft. The more complex and rationalistic society becomes the more the forms of law become divorced from customs, folkways, and mores of the people, and the more important legislative law becomes.[39]

Tönnies assumed man to be, in part at least, a social animal by nature.[40] This led him to conceive a system of law which stood in direct contrast to the individualistic rational law. This contrasting system was based upon common altruism, mutual sympathy, and understanding, mutual recognition of rights and duties—all conditions essential for community solidarity and integration. In such a society there would be no disparity between law and morality, since common property in land and means of production would prevail as it prevails in many agrarian societies.

Under morality are grouped such norms as are interpreted by or relevant to an imaginary judge, who may be God; their range is wide, varying from rules for decent conduct to what is formally polite. Human conscience, reason, and ideals furnish their general basis. In Gemeinschaft these norms are sanctioned by religion through its beliefs, faith, and creeds. In Gesellschaft the norms of morality are sanctioned by public opinion which arises from common interests. In both instances the influence extends to both social and political life.

D. The Fourth Sphere—Social Values[41]

Tönnies divides social values into three groups: economic, political, and intellectual or spiritual values. The real nature of all social values is determined by social and individual will. If a cultural item, such as a piece of art, is produced and used as a mere means to an end, the rational will conditioning such production and use is by no means the same as the natural will which leads to production for the pure joy of creation itself. Land may in one society be a mere good offered for sale with no more ceremony or ado than the exchanging of one denomination of money for another. In another society, however, the land may be the common property of a group, and may represent spiritual values so closely bound up with the integrity and sanctity of group mores that it cannot be transferred.

All social values and ideals have their points of reference in social relationships, collectives, and social organizations. The greater the understanding, harmony, and friendship existing between individuals, the greater the probability that their values will be common and the more the possessions of each will merge into those of the other. The development of the modern spirit of trade and capitalism tends to liquidate original family-like communism based upon liking, habit, and memory.[42] The scientific, individualistic, and rationalistic intellectual attitude has driven the supernatural sanction of social values into the background.

E. Fifth and Last Sphere—Systems of Human Endeavor
     (Bezugsgebilde)

The least-developed phase of Tönnies' theory is his systems of human endeavor grouped under the same three categories used for social values—the economic, political, and intellectual or spiritual. In fact, these systems can be considered as social values, each form having its counterpart in Gemeinschaft and Gesellschaft. Among the economic systems are home industry, city economy, agriculture, national economy, and world economy. Under political systems are listed systems of law, protection, and constitutions. Under the intellectual or spiritual category are listed systems of religion, art, philosophy, science, and education.

Empirical Sociology, or Sociography

Heberle[43] has summarized the important empirical works of Tönnies. The wide range of topics includes the following: the surveys of the socio-economic situation of longshoremen and seamen in Hamburg and other ports, undertaken by Tönnies upon request after a large strike in Hamburg; a study on suicide in Schleswig-Holstein; a study of the relationship between certain moral phenomena and socio-economic conditions in Schleswig-Holstein; a monograph on criminality in Schleswig-Holstein, based upon material collected in the chief prisons of the province; and a study on cyclical changes in marriage rates and in the proportion of male to female births in relation to certain economic data, published during the first year of World War I. This latter was one of the first German contributions to the empirical study of business cycles, and in it Tönnies invented a method of correlation of his own.

PERSONAL BELIEFS AND PHILOSOPHY

For Tönnies the end and meaning of any social order was peaceful relationships among men. So firm was this belief that he excluded negative or antagonistic behavior from his pure sociology.[44] Maladjustments could best be righted peacefully without resort to revolution and the recasting of the institutions and norms of society.[45] Sociology should point the way to the establishment of peaceful human relationships among groups, classes, and nations. However, Tönnies believed that the common people would seek and find the highways and byways which they would follow.[46] This great faith in and sympathy for the common people is in part explained by the remarkable facility with which he made their acquaintance and gained their confidence. He knew their lots and what they were thinking about. He knew that they were as a group generally more realistic, social-minded, and kind-hearted than were the more wealthy and educated classes, who, in order to gain or retain status, relied upon rational action regardless of the fairness or humaneness of such action. This in part explains why Tönnies sided with the laborers in labor disputes. He believed that in siding with the common man he was taking the position which from the long-time point of view was the best for the nation.

As previously stated, Tönnies had, during his own lifetime, experienced the disintegrating influence of commercialization and industrialization in his rural homeland. Moreover, he had witnessed the incorporation of the duchies of Schleswig and Holstein into Prussia, thus changing a political community into a mere administrative district. These experiences, as well as his studies, gave him his sympathy for the common man and that type of state control which would protect him. He hoped that co-operative and trade-union movements of the people themselves might solve many of the maladjustments brought on by the development of rationalism and individualism.[47]

THE APPLICATION OF GEMEINSCHAFT AND GESELLSCHAFT AS RELATED TO OTHER TYPOLOGIES*

THE TYPOLOGICAL TRADITION

Tönnies' use of Gemeinschaft and Gesellschaft resembles in certain respects conceptual forms that are a part of an old tradition of typing social entities antithetically. As Sorokin has pointed out, the tradition may be traced back to the philosophical speculation of the Classical Greeks and to the epoch of Confucius. Notwithstanding the age of the tradition, it still has a marked vitality, and appears to be one of the fundamental approaches to sociological phenomena. Examples of this tradition are such familiar conceptualizations as Maine's status society and contract society; Spencer's militant and industrial forms; Ratzenhofer's conquest state and culture state; Wundt's natural and cultural polarity; Durkheim's mechanical and organic solidarity; Cooley's primary and secondary (implicit) groups; MacIver's communal and associational relations; Zimmerman's localistic and cosmopolitan communities; Odum's folk-state pair; Redfield's folk-urban continuum; Sorokin's familistic vs. contractual relations; Becker's sacred and secular societies; as well as such nonpersonalized but common dichotomies as primitive-civilized; literate-nonliterate; and rural vs. urban.

Obviously these varied polarizations are not interchangeable and do not abstract the "same things" out of the social world, but they do have something in common. Not only do they frequently represent similar "content," but, perhaps more important, they exemplify in common the view that it is necessary to distinguish fundamentally different types of social organization in order to establish a range within which transitional or intermediate forms can be comprehended. The polar extremes in point are clearly ideal or constructed types despite the fact that some of the aforementioned theorists tended to treat their types as ontological entities rather than as conceptual devices. The polar-type

12

formulations, implicitly at first, but in recent years with increasing explicitness, have firmly established the point that the continuum is a vital notion in the comparative analysis of social phenomena. The types establish the "outer limits" or standards by means of which the processes of change or intermediate structural forms can be comprehended from the perspective of the continuum. It is in this sense that Gemeinschaft and Gesellschaft and related typologies remain as an important part of current sociological endeavor. A brief examination of the applicability of some of the type constructs would therefore seem to be pertinent.

*This section of the Introduction was prepared by John C. McKinney, in collaboration with Charles P. Loomis.

1. *Durkheim: Mechanical and Organic Solidarity*

Describing not merely the range of human existence, but what to him appeared as an irreversible historical trend, Durkheim in his study of the division of labor polarized society into two types.[48] The first type is the *mechanically solidary society*, wherein beliefs and conduct are alike. People are homogeneous mentally and morally, hence communities are uniform and nonatomized. It is in this type of society that a totality of beliefs and sentiments common to all men exists, and which Durkheim called the *conscience collective*. This conscience is characterized by the attributes of *exteriority* and *constraint*. Exteriority refers to the fact that the conscience as totality is never a product of the members of society at any one point in time; constraint has reference to the significant point that the membership of a mechanically solidary society cannot morally refute its collective conscience. Offense against the collective conscience is moral offense and is punishable by repressive law.

Durkheim's second polar type, defining the direction of historical development, is the *organically solidary society*, wherein society is held together by the interdependence of its parts. The division of labor is a result of the struggle for existence, and the specialization of labor stimulated individualism and differentiation. People in the society are heterogeneous; their mental and moral similarities have disappeared. Volume and material and moral density of people are the necessary conditions for the division, as they make it possible for more individuals to make sufficient contact to be able to act and react upon one another. This in turn makes possible the contact and interconnection of formerly separate collectivities and breaks down the insulation between them, with resultant diversification. The primary consequence of this whole process is the weakening of the *conscience collective*. Crime ceases to be an offense against common moral sentiments and becomes an offense against personal "rights." Spontaneous relations between individuals are replaced by contractual associations. Offensive acts then lose their sacrilegious character and "repressive" law is replaced by "restitutive" law.

Durkheim's investigation of suicide[49] brought about a fundamental change in his conception of the conscience collective as put forth in *The Division of Labor in Society*. The emphasis on the strong predominance of the *conscience* in the mechanically solidary society and the weakening of the *conscience* in the organically solidary society was supplanted by a recognition of the existence of the *conscience collective* in the differentiated, heterogeneous, organically solidary society as the basis of either egoistic or altruistic order. A more specific definition of its absence was arrived at—the anomic society, wherein the collective beliefs and sentiments no longer effectively regulate social action and society persists only on the basis of a shifting and precarious consensus. The change from mechanical solidarity to organic solidarity does not result in an automatic loss of *conscience collective*, but an alteration in its forms. The "noncontractual basis of contract" is a moral, and hence collective foundation for individualistic and secular association. Durkheim's recognition of this, based upon the research use of his types, has given an undeniable impetus to the specialized sociological study of law, religion, and knowledge due to the now obvious relation of these phenomena to social structure.

2.   *Cooley: The Primary Group*

Cooley, an American contemporary of Durkheim's, maintained that neither the individual nor the group has primacy in social action. Contrary to Durkheim, who gave the group primacy over its individual members, and contrary to Spencer, who asserted that the individual is basic and the group only the sum total of its members, Cooley perceived the importance of interactive process of mutual influence between group and individual. For him the most important groups in the formation of individual human nature and the development of norms and ends are what he called primary groups.[50]

> Type examples of the primary group are the family, or household group, the old-fashioned neighborhood, and the spontaneous play-group of children. In such groups all children everywhere participate, and the intimate association there realized works upon them everywhere in much the same way. It tends to develop sympathetic insight into the moods and states of mind of other people and this in turn underlies the development of both the

flexible type of behavior and the common attitudes and sentiments which we have mentioned. . . .

The chief characteristics of a primary group are:

1) Face-to-face association.
2) The unspecialized character of that association.
3) Relative permanence.
4) The small number of persons involved.
5) The relative intimacy among the participants.

Such groups are primary in several senses, but chiefly in that
they are fundamental in forming the social nature and ideals of
the individual. The result of intimate association, psychologically,
is a certain fusion of individualities in a common whole, so that
one's very self, for many purposes at least, is the common life
and purpose of the group. Perhaps the simplest way of describing
this wholeness is by saying that it is a "we"; it involves the sort of
sympathy and mutual identification for which "we" is the natural
expression. One lives in the feeling of the whole and finds the chief
aims of his will in that feeling.[51]

Cooley's combination of organic theory and psychological orientation which led him to the invention of the concept, "looking-glass" self,
and to say that "self and society are twin born,"[52] resulted in the conceptualization of the primary group, apparently independently of the
other theorists we discuss. He did not use the term "secondary group,"
permitting the implicit type under which groups with characteristics
opposite to the primary groups to go unnamed. Since the time of Cooley
the primary group, in one form or another, has been a focal point of attention in American sociology. From the mid-thirties on, a tremendous
amount of research pertaining to this form of social structure has been
conducted.[53]

3. *Redfield: The Folk-Urban Continuum*

The folk-urban typology of Redfield has been the best-known and most
controversial typological formulation in cultural anthropology for the
past twenty-five years.[54] It has often been criticized, particularly by
idiographically-minded field workers, but it nevertheless has been the
stimulant for a great amount of research.[55]

Redfield has formulated an ideal-type version of folk society by link-
ing together a set of attributes. In the absence of explicit delineation the
"urban" type is simply composed of the opposite attributes, and hence
becomes the polar antithesis.

To Redfield, the folk society is a small collectivity containing no more people within it than can know each other well. It is an isolated, nonliterate, homogeneous grouping with a strong sense of solidarity. Technology is simple, and, aside from the division of function between the sexes, there is little other division of labor; hence the group is economically independent of other groups. The ways in which problems are met by the society are conventionalized by long intercommunication within the group, and these ways have become interrelated with one another to constitute a coherent and self-consistent system: a culture. Behavior is spontaneous, traditional, personal, and there is no motivation toward reflection, criticism, or experimentation. Kinship, its relations and institutions, is central to all experience, and the family is the unit of action. The value of traditional acts and objects is not to be questioned; hence they are sacred. The sacredness of objects is apparent in the ways in which objects are hedged in with restraints and taboos that keep them from being commonplace. All activities, even those of economic production, are ends in themselves. The more remote ends of living are taken as given; hence the folk society exists not so much on the basis of exchange of useful functions as in common understandings as to what is to be done.

Redfield contends that understanding of society in general and of our own modern urbanized society in particular can be gained through consideration of the societies least like our own—folk societies. His scheme defines an ideal type, the *folk society*, which is the polar opposite of urban society. The type is a construct, and no known society precisely corresponds to it. It is "created only because through it we may hope to understand reality. Its function is to suggest aspects of real societies which deserve study, and especially to suggest hypotheses as to what, under certain defined conditions, may be generally true about society."[56] The fact that the typology has served this function to a significant degree is evidenced by the gratifying amount of research done in terms of it since the initial tentative type formulation in 1930 in the study of Tepoztlan.[57]

Redfield explicitly indicates his indebtedness to Maine, Durkheim, and Tönnies and points out that his folk-society type results from a restatement of the conceptions of these three men in the light coming from consideration of real primitive societies.[58] It is less generalized and abstract than any of the sets of concepts formulated by Maine, Durkheim, and Tönnies, but it contains essentially the same attributes. As a consequence, Redfield has succeeded in transferring the central considerations of these concepts to a cross-cultural basis and facilitated the comparative study of societies.

4. *Becker: Sacred and Secular Societies*

The sacred-secular antithesis has been utilized by many people, but it finds its most elaborate construction in the work of Howard Becker.[59] Becker makes it very explicit that sacred and secular societies are constructed types. He has meticulously and skillfully preserved their conceptual character and in so doing has contributed significantly to the methodology of typing.

The *sacred society* is isolated vicinally, socially, and mentally. This isolation leads to fixation of habit and neophobia, relations of avoidance, and traditional in-group-out-group attitudes. The concrete is emphasized at the expense of abstraction; social contacts are primary; and tradition and ritual play a large part in the life of the individual.

There is the dominance of sacredness even in the economic sphere which works toward the maintenance of self-sufficiency, and against any development of the pecuniary attitude. The division of labor is simple. Kinship ties are strong and are manifest in "great family" relationships. All forms of activity are under sacred sanctions, and hence violent social control is at a minimum. The forces of gossip and tradition are powerful tools of control. Nonrational behavior is predominant, with an important element of supernaturalism present. Rationalism, particularly in the form of science, is largely absent. The value system is impermeable.

The *secular society* lies at the opposite pole of the continuum and is vicinally, socially, and mentally accessible. Habit fixation is rendered difficult by the accessibility of the social structure. There is an absence of social barriers. Social circulation is unimpeded. Ends are evaluated in terms of "happiness," and means according to the norm of efficiency. Tradition and ritual are minimal. Rationality is dominant, and science is pervasive and powerful. The kinship group is manifest in the conjugal family form. Innovation is frequent; change is sought after and idealized as progress. Informal sanctions are weak, and formal law prevails. Offense against the law invokes little social disapproval. Legal contracts are the rule. Individuation is prominent in society, and the value system is permeable.

These two constructed types cannot be found except in empirical approximations to the major subtypes derived by Becker. The *folk sacred* society is best exemplified by the old-fashioned and primitive groups in the world. The *prescribed-sacred* finds its closest approximation in the Geneva theocracy of Calvin, the Jesuit state of Paraguay, Fascist Italy, Nazi Germany, and Soviet Russia. The *principled-secular* is an equilibrating society wherein the extreme aspects of the sacred are lost, and yet a principle derived from the sacred value system puts a check on rampant change and reduces the potential of mental accessibility. The *normless-secular* society refers to a society wherein there is confusion, ambivalence, and disagreement with regard to the norms, with resultant social disorganization. Instances are most frequently found in centers of culture contact wherein the devices of communication generate social accessibility.

The primary value of the Becker polarity lies in its use in getting at the sacred or secular aspects of a group relationship conceived of as *system*, and in exposing the process of secularization or sacrilization that might be taking place. In contrast to the preceding typologies there is no notion of irreversible process in the sacred-secular schema. Although the main historical trend has been toward secularization it is equally permissible to speak of specific cases of sacrilization, as for instance in the Nazi movement.[60] Also in contrast to earlier typologists, Becker has recognized the fundamental limitations of the general types: that is, that their construction on a very general level makes them "sponge" types, and hence precludes their use for many specific research purposes. As a consequence, Becker has derived a large number of subtypes incorporating particular combinations of attributes for which empirical approximations can readily be found in quite specific research contexts.[61] Due to the fact that the subtypes are derivations, theoretic articulation is retained, and hence the comparative study of concrete groupings is facilitated. The sacred-secular polarity has been constructed along comprehensive lines, and yet remains versatile and flexible.

5. *Sorokin: Familistic, Contractual and Compulsory Relations*

As Sorokin states in the foreword to the English edition of *Gemeinschaft and Gesellschaft*, these types are reiterated up to and presumably in his own thinking. Sorokin's *familistic* and *contractual* relationships correspond respectively to Gemeinschaft and Gesellschaft and have been used as pairs to accompany these concepts, i.e., *familistic Gemeinschaft* and *contractual Gesellschaft*.[62] Sorokin has himself stated that his third type, *compulsory* relations, represents conceptualization on a different level. Either *familistic* relationships or *contractual* voluntary relationships may be more or less the opposite to compulsory relations. We shall here treat only the *familistic* and *contractual* relationships. For Sorokin, *familistic* relationships are permeated by mutual love, sacrifice, and devotion. They are most frequently found among members of a devoted family and among real friends. Familistic relations represent a fusion of the ego into "we." Both joys and sorrows are shared in common, and those involved need one another, seek one another, sacrifice for one another, and love one another. Norms of such relations require that the participation be all-embracing, all-forgiving, all-bestowing and unlimited.

The *contractual* relationship is limited and specified, covering only one narrow sector of the lives of the parties involved. Typical contractual relationships are those of employer and employee, buyer and seller, plumber and householder. The rights and duties of each party are specified by contract. The unity of such groups is rooted in the sober calculation of advantage. It is self-centered and utilitarian. Typically one member of the relationship tries to get as much from the other as possible with the smallest possible contribution. They may remain strangers to each other, one party little interested in the well-being, activities, and philosophy of the other. There is no fusion to produce a homogeneous "we." Such relations are usually of limited duration, voluntary, and stand in contrast to those which are compulsory.[63] Relationships may develop from familistic to contractual or vice versa.[64]

6. *Weber: Types of Action Orientation*

Although not following properly in the tradition of dichotomously typing society, the types of action constructed by Weber are directly relevant to the Tönnies' formulation, the Parsons' formulation which is to follow, and the present context in general. All the relationships discussed here, indeed all relations, are based upon a continuity of social action.[65] Weber starts by typing the action context, and then constructs his varied relationship types on the basis of the underlying typical lines of action. Action is typed:

> ... in terms of rational orientation to a system of discrete individual ends *(zweckrational)*, that is, through expectations as to the behavior of some objects in the external situation and of other human individuals, making use of these expectations as "condition" or "means" for the successful attainment of the actor's own rationally chosen ends; (2) in terms of rational orientation to an absolute value *(wertrational)*; involving a conscious belief in the absolute value of some ethical, aesthetic, religious, or other form of behavior, entirely for its own sake and independently of any prospects of external success; (3) in terms of affectual orientation *(affektuell)*, especially emotional, determined by the specific affects and states of feeling of the actor; (4) as traditionally oriented *(traditional)* through the habituation of long practice.[66]

It may be seen that *zweckrational* is essentially expedient rationality and denotes a system of action involving an actor's motives, conditions, means, and ends wherein the actor weighs the possible alternative ends and means available to him in terms of his purposes and selects the course of action most expedient to him. A system of discrete ends exists for the actor, and an orientation toward them involves such considerations as "efficiency," "counting the cost," "undesirable consequences," "amount of return," and "figuring the results" which condition the otherwise unrestrained adaptation of means to the achievement of ends. This form of rationality plays a dominant role in Weber's over-all sociological analysis.

Wertrational orientation is differentiated from expedient rationality by Weber through the inclusion of an "absolute value" which eliminates the possibility of the actor's selection from alternative ends, and ultimately, therefore, bars the possible selection of certain means. This is a sanctioned form of rationality wherein the actual adaptation of means toward the achievement of the absolute, or ultimate end (value), may comply with the criteria of expedience but cannot in itself be *zweckrational* in view of the lack of a discrete system of ends and the possibility of weighing them in terms of available means and prevailing conditions. The sole important consideration of the actor is the realization of the value.

Affectual action is actually treated by Weber as a form of nonrationality (possibly even irrationality) wherein means and ends become fused, and therefore insusceptible of delineation in behavior. This form of action is dominated by emotional states of feeling of the actor and involves an impulsive or uncontrolled reaction to some exceptional stimulus. It occurs as a release from tension, and therefore the later phases of an affectual act may become increasingly "rational."

Traditional action is also treated by Weber as a deviation from rational orientation in that the means involved become ends in themselves or hold the same rank as ends. This type of action is an almost automatic reaction to habitual stimuli which guide behavior in repeatedly followed and prevailing courses. Typically this means a conformity with the accepted and prevalent ways of behavior, with little evaluation or consideration of their expedience.

These four ideal-typical modes of social action were formulated by Weber for purposes of comparison with actual occurrences of behavior. Such behavior of course shades across the types in various degrees of approximation. It is important to note, however, that in Weber's actual analysis of empirical occurrences there is a marked tendency on his part to utilize the *zweckrationale* orientation as the basis for "understanding" and "interpreting" behavior, thereby reducing the other forms to the status of residual categories. In effect, this produces an implicit rational-nonrational dichotomy underlying the action types, which in turn results in the conceptualization of relationships in these terms. Weber's *Vergemeinschaftung* and *Vergesellschaftung* are directly modeled upon Tönnies' formulations, although Weber does introduce a third category of kampf (conflict) that is not provided for in Tönnies' system. *Zweckrational* may be compared with Tönnies' *Kürwille* and the resulting Gesellschaft, whereas *wertrational*, *affectual*, and *traditional* behavior may be identified with Tönnies' *Wesenwille* and the resulting Gemeinschaft. It is easy to see then how Weber reached his conclusion that the main trend of history was that of increased rationalization. This compares directly with Tönnies' conclusions regarding the trend toward *Gesellschaft,* and also with the related conclusion of Sorokin, Becker, Durkheim, and Redfield.

7. *Parsons: The Pattern Variables of Action Orientation*

The pattern variables of action orientation (or of value orientation or role definition, as they are variously called) constitute the most persistent link between personal, cultural, and social systems in Parsons' theory of social action.[67] As a consequence they are of central importance in articulating the scheme. It is apparent that the pattern variables were born as a negative reaction to what Parsons conceived of as the inadequacies of Weber's types of action and Tönnies' polar types. Parsons ends his classic discussion of Gemeinschaft and Gesellschaft with the following comment:

> . . . this discussion of *Gemeinschaft and Gesellschaft* should not be taken to mean that these concepts are unreservedly acceptable as the basis for a general classification of social relationships or, indeed, that it is possible to start from any dichotomy of only two types. The basic types cannot be reduced to two, or even to the three that Weber used. To attempt to develop such a scheme of classification would be definitely outside the scope of the present study. Such an attempt would, however, have to make a critical examination of the schemes of Tönnies, Weber and some others one of its main tasks.
>
> However, the aspects of Tönnies' classification with which this discussion has been concerned do involve distinctions of basic importance for any such scheme and would hence have to be built into the wider scheme, which would probably involve considerable alteration in their form of statement.[68]

At base the attitude of Parsons indicated a recognition of the fact that general "sponge" types had inherent limitations with respect to the handling of many specific problems. Weber manifested some recognition of this; Becker has been acutely aware of it; and the present writers among others in recent years have been directly concerned with the problem. Whereas Becker approached the problem by deriving a series of subtypes for empirical purposes, Parsons, in line with his propensity for systematic theory, chose the approach of deriving the components of action orientation directly from the structure of social action.

In starting his analysis with an actor in a situation, Parsons contends that any actor must make five separate choices before the action will have a determinate meaning for him. Meaning does not automatically emerge in a situation, but rather, is based upon the actor's selections from the five sets of alternatives posed for him in any situation. These dichotomies are termed the pattern variables of action orientation, and the problems of choice between them are termed the dilemmas of action. The pattern variables are listed as follows:

> Affectivity --------- Affective neutrality
> Particularism ----- Universalism
> Ascription --------- Achievement
> Diffuseness -------- Specificity
> Collectivity-
> Orientation -------- Self-Orientation

Affectivity vs. *affective neutrality* is the gratification-discipline dilemma and involves the problem of accepting an opportunity for gratification without regard for its consequences, or conversely, evaluating it with regard for its consequences. It is a matter really of whether evaluation will take place or not in a given situation.

Particularism vs. *universalism* is the dilemma of choice between types of value standards, and involves evaluating an object of action in terms of its relations to the actor and his specific object relationship situation, or in terms of its relations to a generalized frame of reference. This dilemma is one concerning primacy of cathectic or cognitive standards.

Ascription vs. *achievement* is the dilemma of choice between "modalities" of the social object, and involves the actor's seeing the social object as a composite of ascribed qualities, or conversely, as a composite of performances. This dilemma concerns the conception of objects as "attribute" or "action" complexes.

Diffuseness vs. *specificity* is the dilemma of the definition of the scope of interest in the object, and involves the concession to a social object of an undefined set of rights to be delimited only by conflicting demands, as over against the concession to a social object of a clearly specified and limited set of rights. This dilemma concerns the scope of significance of the object in action.

Collective-orientation vs. *self-orientation* is the collective-interest vs. private-interest dilemma and involves the problem of considering an act with respect to its significance for a collectivity or a moral code, or with respect to its personal significance. This dilemma concerns the primacy of moral standards in a procedure of evaluation.[69]

Parsons contends that these pattern-variables are the single most important thread of continuity in the action frame of reference and that they enter in at four different levels. On the concrete level of empirical action they exist as five discrete choices an actor must explicitly or implicitly make before he can act. They enter on the collectivity level as aspects of role definition wherein actions of role-incumbents tend to be specified in terms of one side or another of a dilemma. The variables also enter on the cultural level as aspects of value-standards; in that value-standards are rules governing action, and insofar as an actor is committed to a standard he will habitually choose the horn of the dilemma specified by adherence to that standard.

In view of their history, derivation, and content, it seems justifiable to conclude that the pattern-variables represent a further and more elaborate specification of the aspects of society dealt with by Gemeinschaft and Gesellschaft.[70] In our judgment, then, it is legitimate to speak of them as theoretical components of the more general types. On the basis of our analysis we feel that it is possible to take Parsons' first four variables, add Sorokin's familistic-contractual dichotomy, and Weber's rational-traditional pair and conceive of them as subtypes of Gemeinschaft and Gesellschaft or Becker's sacred-secular society. In our judgment all the major implications and content of these two typologies are covered, and in addition the advantage of having more specific categories to work with is gained. The fit with the Durkheim, Cooley, and Redfield typologies is not as good because of the differences in construction and levels of abstraction, but nevertheless it seems obvious that there are basic similarities between all the typologies treated here; hence the things that can be empirically said about Gemeinschaft and Gesellschaft or sacred and secular at least have implications for the other typologies. We shall attempt an operational demonstration of our type usage.

APPLICATION OF TYPES USED BY PARSONS, SOROKIN,
WEBER, AND BECKER IN RELATION TO TÖNNIES'
GEMEINSCHAFT AND GESELLSCHAFT

In a recent article the authors of this "Introduction" attempted to describe what they considered to be essential differences in the systemic attributes of communities of family farms and large estates through a tentative demonstrational analysis of two communities in Costa Rica.[71] Both the concrete and abstract or typological attributes were presented, but we shall here concern ourselves primarily with the application of Tönnies' concepts Gemeinschaft and Gesellschaft and pertinent concepts as used by other theorists. The two communities to be described are Atirro, a hacienda community with 65 families, and San Juan Sur, a near-by community of family farms including 75 families. Both these communities are located in the Turrialba Canton of Costa Rica 6 miles and 3 miles respectively from the town Turrialba in which 6,500 people live. They are, we believe, typical communities of rural Latin America. If they are typical, the differences are all the more significant in view of the ideological struggles going on in the world today concerning the relative merits of various forms of land tenure and settlement form. We shall attempt to establish their *type differences* in terms of the theory of social systems.[72]

    A.   *The Procedure.* In an attempt to avoid some of the shortcomings of previous typological descriptions of communities, we have introduced the following innovations: First, what we believe to be the important subtypes of the major general types have been introduced as continua. Second, in the analysis we use subtypes in the form of variable polar components of more general types. These subtypes, although varied and to a certain unavoidable degree overlapping, represent similar levels of abstraction. Third, we have used the concept of the "social system" and consequently are able to treat these subtypes as systemic attributes. This establishes the theoretical possibility of finding similar attributes in apparently different empirical groups. Fourth, we apply the types to only one social system or reference group at a time. We do not attempt to apply the types to many reference groups, such as the family, church groups, occupational groups, political systems, etc., simultaneously. The level of abstraction is thereby held constant. It should also be noted that our types are applied to social systems, not cultural systems or personality systems.[73] Fifth, we apply the types to specific and comparable status-*roles* in specific social systems. Sixth, to standardize the typing of the relationships, a specific category of action is supplied.

In order to make our hypothetical treatment of these systems pertinent to intercultural accessibility or to resistance to change, we are considering changes which require community action, not "normal" or gradual infiltration of ideas or techniques. On the contrary, we are referring to instigated change involving the articulation of the entire community in a common course of action, such as proposals to introduce organized sanitation to prevent spread of communicable diseases or quarantine regulations of sick persons with such diseases, or to set up community-wide co-operatives, schools, and the like.

B.   *The Social Relationships to Be Compared*. In order to arrange for typing of communal action, we chose a status-*role* in each community which articulated the power structure of the whole social system. The status-*role* of the administrator was chosen as the subject, and the status-*role* of an immediate subordinate, the supervisor, was chosen as object on the large estate, Atirro. The administrator initiates action continuously to the supervisor, who is in daily contact with most families in the hacienda community.

Since the power structure of San Juan Sur is articulated only during fiestas and times of crises and since there are no formally elected or appointed governmental administrative officials, obviously there are no status-roles exactly comparable to those of the administrator and supervisor at Atirro. The local informal leader of the community, the *gamonal*,[74] most frequently initiates action in the community as a whole. The following will perhaps best provide an idea of the leadership of the *gamonal* in San Juan Sur:

> During a heavy rain in the wet season one of the children of San Juan Sur fell in a bridgeless river when returning from school. She was drowned. The river is now bridged because Sr. Torres rallied all villagers and their families to walk to the trade center town to demand that the *Jefe Politico* make funds available to bridge the river. This leader has led the community members in several such events.[75]

In our typology the *gamonal* is considered as subject, and a fellow community member whom he chose to help him is considered as object.

C.   *The Specific Category of Action.* Several social scientists[76] who are Latin-American specialists were asked to function as "judges" in the typing of the two communities under consideration. Each is intimately acquainted with Atirro and San Juan Sur. The instructions that they followed, as well as one example of the continua offered them, are seen in Figure 1, continua which we believe may be communicated across cultures.

D.   *Subtypes or Component Continua of the General Types.* On hypothetical grounds we have accepted the Gemeinschaft and Gesellschaft types as the most general forms relevant to our problem. Figure 2 provides the subtypes or component continua which we believe are the chief constituents of these general types. In typing the relationships as presented in Figure 2, an attempt was made to communicate the meaning of the continua through characteristics of their poles.

The judges' reactions are portrayed schematically in Figure 2. Different "profiles" emerged for the two communities. These are marked F and H. The two systems tended to scale out toward opposite poles of the typology, sharp and significant differences being thereby established.[77]

CONCLUSIONS

Insofar as a specific manifestation of the employment of power in San Juan Sur tended toward the affectivity, particularistic, ascription, diffuseness, traditional, and familistic poles, it becomes subject to the hypotheses and statements made about Gemeinschaft or sacred communities.

On somewhat more tenuous grounds, and with the proper interpretive care, it also becomes subject to many of the hypotheses and statements typically related to the primary group, and mechanical and folk societies.

In contrast, Atirro under comparable conditions tended toward the opposite poles of affective neutrality, universalism, achievement, specificity, rationality, and contractual, and hence becomes subject to hypotheses and statements made about Gesellschaft or secular communities. Again, with the proper interpretive care and recognition of limitations of transfer, it also becomes subject to treatment in terms of secondary, organic, and urban theory.

It is now a commonplace in the sociology of knowledge that different types of knowledge, as well as the techniques and motivations for extending knowledge are bound up with particular forms of groups. Gemeinschaft types of society have a traditionally defined fund of knowledge handed down as conclusive and final; they are not concerned with discovering new ideas or extending their spheres of knowledge.

FIGURE 1

THE SCHEDULE: AN ILLUSTRATION*

INSTRUCTIONS: Assume that in both the community of family-sized farms (San Juan Sur) and the large estate community (Atirro) two leaders are organizing a reception for the national president who has just informed the leader in the subject role that he will arrive on the next day. The status-*roles* which structure the interaction which is to be placed on the continua are the following: Hacienda community—Subject is the administrator and object the next subordinate, e.g., the supervisor; community of family-sized farms—Subject is the most powerful informal leader, the *gamonal*, and the object

whoever helps him most in the execution of the act. In both cases the initiator of the action is the subject, administrator on the hacienda community and *gamonal* in the community of family-sized farms.

Place an H on each continuum below for the above-described action between the specified roles for the event and situation as indicated, for the hacienda community. Place an F on each continuum to indicate how the interaction event and situation for the roles specified would compare in the community of family-sized farms.

NORMS OF ORIENTATION OF THE SUBJECT TO OBJECT

1. AFFECTIVITY   AFFECTIVE NEUTRALITY

5	4	3	2	1	0	1	2	3	4	5

Note: Position No. 5 as the polar type represents action determined completely by emotions—love, hate, fear and other emotions. Examples of interaction which would fall toward this pole are the following: Mother as subject loving her child, Damon as subject pleading to die for his friend Pythias.

Position No. 5 as a polar type represents action completely devoid of feeling. Examples of hypothetical interaction which would fall close to this pole are the following: A robot commanding another actor; the hired gunman "cold-bloodedly" shooting his victim, a telephone operator giving the object the time of day at the response to a dial signal, etc.

* Other component subtypes were similarly polarized and illustrated. The complete schedule can be seen in Charles P. Loomis and John C. McKinney, op. cit. pp. 410-411.

FIGURE 2

PROFILES TYPING THE NORMS OF ORIENTATION OF SUBJECT TO OBJECT IN AN ACTION CONTEXT

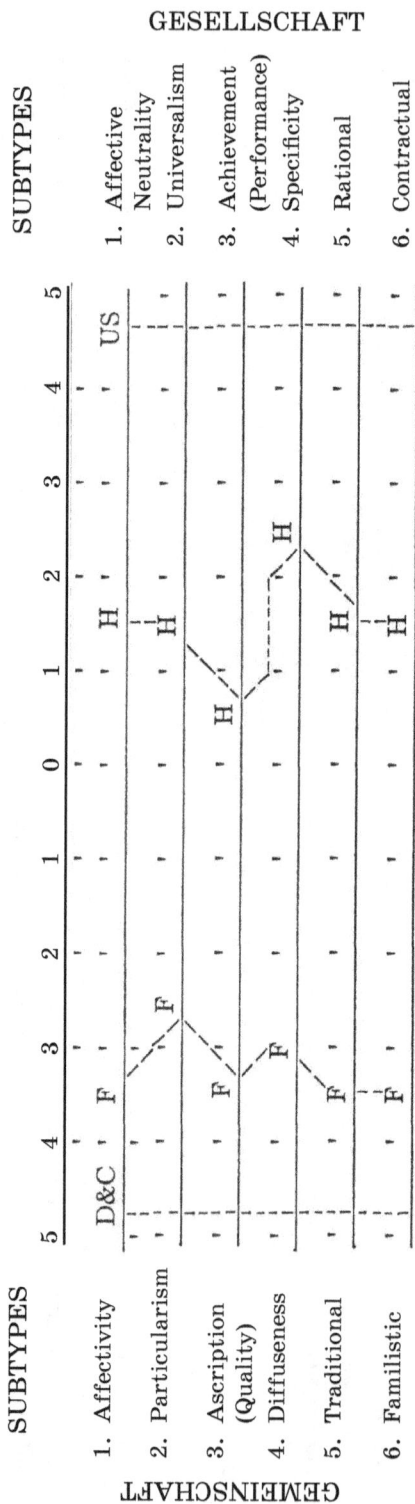

GESELLSCHAFT

SUBTYPES

1. Affective Neutrality
2. Universalism
3. Achievement (Performance)
4. Specificity
5. Rational
6. Contractual

SUBTYPES

1. Affectivity
2. Particularism
3. Ascription (Quality)
4. Diffuseness
5. Traditional
6. Familistic

GEMEINSCHAFT

F   designates the profile of the relationship of informal community leader and an assistant in a community of family-sized farms.

H   designates the profile of the relationship of the manager to an immediate superordinate, the supervisor, in the large-estate community.

D   and C designate the profile of the relationships of president and cabinet subordinate in the Dominican Republic and the Republic of Cuba.

US designates the profile of the relationship of the president and a cabinet subordinate in the United States.

Any effort to test the traditional knowledge, insofar as it implies doubt, is ruled out on moral grounds. In such a group, the prevailing methods are ontological and dogmatic; its mode of thought is that of conceptual realism. In contrast, Gesellschaft types of organization institutionalize techniques for the attainment and codification of knowledge. In such a group the methods are primarily epistemological and critical; the mode of thought nominalistic.

If the communities of Atirro and San Juan Sur are actually representative of other large-estate and family-farm communities in Latin America, then we have solid grounds for saying that the large-estate community possesses a different order of accessibility, socially and culturally, than the family-farm community. Moreover, we are justified in saying that the instigation of any change will necessarily have to follow different procedures, adapted to the two distinctly different social structures.

The specific and very limited problem we have dealt with here with respect to these communities is part of a much larger problematic area, that of *social change*. If sociology is to play a key role in contemporary research, then the major inquiries must be made in a world where the patterns of the past are under increased pressure from a dynamic future. The frames of reference utilized in the past to analyze social change appear to be either oversimplified, too much identified with Western ideologies, or overly impressed with an inevitable one-way direction of progress. From out of this heritage it seems possible, however, to salvage a fundamental starting point—the idea of the societal continuum. The dynamics of a societal continuum so formulated as to comprehend the concept of constant polarity and transitional society in which empirical regularities, constant societal denominators, and universal norms can be recognized cannot be sterile. Tönnies' analysis of Gemeinschaft and Gesellschaft and the related work of other theorists attacking similar problems is still relevant, and continues to pose pertinent problems for contemporary sociologists.

At the beginning of a great but deep work perhaps a few suggestions to readers from the translator are in order. As Rudolf Heberle so aptly stated in his Preface, "Certainly, this is an intricate work which makes great demands on the reader." Because of its relative clarity and simplicity, the reader may find the introduction to Tönnies made somewhat easier by turning to the synopsis in Part Five, which we have called "The Summing Up." This section is a translation of a separate article called "Gemeinschaft und Gesellschaft," which was printed almost half a century after the first appearance of the original volume and five years before the author's death.

"Notes on Tönnies' Fundamental Concepts," which comprise the last section of this volume, contain various terms as used by Tönnies, systematically classified and related to one another. The reader will find these many concepts and expressions throughout the book. Again as Heberle pointed out, "The meaning of these concepts, and their function in the system are not so easily understood, largely because their author developed them against a background of contemporary thought which has lost a good deal of its relevance to present-day sociology." But Gemeinschaft und Gesellschaft is one of "the few classic treatises in sociology—a classic in both form and content." This translation has tried to preserve both.

Gemeinschaft
und
Gesellschaft

FERDINAND TÖNNIES

PART ONE

General Statement of the Main Concepts

SUBJECT OF INVESTIGATION

1. *Relations Between Human Wills — Gemeinschaft (Community)
    and Gesellschalt (Society) from a Linguistic Point of View*[1]

Human wills stand in manifold relations to one another. Every such relationship is a mutual action, inasmuch as one party is active, or gives, while the other party is passive, or receives. These actions are of such a nature that they tend either toward preservation or destruction of the other will or life; that is, they are either positive or negative. This study will consider as its subject of investigation only the relationships of mutual affirmation. Every such relationship represents unity in plurality or plurality in unity. It consists of assistance, relief, services, which are transmitted back and forth from one party to another and are to be considered as expressions of wills and their forces. The group which is formed through this positive type of relationship is called an association *(Verbindung)* when conceived of as a thing or being which acts as a unit inwardly and outwardly. The relationship itself, and also the resulting association, is conceived of either as real and organic life—this is the essential characteristic of the Gemeinschaft (community); or as imaginary and mechanical structure—this is the concept of Gesellschaft (society).

Through the application of these two terms we shall see that the chosen expressions are rooted in their synonymous use in the German language. But to date in scientific terminology they have been customarily confused and used at random without any distinction. For this reason, a few introductory remarks may explain the inherent contrast between these two concepts.

All intimate, private, and exclusive living together, so we discover, is understood as life in Gemeinschaft (community). Gesellschaft (society) is public life—it is the world itself. In Gemeinschaft with one's family, one lives from birth on, bound to it in weal and woe. One goes into Gesellschaft as one goes into a strange country. A young man is warned against bad Gesellschaft, but the expression bad Gemeinschaft violates the meaning of the word. Lawyers may speak of domestic *(häusliche)* Gesellschaft, thinking only of the legalistic concept of social association; but the domestic Gemeinschaft, or home life with its immeasurable influence upon the human soul, has been felt by everyone who ever shared it. Likewise, a bride or groom knows that he or she goes into marriage as a complete Gemeinschaft of life *(communio totius vitae)*. A Gesellschaft of life would be a contradiction in and of itself. One keeps or enjoys another's Gesellschaft, but not his Gemeinschaft in this sense. One becomes a part of a religious Gemeinschaft; religious Gesellschaften (associations or societies), like any other groups formed for given purposes, exist only insofar as they, viewed from without, take their places among the institutions of a political body or as they represent conceptual elements of a theory; they do not touch upon the religious Gemeinschaft as such. There exists a Gemeinschaft of language, of folkways or mores, or of beliefs; but, by way of contrast, Gesellschaft exists in the realm of business, travel, or sciences. So of special importance are the commercial Gesellschaften; whereas, even though a certain familiarity and Gemeinschaft may exist among business partners, one could indeed hardly speak of commercial Gemeinschaft. To make the word combination "joint-stock Gemeinschaft" would be abominable. On the other hand, there exists a Gemeinschaft of ownership in fields, forest, and pasture. The Gemeinschaft of property between man and wife cannot be called Gesellschaft of property. Thus many differences become apparent.

In the most general way, one could speak of a Gemeinschaft comprising the whole of mankind, such as the Church wishes to be regarded. But human Gesellschaft is conceived as mere coexistence of people independent of each other. Recently, the concept of Gesellschaft as opposed to and distinct from the state has been developed. This term will also be used in this book, but can only derive its adequate explanation from the underlying contrast to the Gemeinschaft of the people.

Gemeinschaft is old; Gesellschaft is new as a name as well as a phenomenon. This has been recognized by an author who otherwise taught political science in all its aspects without penetrating to its fundamentals. "The entire concept of Gesellschaft (society) in a social and political sense," says Bluntschli *(Staatswörterbuch IV),* "finds its natural foundation in the folkways, mores, and ideas of the third estate. It is not really the concept of a people *(Volks-Begriff)* but the concept of the third estate ... Its Gesellschaft has become the origin and expression of common opinion and tendencies . . . Wherever urban culture blossoms and bears fruits, Gesellschaft appears as its indispensable organ. The rural people know little of it." On the other hand, all praise of rural life has pointed out that the Gemeinschaft among people is stronger there and more alive; it is the lasting and genuine form of living together. In contrast to Gemeinschaft, Gesellschaft is transitory and superficial. Accordingly, Gemeinschaft should be understood as a living organism, Gesellschaft as a mechanical aggregate and artifact.

2.   *Organic and Mechanical Formations*

Everything real is organic insofar as it can be conceived only as something related to the totality of reality and defined in its nature and movements by this totality. Thus, the power of attraction in its manifold forms makes the universe, insofar as it is accessible to our knowledge, into a totality. Therefore, considering any two bodies in the system, a change in the position of one will effect the position of the other. But for observation and scientific theory based thereupon, a totality must be limited to be effective, and each such totality will consist of smaller totalities which have a certain direction and speed in relation to each other. The power of attraction itself remains either unexplained (as force in space) or is understood as mechanical force (by exterior contact) making itself effective, perhaps in some unknown manner.

Thus, the masses of matter may be divided into homogeneous molecules which attract each other with more or less energy and which in their aggregate state appear as bodies. The molecules are divided into dissimilar (chemical) atoms, the dissimilarity of which remains to be explained by further analysis of the different arrangement which similar atom constituents take within the atom. Pure theoretical mechanics, however, presupposes the existence of centers of force without dimension as sources of real actions and reactions. The concept of these centers is very close to the concept of metaphysical atoms and it excludes from the calculation all influence of the movements, or tendencies thereto, of the parts. For all practical applications, the physical molecules, when thought of in relation to the same body as their systems, can be considered equally well as carriers of energy, as substance itself, since these molecules are equal in size and no attention is given to their possible subdivision. All real masses may be compared by weight and expressed as quantities of a similar definite substance when their parts are conceived as being in a perfectly solid state of aggregation.

In every case the unit, which is assumed as the subject of a movement or as an integral part of a totality (a higher unit), is the product of a fiction necessary for scientific analysis. Strictly speaking, only the ultimate units, metaphysical atoms, could be accepted as their adequate representatives; somethings which are nothings or nothings which are somethings *(Etwasse, welche Nichtse, oder Nichtse, welche Etwasse sind).* But, in so reasoning, the relative meaning of all concepts of size must be kept in mind.

In reality, however, even if they may be anomalies in the mechanical concept, there exist bodies other than these combinable and combining particles of matter conceived of as dead. Such bodies appear to be natural totalities which, as totalities, have movement and action in relation to their parts. These are the organic bodies. We human beings, who strive for knowledge and understanding, represent them. Each of us has, in addition to imparted knowledge of all possible bodies, an immediate knowledge of his own. We are driven to the conclusion that psychic life is connected with every living body, existing as an entity in the same way as we know ourselves to exist. But objective observation teaches not less clearly that in the case of a living body we deal each time with a totality which is not a mere aggregation of its parts but one which is made up of these parts in such a manner that they are dependent upon and conditioned by the totality, and that such a body as a totality and hence as a form possesses reality and substance.

As human beings we are able to produce only inorganic things from organic materials, dividing and recombining them. In the same way things are also made into a unity through scientific manipulation and are a unity in our concepts. Naïve interpretation or attitudes and artistic imagination, folk belief, and inspired poetry lend life to the phenomena. This creative element is also apparent in the fictions of science. But science also reduces the living to the dead in order to grasp its relations and conditions. It transforms all conditions and forces into movements and interprets all movements as quantities of labor performed, i.e., expended energy, in order to comprehend processes as similar and commensurable. This last is true to the same extent that the assumed units are realities, and the possibility for thought is unlimited. Thus understanding, as an end, is attained, and therewith other objectives.

However, the tendencies and inevitableness of organic growth and decay cannot be understood through mechanical means. In the organic world the concept itself is a living reality, changing and developing as does the idea of the individual being. When science enters this realm it changes its own nature and develops from a logical and rational to an intuitive and dialectic interpretation; it becomes philosophy. However, the present study does not deal with genus and species, i.e., in regard

to human beings it is not concerned with race, people, or tribe as biological units. Instead, we have in mind their sociological interpretation,
which sees human relationships and associations as living organisms
or, in contrast, mechanical constructions. This has its counterpart and
analogy in the theory of individual will, and in this sense to present the
psychological problem will be the text of Part Two.

SECTION ONE: Theory of Gemeinschaft

1. *Embryo or Emergent Forms*

In accordance with the preliminary explanations, the theory of
Gemeinschaft starts from the assumption of perfect unity of human
wills as an original or natural condition which is preserved in spite of
actual separation. This natural condition is found in manifold forms
because of dependence on the nature of the relationship between individuals who are differently conditioned. The common root of this natural condition is the coherence of vegetative life through birth and the
fact that the human wills, insofar as each one of these wills is related
to a definite physical body, are and remain linked to each other by pa-
rental descent and by sex, or by necessity become so linked. This close
interrelation as a direct and mutual affirmation is represented in its
most intense form by three types of relationships, namely: (1) the relation between a mother and her child; (2) the relation between husband
and wife in its natural or general biological meaning; (3) the relation
among brothers and sisters, that is, at least among those who know each
other as being the offspring of the same mother. If in the relations of
kindred individuals one may assume the embryo of Gemeinschaft or
the tendency and force thereto, rooted in the individual wills, specific
significance must be attributed to the three above-mentioned relationships, which are the strongest and most capable of development. Each,
however, is important in a special way:

(A) The relation between mother and child is most deeply rooted
in liking or in pure instinct. Also, in this case the transition from an
existing physical to a purely psychic bond is evident. But the younger
the child, the more apparent is the physical element. The relationship
implies long duration, as the mother has to feed, protect, and educate
the child until it becomes capable of doing this alone. With this development the relation loses in essentiality, and separation of mother and
child becomes more probable. This tendency toward separation, how
ever, can be counterbalanced, or at least restrained, by other tendencies,
namely, through the mother and child becoming accustomed to one
another and through remembrance of the pleasures which they have

given each other, especially the gratitude of the child for the care and painstaking attention of the mother. To these direct mutual relations, other common and indirectly binding relations involving other things are added: pleasure, habit, remembrance of objects in the environments which were, or have become, pleasant. The same holds also for shared remembrances of intimate, helpful, beloved persons such as the father, if he lives with the mother, or the brothers and sisters of the mother or child, etc.

(B) Sexual relationship does not in any way necessitate a permanent living together. Moreover, in the beginning it does not lead so much to a fixed mutual relationship as to one-sided subjugation of the woman who, weaker by nature, can be reduced to an object of mere possession or to servitude. For this reason, the relationship between man and wife, if considered independent from kinship and from all social forces based thereupon, has to be supported mainly by habituation to one another in order that the relationship may shape itself into one of mutual affir-mation. Besides this, there are, as will be readily understood, the other previously mentioned factors which assist in strengthening the bond; the children as common possession, and, further, the common posses-sions and household.

(C) Among brothers and sisters there is no such innate and in-stinctive affection and natural liking or preference as between mother and children or between husband and wife. This is true even though the husband-wife relationship may resemble that among brothers and sisters, and there are many reasons to believe that this has frequently been the case with some tribes in an earlier period in the history of man. It must be remembered, however, that among such tribes, as long as descent was reckoned only from the mother, the relationship between brothers and sisters was extended in name, as well as in its emotional aspects, to the corresponding generations of cousins. This practice was so general that the more limited meaning of the concept was developed only in a later period. It was through a similar development in the most important ethnic groups that marriage between brothers and sisters came to be regarded as illicit; and, where exogamy prevailed, marriage and clan membership (but not kinship) also became mutually exclu-sive. Therefore, one is justified in considering love between brother and sister, although essentially based upon blood kinship, as the most "human" relationship between human beings. The intellectual quality of this relationship, as compared to the two others discussed above, is also apparent from the fact that, while instinct plays only a small part, the intellectual force of memory is the foremost in creating, con-serving, and consolidating this bond of hearts. For where children of the same mother, in living with her, are also living together with each other, the reminiscences of each of them about pleasant impressions and experiences will necessarily include the persons and activities of their brothers or sisters. This all the more so, the more closely the group is united, especially where, endangered from the outside, it is compelled to strive and act as a group. Thus habit makes such life easier and dearer. At the same time the greatest possible similarity of nature and equality of strength may be expected among brothers even though differences in intelligence and experience, as a purely human or mental element, may easily be perceived.

2. *Their Unity*

Many other less intimate relationships are linked to these most fundamental and familiar types. They find their unity and perfection in the relationships between father and children. The existence of an organic basis which keeps the intelligent father connected with the offspring of his body makes this relationship similar to the mother child relationship in the most important aspect. It differs in that the instinctive part of it is so much weaker. Thus, it resembles more closely the husband-wife relationship and is, therefore, more readily conceived as merely coercive. But while the affection of the father, as to duration more than as to intensity, is inferior to that of the mother, the love of a father differs from the love of a mother in the opposite direction. If present to any considerable degree, therefore, it is similar through its spiritual nature to the affection among brothers and sisters, but, in contrast to the latter, it is defined by an inequality of nature, especially that of age and intellectual power.

Thus, the idea of authority is, within the Gemeinschaft, most adequately represented by fatherhood, or paternity. However, authority, in this sense, does not imply possession and use in the interest of the master; it means education and instruction as the fulfillment of procreation, i.e., sharing the fullness of one's own life and experiences with the children, who will gradually grow to reciprocate these gifts and thus to establish a truly mutual relationship. In this regard the first-born son has a natural preference: He is the closest to the father and will occupy the place which the aging father leaves. The full authority of the father is, therefore, at least implicitly, passed on to the first-born son at his very birth. Thus, the idea of an ever-renewed vital force finds its expression in the continuous succession of fathers and sons. We know that this rule of inheritance is not the original one. Apparently the patriarchate has been preceded by the matriarchate and the rule of the brother on the mother's side, and even if collateral succession (the system of tanistry) has precedence over primogeniture, this is based only on the relation to a former generation; the succeeding brother does not derive his right from the brother but from the common father.

3. *Enjoyment and Labor*

Wherever people live together there is, or develops, according to general conditions, some difference and division of enjoyment and labor, which produces a reciprocal relation between them. This is most directly evident in mother-child relationships. Here the enjoyment surpasses work in importance. The child enjoys protection, nutriment, and instruction; the mother enjoys possession, later on obedience, and finally intelligent assistance. To a certain degree a similar mutuality exists also between husband and wife—a mutuality which is based, however, in the first place upon sexual difference and only secondly upon difference in age. Relevant to the sex difference, the difference in natural strength becomes evident in the division of labor. In defending their common property the task of the woman is the protection of valued possessions; the man has to keep off the enemy. To obtain and provide the necessities of life is the field of the man; to conserve and prepare them as far as food is concerned, that of the woman. And when other work and the instruction of children is needed, we find that the masculine energy is directed toward the outside, fighting and leading the sons. The woman, on the other hand, remains confined to the inner circle of home life and is attached to the female children. Real helpfulness, mutual aid, and advancement exist in the purest form among brothers and sisters because they tend toward the same common activities. Besides difference in sex, difference in mental capacity necessarily becomes apparent in the brother-sister relationship. Accordingly, one side will be more concerned with brainwork, thinking and planning, while to the other side is given the manual labor, the task of execution. But such division of labor may also be regarded as a relation between guidance and leadership, on the one hand, and compliance and obedience on the other. It must be recognized that all these differentiations follow a pattern of nature; however, often these inherent regular tendencies, like all others, may be interrupted, counterbalanced, or reversed.

4. *Dominance and Balance*

In each of these relationships, individual wills mutually direct and serve each other so that the relationship may be presented as an equilibrium of forces. If, however, this is true, everything that gives dominance to one will has to be counterbalanced by a stronger influence from the opposite direction.

The ideal equilibrium would be attained if greater enjoyment derived from the relationship corresponded to harder work for it, i.e., work which requires greater effort or rarer abilities. Vice versa, easier work would be balanced by lesser enjoyment. For even though toil and struggle be in themselves pleasure, the exertion of forces necessitates subsequent relaxation: Energy spent must be restored; motion must be followed by rest.

The greater satisfaction of the stronger individuals is partly the feeling of superiority itself, of power and command; whereas, on the contrary, being led and protected and having to obey—the feeling of inferiority—is always felt with some displeasure as a kind of pressure and constraint even though it may be alleviated by affection, habit, and gratitude.

The relation of forces among the individual wills is made still clearer by the following reasoning: All superiority carries with it the danger of haughtiness and cruelty and, therefore, of a hostile, coercive treatment if, accompanying increasing superiority, the tendency to benefit those dominated is not greater or does not also increase. And this happens to be a natural inherent tendency: Greater force and power entail also greater ability to aid. If such an intention or will is at all existent, it will be all the stronger and more decided because of the feeling of power which in itself is will. Thus, we find, especially in the realm of these physical-organic relationships, an instinctive and naïve tenderness of the strong for the weak, a desire to aid and to protect, which is closely connected with the pleasure of possession and the enjoyment of one's own power.

5. *Three Types of Authority*[2]

A superior power which is exercised to the benefit of the subordinate and which, because in accordance with his will, is accepted by him, I call dignity or authority. We distinguish three kinds: authority of age, authority of force, and authority of wisdom or spirit. These three are united in the authority of the father who is engaged in protecting, assisting, and guiding his family. The danger inherent in such power causes fear in the weaker ones, and this by itself would mean nothing but negation and repudiation (except in so far as mingled with admiration). Beneficence and good will, however, bring forth the will to honor; and the sentiment of reverence is born in a situation where will to honor predominates. Thus, as a result of this difference in power, tenderness corresponds to reverence or, in a lesser degree of intensity, benevolence to respect; they represent the two poles of sentiment on which Gemeinschaft is based, in case there exists a definite difference of power. The existence of such motives makes possible and probable a kind of Gemeinschaft even between master and servant, and this is the rule especially if it is supported and fostered, as in the case of kinship, by an intimate, lasting, and secluded common life in the home.

6. *Gemeinschaft by Blood—of Place—of Mind— Kinship—Neighborhood—Friendship*

The Gemeinschaft by blood, denoting unity of being, is developed and differentiated into Gemeinschaft of locality, which is based on a common habitat. A further differentiation leads to the Gemeinschaft of mind, which implies only co-operation and co-ordinated action for a common goal. Gemeinschaft of locality may be conceived as a community of physical life, just as Gemeinschaft of mind expresses the community of mental life. In conjunction with the others, this last type of Gemeinschaft represents the truly human and supreme form of community. Kinship Gemeinschaft signifies a common relation to, and share in, human beings themselves, while in Gemeinschaft of locality such a common relation is established through collective ownership of land; and, in Gemeinschaft of mind, the common bond is represented by sacred places and worshiped deities. All three types of Gemeinschaft are closely interrelated in space as well as in time. They are, therefore, also related in all such single phenomena and in their development, as well as in general human culture and its history. Wherever human beings are related through their wills in an organic manner and affirm each other, we find one or another of the three types of Gemeinschaft. Either the earlier type involves the later one, or the later type has developed to relative independence from some earlier one. It is, therefore, possible to deal with (1) kinship, (2) neighborhood, and (3) friendship as definite and meaningful derivations of these original categories.

The house constitutes the realm and, as it were, the body of kinship. Here people live together under one protecting roof. Here they share their possessions and their pleasures; they feed from the same supply, they sit at the same table. The dead are venerated here as invisible spirits, as if they were still powerful and held a protecting hand over their family. Thus, common fear and common honor ensure peaceful living and co-operation with greater certainty. The will and spirit of kinship is not confined within the walls of the house nor bound up with physical proximity; but, where it is strong and alive in the closest and most intimate relationship, it can live on itself, thrive on memory alone, and overcome any distance by its feeling and its imagination of nearness and common activity. Nevertheless, it seeks all the more for physical proximity and is loath to give it up, because such nearness alone will fulfill the desire for love. The ordinary human being, therefore—in the long run and for the average of cases— feels best and most cheerful if he is surrounded by his family and relatives. He is among his own *(chez soi)*.

Neighborhood describes the general character of living together in the rural village. The proximity of dwellings, the communal fields, and even the mere contiguity of holdings necessitate many contacts of human beings and cause inurement to and intimate knowledge of one another. They also necessitate co-operation in labor, order, and management, and lead to common supplication for grace and mercy to the gods and spirits of land and water who bring blessing or menace with disaster. Although essentially based upon proximity of habitation, this neighborhood type of Gemeinschaft can nevertheless persist during separation from the locality, but it then needs to be supported still more than ever by well-defined habits of reunion and sacred customs.

Friendship is independent of kinship and neighborhood, being conditioned by and resulting from similarity of work and intellectual attitude. It comes most easily into existence when crafts or callings are the same or of similar nature. Such a tie, however, must be made and maintained through easy and frequent meetings, which are most likely to take place in a town. A worshiped deity, created out of common mentality, has an immediate significance for the preservation of such a bond, since only, or at least mainly, this deity is able to give it living and lasting form. Such good spirit, therefore, is not bound to any place but lives in the conscience of its worshipers and accompanies them on their travels to foreign countries. Thus, those who are brethren of such a common faith feel, like members of the same craft or rank, everywhere united by a spiritual bond and the co-operation in a common task. Urban community of life may be classified as neighborhood, as is also the case with a community of domestic life in which nonrelated members or servants participate. In contradistinction, spiritual friendship forms a kind of invisible scene or meeting which has to be kept alive by artistic intuition and creative will. The relations between human beings themselves as friends and comrades have the least organic and intrinsically necessary character. They are the least instinctive and are based less upon habit than are the relationships of neighborhood. They are of a mental nature and seem to be founded, therefore, as compared with the earlier relationships, upon chance or free choice. But a similar differentiation has been pointed out already for the relations of pure kinship and leads to the following statements.

7. *Judicial—Feudal—Sacerdotal Functions*

The neighborhood may be compared with the kinship type in the same way as the husband-wife relationship; therefore, affinity in general may be compared with the mother-child relationship. What is achieved only by mutual liking in the mother-child relationship must be made up for by habit in the neighborhood type. As the relation among brothers and sisters—therefore, also all cousins and other relations of similar consanguinity—are comparable to the other organically conditioned relationships, so in the same manner friendship is comparable to neighborhood and kinship. Memory creates gratitude and faithfulness. The specific truth of such relationships must manifest itself in mutual trust and belief. As the foundations of these relationships are no longer spontaneous and so self-evident and as the individuals know and determine their own will and ability more definitely, these relationships are the most difficult to preserve and the most susceptible to disturbances—such as disputes and quarrels, which will happen in almost all group life. Not only does constant proximity and frequency of contacts mean mutual furtherance and affirmation, but inhibition and negation also become real possibilities or probabilities of a certain degree. Only as long as mutual furtherance and affirmation predominate can a relation really be considered Gemeinschaft. Thus, it is explained that, in conformity with many experiences, such purely mental or psychological brotherhoods can stand only to a certain limit the frequency and narrowness of physical proximity of real joint life. They have to find their counterpoise in a high degree of individual freedom.

Within kinship, all natural authority is concentrated in paternal authority; where the social grouping is based on neighborhood, this paternal authority is transformed into the authority of the prince and as such retains its importance. Under this form it is based more upon power than upon age and fatherhood. It is most clearly evident in the influence of the master over his people, of the landlord over his copyholders, of the feudal lord over his serfs. When friendship is based on common devotion to the same calling or the same craft, such dignity and authority expresses itself as the authority of the master toward his disciples, pupils, apprentices.

Judicial functions and the element of justice befit the authority of age, for youthful irascibility and passions of all kinds give rise to violence, revenge, and dispute. The aged man is a speculator, above such frailties, and less disposed to help one against another because of predilection or hatred. He will try to discover by which side the evil was started and whether there existed sufficient provocation for a normal, moderate person. He will also decide through what action or suffering the excessive deed is to be compensated.

The authority of power must shine forth in battle—it must be proven by courage and bravery. Therefore, it attains its consummation in the feudal authority. To the lord falls the task of rallying the fighting forces, leading the march against the enemy, directing all energies toward the attainment of the goal and the warding off of evil forces.

The enlightened is endowed with the gift to divine and surmise, in most decisions and measures, more of what is right and wholesome than anyone else is able to see with certainty. As the future is hidden and often stands menacing and terrible before us, among all human arts pre-eminence seems to be accorded to that which enables one to know, to interpret, and to impel the will of the invisible. Thus, the authority of wisdom surpasses all others as sacerdotal authority, in which form God himself seems to dwell in person among the living and in which the immortal and eternal force is believed to reveal and communicate itself to those surrounded by dangers and mortal fear.

These various directing and leading activities and virtues require and complement each other. The above-mentioned kinds of authority can, essentially, be conceived of as connected with every superior position as far as such is derived from the unity of a Gemeinschaft. Thus, the judicial authority is consistent through its origin with the position of the family father, while the authority of the duke or knight or feudal lord corresponds to the rank of the patriarch, and finally the sacerdotal authority befits best the rank of the master. Feudal authority, however, is also due, quite naturally, to the paterfamilias, especially when unity against enemies requires submission. That applies to the leader of a clan, as the head of the oldest among a group of related families, and, in the most forceful way, to the chief of an unorganized tribe who takes the place of the mythical common ancestor. And this feudal authority again is raised to the divine sacerdotal authority. For the ancestors are, or will become, deities. The deities, on the other hand, are believed to be ancestors and fatherly friends. Thus, we find deities of the home, of the family, of the tribe, and of the folk community *(Volks-Gemeinde)*. In them the force of such a Gemeinschaft exists in the most eminent way: They are capable of bringing about the impossible; their workings are supernatural. Therefore, they will help if nourished and worshiped with piety and humility; they do harm and punish if forgotten or despised. They themselves are, as fathers and judges, lords and leaders, taskmasters and teachers, the original possessors and examples of these human dignities. The feudal authority requires the holder to be a judge, for a common fight against the enemy requires undisputed decisions in settling internal quarrels. The sacerdotal office is qualified to consecrate such decisions as sacred and inviolable. The gods themselves are honored as creators of law and judicial wisdom.

8. *Authority and Service—Inequality and Its Limits*

All authority or office is characterized by particular and enhanced free-dom and honor, and thus represents a specific sphere of will. As such it must be derived from the general and equal sphere of will of the Gemeinschaft. It finds its corollary in service as a particular and dimin-ished freedom and honor. Each office or authority can be regarded as service and each service as office or authority, provided the particular-ity involved is taken into consideration. The realm of will and, therefore, the will of the Gemeinschaft is a mass of determined force, power, or right. And right is, in essence, will to initiate action, to allow action to be initiated, to obey and accept responsibility. This is the nature of all derived realms of will in which rights and duties are the two correspond-ing aspects of the same thing, or nothing but the subjective modalities of the same objective substance of right or force. In this way, through increased and diminished duties and rights, real inequalities exist and develop within the Gemeinschaft through its will. These inequalities can be increased only to a certain limit, however, because beyond this limit the essence of the Gemeinschaft as the unity of unequal beings would be dissolved: In case the superiors' legal power would become too great, their relation to the common sphere of right would become indifferent and without value, and the inferiors' legal power would be-come too small and their relationship thereto unreal and insignificant.

The less human beings who remain or come into contact with each other are bound together in relation to the same Gemeinschaft, the more they stand opposite each other as free agents of their wills and abilities. The less this freedom is dependent upon a preconditioned will of the individual himself, which is to say the less this will is dependent upon or influenced by a common will, the greater is the freedom. For, besides the inherited forces and instincts, the influence of a community as an educating and guiding will is the most important factor determining the condition and formation of every individual habit and disposition. Especially is the family spirit *(Familiengeist)* important, but so also is every spirit *(Geist)* which is similar to it and has the same effects.

9. *Common Will—Understanding—Natural Law—*
    Language—Mother Tongue—Concord

Reciprocal, binding sentiment as a peculiar will of a Gemeinschaft we shall call understanding *(consensus)*.[3] It represents the special social force and sympathy which keeps human beings together as members of a totality. As everything instinctive in man is related to reasons and re-quires the capacity of speech, this mentality can be regarded also as the reason and significance of such a relationship. This mentality exists, for instance, between the parent and the child only to the degree in which the child is conceived as possessing speech, intellect, and reason. In the same way it can be said that everything that conforms to the conception of a Gemeinschaft relationship and what in and for this situation has meaning forms its laws. Everything that conforms to the conception of this Gemeinschaft relationship is to be considered as the proper and real will of those bound together. Insofar as enjoyment and labor are differentiated according to the very nature and capability of individuals—especially in such a manner that one part is entitled to guidance, the other bound to obedience —this constitutes a natural law as an order of group life, which assigns a sphere and function, incorporating duties and privileges, to every will. Understanding is based upon intimate knowledge of each other insofar as this is conditioned and advanced by direct interest of one being in the life of the other, and readiness to take part in his joy and sorrow. For that reason, the more the constitution and experience or natural disposition, character, and intellectual attitude are similar or harmonize, the more probable is understanding.

The real organ of understanding, through which it develops and improves, is language. Language, by means of gestures and sounds, enables expressions of pain and pleasure, fear and desire, and all other feelings and emotions to be imparted and understood. Language has —as we all know—not been invented and, as it were, agreed upon as a means and tool by which one makes oneself understood. It is itself the living understanding both in its content and in its form. Similar to all other conscious activities of expression, the manifestation of language is the involuntary outcome of deep feelings and prevailing thoughts. It is not merely an artificial means of overcoming a natural lack of understanding, nor does it serve merely the purpose of enabling one to make oneself understood. Language can be used, however, among those who do understand each other, as a mere system of symbols, the same as other symbols which have been agreed upon. All these manifestations can be expressions of hostile as well as friendly passions. This justifies the general statement that friendly and hostile moods and passions underlie the same or very similar conditions. We must, however, distinguish between the hostility which springs from the rupture or loosening of natural and existing ties and the other type of hostility which is based upon strangeness, misunderstanding, and distrust. Both are instinctive, but the first one is anger, hatred, displeasure; the second one is fear, abhorrence, dislike. The first one is acute; the second one, chronic. Of course, language, like any other means of communication between minds, did not spring from either of these two kinds of hostility—which is only an unnatural and diseased state—but from intimacy, fondness, and affection. Especially from the deep understanding between mother and child, language should develop most easily and vigorously. Underlying the open hostility associated with an intimate understanding, on the contrary, we can always think of a certain friendship and unity.

The real foundation of unity, and consequently the possibility of Gemeinschaft, in the first place is closeness of blood relationship and mixture of blood; secondly, physical proximity; and, finally, for human beings, intellectual proximity. In this gradation, therefore, are to be found the sources of all kinds of understanding.

We may now establish the great main laws of Gemeinschaft: (1) relatives and married couples love each other or easily adjust themselves to each other. They speak together and think along similar lines. Likewise do neighbors and other friends. (2) There is understanding between people who love each other. (3) Those who love and understand each other remain and dwell together and organize their common life. A mixed or complex form of common determinative will, which has become as natural as language itself and which consists of a multitude of feelings of understanding which are measured by its norm, we call concord *(Eintracht)* or family spirit *(concordia* as a cordial allegiance and unity). Understanding and concord are one and the same thing; namely, will of the Gemeinschaft in its most elementary forms, including understanding in their separate relations and actions and concord in their total force and nature.

10. *Structure of the Natural Elements*

Understanding is, as we saw, the simplest expression for the inner nature and the reality of all genuine living, dwelling, and working together. This, therefore, applies in its primary and most general meaning to home life, since the basis of home life exists in the bond and unity between man and wife for raising and educating children. So in this connection marriage as a lasting relationship has this meaning. The tacit understanding, as we might term it, concerning duties and rights, as well as good and evil, could be compared with an agreement or contract, but such a comparison would only serve the purpose of more vigorously emphasizing the contrasting features. For one could also say that words were agreed-upon, arbitrary symbols, and yet the contrary is true.

Agreement and contract are unification which is planned and decided upon; exchange of promise, therefore, requires language and mutual comprehension and acceptance of actions offered for the future, which must be expressed in definite terms. The agreement can be imputed to have actually come into being if the result is the same as if there were such agreement. The agreement can also be tacit, by chance *(per acci-dens)*. Understanding is, however, according to its very nature, tacit. This is because the contents of mutual understanding are inexpressible, interminable, and incomprehensible. Just as language cannot be made by agreement, even though through language there exist many systems of symbols representing concepts, real concord cannot be artificially produced. This is not to say, however, that many kinds of agreement are not arrived at artificially. Understanding and concord grow and blossom forth from existing buds if the conditions are favorable. As one plant springs from another, so one home (as a family) generates from another. In the same way marriage develops from concord and the folkways and mores.

Understanding and concord are conditioned and effected not solely by their own kind which went before but also by a universality contained in them and by the form in which they appear. Therefore, we find also in larger groups this unity of will as the psychological expression of blood relationship, although in a weaker form and expressing itself to individuals only in an organic order. In the same way as the general use of common language, making possible understanding through speech, brings nearer and binds human minds and hearts, so we find a common state of mind which in its higher forms—common custom and common belief—penetrates to the members of a people *(Volk)*. It means the unity and peace of life of a people, although not guaranteeing it. As one passes from the consideration of the people to the tribe, one finds this common state of mind to be of growing intensity, extending to the branches and twigs. Finally, it is found in the most perfect development in the related families of the early and important formation of organic life, the clan or tribe which may be said to be the family before the family. From these groups, and above them, develop, as their modifications, the complexes defined by field and soil. We distinguish, in a general graduation: (a) the country, (b) the district or the province, and (c) the village, as the most intimate form of this kind. Partly from the village, partly independent of it, develops the town, which, in its perfection, is held together not so much by common objects of nature as by common spirit. According to its exterior aspect, the town is nothing but a large village, a multitude of neighboring villages or a walled-in village. In the next stage a town will dominate a surrounding territory, thereby representing a new organization of the district within the larger unit of the country, and thus changing or reforming the structure of a tribe or a people. Within the town we find as its typical products or fruits the fellowship of work, the guild or corporation, and the fellowship of cult, the fraternity, the religious community. These are together the last and highest expression of which the idea of Gemeinschaft is capable. In the same way, however, the entire town, a village, a people, tribe, generation, or finally, a family, can be represented or conceived as a special kind of guild or religious community. And vice versa, in all these manifold formations are contained and from them spring the idea of the family as the most general expression of the reality.

11. *Possession and Enjoyment—Field and House*

Life of the Gemeinschaft is mutual possession and enjoyment and also possession of and enjoyment of common goods. The will of possession and enjoyment is the will of protection and defense: Common goods— common evils; common friends—common enemies. Evils and enemies are not objects of possession and enjoyment, not of positive, but of negative will, indignation and hatred; therefore, objects of common will for destruction. Objects of wish or desire are not something hostile but are imagined as being possessed and enjoyed even if the acquisition of them may be dependent upon hostile activity. Possession is, in itself, will for preservation; it is enjoyment in the same sense as satisfaction and realization of will are comparable to the inhalation of atmospheric air. This is true also for possession and interest which human beings have in each other. However, to the extent that enjoyment differs from possession through special acts of use, it can be conditioned by destruction, as, for instance, the killing of an animal for consumption. The hunter and fisher do not want so much to possess their prey as to enjoy it, although a part of their use may take a lasting form as possession, as, for instance, the use of skins or of an assembled stock. But the hunting itself, as repetitive action, depends upon the possession of a hunting ground, even though the latter be indefinite. The hunt is enjoyment made possible by the possession of these hunting grounds. An intelligent being should try to maintain the general condition or increase the contents of these grounds, since it is the substance of which the prey is the product. This holds true for the substance of the tree which provides fruit or of the soil which supports the growth of edible blades. The domesticated, fed, and well-kept animal itself gains the same quality, whether to be used as servant and helper or to yield parts of its body for consumption. To this end, animals are bred. The breeding of animals involves a similar relationship to those described. The species or herd remains and is to be preserved, in this sense representing the possession, whereas the single animal is destined to be consumed. The keeping of herds means a special relation to the earth, to the pastures which provide food for the cattle. But hunting grounds and pastures in free territory can be changed if exhausted. The human beings with all their belongings, including the animals, of course, leave them to look for better ones. It is first the broken fields, in which man by his own labor plants seeds, which tie his feet. This plowed land becomes the possession of successive generations and, through its cultivation by the ever-rejuvenated human energies, becomes thus an inexhaustible treasure. It gains its full value only gradually through accumulative experience, increasingly intelligent management, preservation, and care. With the cultivated field, the domicile also becomes fixed. From a house which, like human beings, animals, and things, is movable, the domicile becomes immovable like earth and soil. The human being becomes bound in a twofold way, through cultivated fields and through the house in which he lives; that is to say, he is tied down by his own work.

12. *Scheme of Development*

Life of the Gemeinschaft develops in permanent relation to land and homestead. It can be explained only in terms of its own existence, for its origin and, therefore, its reality are in the nature of things. Gemeinschaft as such exists among all organic beings, rational human Gemeinschaft among human beings. One distinguishes between animals which live together and those which do not, i.e., between social and unsocial animals. This distinction is correct, but the fact is overlooked that it refers only to different stages and types of collective life. Such difference exists, for instance, between the collective life of birds of passage and that of predatory animals. Furthermore, it is also forgotten that staying together is a natural phenomenon, while in every instance special reason has to be given for separation. This means that specific causes lead sooner or later to separation, to the dissolution of larger groups into smaller ones. But the larger group exists prior to the smaller one, as growth comes before procreation (which is conceived of as a superindividual growth). And each of these larger groups tends and is able to persist in spite of the division, the separated parts forming its members. Thus, it can still exert influence and act through its representative members.

If we, therefore, assume a scheme of development with lines radiating from a center into different directions, that center itself represents the unity of the whole. The whole, as will, is related to itself, and such will must, therefore, be present in that center in an eminent way. But new centers come into existence at points along the radii. The more energy they need to expand into this periphery and to maintain themselves, the more they will drain away from the former center. Consequently, this will necessarily become weaker and less able to exert influence in other directions, unless it can in turn derive energy from some original center.

But let us assume that the unity (unity and connection) is maintained and keeps its strength and tendency to express itself as a living entity in the relations of the primary center to the secondary centers directly derived therefrom. Each center (a separate identity) is represented by an entity or self which is recognized as the head in relation to its members. But as the head, it is not the whole. However, it becomes more similar to the whole if it assembles its subordinated centers as represented by their heads. They are, ideally, always present in the center from which they derive. Therefore, they fulfill their natural distinction or calling if they approach it corporally and assemble in one place. That will be necessary if circumstances demand concerted action for mutual aid within or without. Therein lies a power and authority which extends, by whatever means, over life and limb of all.

The possession of all goods is also primarily vested in the whole and its primary center, insofar as it is conceived as the whole. It is from there that the subordinate centers derive their possessions; they assert their right to them in a more positive way, by use and consumption. Other centers, still lower on the scale, also share in the process of derivation. In this way we arrive finally at the last unit, the family or the homestead (house) and its collective property, use, and consumption. Here the power wielded directly affects the individuals who alone, as ultimate units, can derive for themselves freedom and property therefrom. Every larger unit resembles a divided house. Even if this one is less perfect, it must be assumed to embody the rudiments of all organs and functions which the perfect organism comprises. The study of the home is the study of the Gemeinschaft, as the study of the organic cell is the study of life itself.

13. *Home Life—The Three Strata*

The essential features of home life have already been described, but, combined with new ones, will be set forth again here. The house consists of three strata, or spheres, which are grouped, so to speak, in concentric circles. The innermost sphere is the oldest: the master and mistress of the house and the other wives, if they all are of equal rank. The descendants follow in the next sphere, and they may remain in it even after their marriage. The servants, male and female, form the outermost circle. They represent, as it were, the newest stratum, accretions of more or less similar substance. They belong to the Gemeinschaft not as mere objects of compulsion but, in so far as they are assimilated by the common spirit and will, they acquiesce in it in contentment and of their own free will. Similar in kind is the relationship of the wives who have been brought to the group, to their husbands. Their children, who are a bond between them, represent, as descendants and dependents, an intermediate stage between master and servant.

Of these elements of the house, the servant group is the least indispensable. However, it provides the necessary form under which enemies or strangers may participate in the life of a house. This does not, however, hold for strangers who are deemed worthy to share as guests all the house can offer. Such sharing is, by its very nature, only temporary, but while it lasts it approximates a participation in the power and authority of the master, the more the guest is received with reverence and love. The less the guest is esteemed, the more this form of relationship approaches that of servitude. The status of the servant itself may become similar to that of the child, but it also can change into slavery if his treatment violates human dignity. A prejudice as deep as it is thoughtless considers servitude itself as a disgrace of humanity because it violates the principle of the equality of men. In reality, a human being, because of a servile demeanor caused either by fear, whether habitual or superstitious, or through calculation and appraisal of his own interest, can degrade himself in his manifold relations to another just as subordinates, even if formally under a free contract, can be oppressed and tortured by the arrogance and ruthlessness of a tyrannical or greedy master. Both phenomena are a likely though not necessary feature of servitude. If the constantly ill-treated person and the sycophant are morally slaves, in contrast the servant who shares the weal and woe of the family, who pays his master the respect of a grown son and who enjoys the confidence accorded to a helper or even an adviser, is morally, although not legally, a free person. The legal institution of slavery is wrong, because law aspires and ought to be something rational, and therefore demands that there be a distinction between person and thing, or the recognition of an intelligent being as a person.

14. *Household—Hearth and Board*

The organization of the house is primarily important from its economic aspect, i.e., as domestic economy and as community co-operating in work and consumption. The taking of food is repeated with the regularity of breathing; the production and preparation of food and beverages, therefore, is necessary and regular work. That labor is divided between the sexes has already been mentioned. While woods, meadows, and fields are the natural outer sphere, the hearth and its living fire are, as it were, the core and the very essence of the house, the place around which husband and wife, young and the old, master and servant, gather to share the meal. Thus, hearth fire and table attain symbolic significance—the former as the vital force of the house everlasting through the generations, the latter as the factor uniting the present members for the support and restoration of body and soul. The table is the house itself insofar as everyone has his place there and is given his proper share. Although in the interest of concerted work, the members of the house are separated and dispersed, they are reunited around the table for the necessary distribution of the fruits of their labor. And similar to this is the common and separate enjoyment of all other goods which have been produced by divided or common labor.

But real exchange (or barter) is contrary to the essential character of the house except as it takes place after the property division and as individuals are granted their share of independent property and of those things which everybody must produce for himself outside of the common production enterprise. The house, as an entity in itself, through its master or manager can change a surplus of its own products for more useful goods. Such exchange can take place regularly and within a community of houses, which is itself like a more comprehensive house (as for instance in the village, in the city, or between town and village within a province or the territory of a city-state). If, under these conditions, exchange is conducted peacefully and in accordance with rules which understanding can accept as just, then it must be conceived of simply as a form of regular distribution and, as it were, of participation in the feast at the table. It should be noted that this always remains the underlying idea of exchange and of simple commodity circulation, regardless of the extent to which it may be concealed. However, the phenomena involved in exchange may deviate so far from this original conception that, in order to comprehend fully these phenomena, it is necessary to take them by themselves and explain them from the needs and wills of the individuals.

15. *Town and Country as Complementary Poles —*
    Form of Exchange

Considering the real house in its physical aspects, three types can be distinguished:

(1) The detached house, i.e., the house which does not belong to a system of houses. In this category belongs the movable tent of the nomads. The detached house was also found in the age of agriculture in the form of the isolated farm dwelling, which is the type of housing characteristic and typical of mountainous regions and the marshes of the lowlands. In the same way the isolated farmhouse continued to exist as manor house or family seat outside and above the village, which was bound by custom to contribute services to the house as its creator and protector, so to speak.

(2) The peasant house in the village is the well-founded and, in a normal agricultural system, appropriate seat of a household which, for all its essential demands, is self-sufficient or can supplement its resources through the co-operation of its neighbors and assistance from communal helpers (as, for instance, the village blacksmith and other artisans). The peasant household can, however, encompass all these workshops in unbroken unity, if not under one roof, at least under one management. This is the type of the classical Greco-Roman house which is characterized by an authority on the subject (Rodbertus) with the following statement: *Nihil hic emitur, omnia domi gignuntur* (Nothing is bought, everything is produced in the house).

(3) The town house, which we think of primarily as the house of the master craftsman, is, on the contrary, dependent on exchange even for the necessities of life. What the master craftsman himself produces (for instance, shoes) is, largely, not for his own use. If the town as a whole is conceived of as a community of guilds which, through mutual co-operation, provides the houses of the burghers and thus itself with useful and beautiful things, it has, nevertheless, constantly to produce a surplus of goods in order to supply itself with the necessary foodstuffs from the neighboring farmhouses, unless the town itself or its burghers own and cultivate land.

Thus develops exchange of goods between town and country, which is most important for a general theory of the phenomena of culture. In this relationship the country, unless it needs tools and other implements of farming, enjoys the obvious advantage which rests with the possession of necessary rather than more dispensable goods. The town has the advantage of producing rare and beautiful goods, whereby it is assumed that in a large rural area only a select group of its population is concentrated in the town, and therefore the number of workers who produce surplus grains and meat are in the ratio of two to one to those who make objects of handicraft and art for purposes of exchange. It is, by the way, assumed that none of these is a professional trader who, in competition with others, tries his hardest to sell his goods, or that any of them is a monopolist who, in order to obtain the highest possible price, waits for the need of his customers to become more urgent and their offers in consequence more favorable. There are no doubt such possibilities, but they will materialize only to the degree that nonworking middlemen take hold of things.

The presumption seems justified that, in spite of the natural desire to keep one's own or to obtain the largest possible quantities of other people's goods, a brotherly spirit of give and take will remain alive in the relationship of town and country, which, outside of those barter activities, is fostered by manifold bonds of friendship and kinship, and for which shrines and meeting places provide the rallying points.

A similar relation is probably also maintained in the livelier exchange between town and town, although less favored with a collective spirit in so far as kinship, proximity, and the noncommercial character of rural people contribute to such. Furthermore, the higher functions of such a social body—i.e., those of animal and mental direction—can, if they form a whole, in no way be conceived as offering and selling of commodities. These functions are, on the contrary, organically maintained, fed, and fostered by a common will and thence by the forces at its disposal in the form of honorary gifts, fees, and compulsory services. The exchange of these for services, if those functions present themselves as such, is nothing but a form in which the mutual character of this relationship can express itself. But it is possible that, in the course of further development, such expression itself must be considered an adequate one. This adequacy may exist within the same limitation within which the ability and the ensuing desire to perform certain functions may be deemed equal to a commodity on the market.

16. *Analogy of the House—Manor—Conditions of Property*

In analogy to the house, village and town are considered the most clearly delimited formations of collective ownership and communal consumption. The clan is prior to the duality of house and village and has already been described as an antecedent of the family (family before the family), but can in the same way, although with less clarity, be conceived as an antecedent of the village (village before the village). This is because the clan comprises in itself these two main forms as potentialities. In the clan the patriarchal character (which stands for all authority based on procreation) is, therefore, as it were, mixed with the fraternal character (which is based on the equality of brothers and sisters). Likewise, the elements of authority on the one hand and fellowship among equals on the other are both inherent in the institutions of the clan. In the house community the former is prevalent, while in the village community the latter dominates. However, brotherly spirit is not lacking in the house any more than is paternal rule in the village. But the paternalistic principle alone, which is an important factor in a system of village organizations, is of significance for the conceptual theory of history, namely as the basis of feudalism. For in this principle, the belief in the natural dignity and authority of an eminent house as a noble and aristocratic one, lives on even after the roots of such belief wither away: It is the respect for old age and noble lineage which connects the chief of the clan in fact or fiction directly (by lineal descent) with the common ancestor of the whole clan and seems to guarantee him divine origin and, consequently, quite readily divine authority. But also for the sake of his leadership, honor and gratitude are accorded to the man of noble birth. Thus, it is quite natural that the first fruits of the fields and the first-born of the domestic animals are given as offerings to him. When, under his leadership, new land is occupied and divided up, it is also natural that before the allotting takes place the nearest and choicest plots of arable land are, by general consensus, added to his holding, first for alternate and finally for permanent possession. His share in the land is, moreover, often several times that of the other clansmen, or, if the clan has split up into several villages, the chief is given an equal share in each (that was the most common procedure in the German agricultural system). Thus, his house and his demesne remain in the middle of the village (or villages), or, in mountainous country, his castle towers above the village.

But the feudal lord acquires real power only when he, in the name of the community, performs functions, the results of which mainly serve his own interest. It follows therefrom that in the end these functions appear to be performed only in his own name. This has special bearing on the administration of the undistributed land, which is the more readily left to him the less useful and exhaustible it is. This holds, therefore, more for woodlands than for pasture, more for waste lands than for woodlands. Indeed, the waste lands are not even considered part of the communal fields; they belong to a higher unit (the district or the country) administered by the rulers of these same higher units and given as fiefs to the lesser barons. These barons settle their people on the part of the land which seems to ensure profitable cultivation. With population increasing, the baron, as knight of war or hunt, is able to gather around his manor an ever-growing following of retainers who, however, consume more than the hunter's bag and the spoils of war, together with tribute payments and the yields of the lord's own land, can provide. The retainers themselves become, therefore, peasants and cattle raisers and are furnished by the baron with implements, seed, and stock (from which the name "feod" is derived). Thus, they remain all the more closely bound to the lord of the manor and under obligation to render services for his demesne and follow his colors in case of war. They have property of their own. But unlike the property of the yeomen it is not derived from their own group, i.e., from the community, but from their relationship (Gemeinschaft) with their lord, and it remains at his disposal by a superior right of property wherein the subsequently separated ideas of feudal lordship and landed property have their common origin. Such seigniorial property belongs—by correct definition, i.e., one based on the nature of things and on tradition (concord, folkways, and mores)—to the Gemeinschaft, the community unit and the lord. Nevertheless, the latter may be given the opportunity or be tempted to consider these property rights as an exclusive prerogative of his own, especially when the less valuable parts of the land are concerned. This may in the end lead him to degrade the free landholders (yeomen), together with their dependents, to a status similar to that of his serfs and to change their property rights to mere rights of use (*dominium utile*). In need of protection and of alleviation of their duties to the higher organizations, the freeholders (yeomen) themselves may favor such development.

In the extreme case, the feudal lord has no longer relative, Gemeinschaft-like, and divided property, but his property appears to be absolute, individual, and exclusive. On the other side this results either in complete serfdom, if unlimited services and contributions are demanded, or in free contractual tenancy, if these are limited, though perhaps excessive. It is possible that with the employment of capital and the higher education of the tenant such tenancy can, in reality, develop into the exact opposite of serfdom. Under different conditions, however, it may mean nothing more than another name for and a new legal form of the same institution.

On the other hand, the dependence of all restricted or peasant property can be abolished by the will of the feudal lord himself or through the influence of legislation compelling him to forfeit rights. It will then be declared individual and absolute property in the same sense as the seigniorial property. In all these cases a definite separation, which is at first only of a legal nature, takes place. In reality, Gemeinschaft-like conditions may persist where they have existed before. But pressure and resistance, which correspond to domination on the one hand and dependence on the other, will also continue and be constantly renewed if domination can assert itself by virtue of the superiority of large over small landed property.

17. *Village Community and Common Land— Community as Household—Economic Communal Organization*

The great variety of these relationships, which become considerably modified if an ecclesiastic body, monastery, or other corporation takes the place of the feudal lord, cannot even be given in outline here. It is only important to note to what a great extent in the culture of the village and the feudal system, which is based upon it, the idea of a natural distribution, and of a sacred tradition which determines and rests upon this natural distribution, dominates all realities of life and all corresponding ideas of its right and necessary order, and how little significance and influence attach to the concepts of exchange and purchase, of contract and regulations. The relationship between community and feudal lords, and more especially that between the community and its members, is based not on contracts, but upon understanding, like that within the family. The village community, even where it encompasses also the feudal lord, is like one individual household in its necessary relation to the land. The common land is the object of its activity and care and is intended partly for the collective purposes of the unit itself, partly for the identical and related purposes of its members. The former purposes are more apparent in the case of common woodlands, the latter in the case of common pasture. But even the allotted fields and pastures belong to the individual family only for the period of cultivation; after the harvest the fences are torn down, the land is turned into pasture, and, as such, again becomes common land. Also during the individual usage, the villager is

...limited in many respects by the superior common right, as the rules and regulations of the common order bind him in the cultivation of his meadows, fields, and vineyards. In order that the individual peasant will hold to the traditional crop rotation, traditional planting and harvesting seasons, there is scarcely required an expressed regulation. This is because it is for him a factual and economic impossibility to emancipate his private economy, which cannot survive without being complemented or even created by the law of the Gemeinschaft, from the community economy. The detailed rules, especially those concerning the open and closed period of the fields and meadows, have mostly been fixed by ancient custom. If these are not sufficient or have to be changed, such change is made by community decision. The community, therefore, opens and closes the meadows and fields, determines the fields for winter and summer crops and for fallow, regulates the time for seeding and harvesting, regulates the grape picking, and later fixes even the wages for the harvest. It also exercises control in such a manner that the usual usage of the fields under common regulation is not changed arbitrarily, so that the Gemeinschaft of the fields would not be disturbed. ... In the laws of the entity are also rooted all the limitations and obligations of individual property in the field mark which are caused by the scattered location of the individual pieces of land. . . . Here also belongs, according to its origin, the whole of law concerning neighborhood relations, because this was more a result in the beginning of the common ties of the mark organization than of an individual modification of (absolute) ownership caused by the special title of a neighboring piece of land. (O. Gierke: *Das deutsche Genossenschaftsrecht, Zweiter Band: Geschichte des deutschen Korperschaftsbegriffs*, pp. 216-218)

An authority on Indian peasantry describes it as similar to the primitive institutions of the West, and the community as an organized, independent, and active being.

They, in fact, include a nearly complete establishment of occupations and trades for enabling them to continue their collective life without assistance from any person or body external to them. Besides the Headman or Council exercising quasi-judicial, quasi-legislative, power, they contain a village police, . . . They include several families of hereditary traders; the Blacksmith, the Harness-maker, the Shoemaker. The Brahmin is also found for the performance of ceremonies, and even the Dancing-Girl for attendance at festivities. There is invariably a Village-Accountant, ... the person practising any one of these hereditary employments is really a servant of the community as well as one of its component members. He is sometimes paid by an allowance in grain, more generally by the allotment to his family of a piece of cultivated land in hereditary possession. Whatever else he may demand for the wares he produces, is limited by a customary standard of price, very rarely departed from. It is the assignment of a definite lot in the cultivated area to particular trades, which allows us to suspect that the early Teutonic groups were similarly self-sufficing. (H. S. Maine, *Village-Communities in the East and West*, pp. 125 ff.)

This is confirmed in a description of the German mark:

According to the modern conception, to the extent that the common land was used also for payment and compensation for the directing supervisors, officials, and employees of the community, the purposes of this community were related to the common land. Sometimes special office fiefs were granted the community officials and employees out of the mark. Almost everywhere they were granted special usages of forests and pastures which had the character of remunerations. To this belonged, until they changed their character with the change of the office into a seigniorial right, the usage-privileges of officials, forest commissioners, forest judges, etc. The same was also true for the official usages or privileges of the village and peasant judges. Especially, however, the privileges of jurors, assessors, foresters, mill controllers, guardians of woods, bailiffs, herdsmen, and other communal officials, which are often expressly described and considered as a result of discharging of official duties which served the community, entailed the use of common land as compensation. The privileges of priests and teachers are often looked upon in a similar fashion. Finally, also the use of the common land, which was a privilege of the artisans who were permitted by the community or the lord to carry on their trades in the mark, was of similar character. The artisans were regarded as employees of the community, and were as such not only entitled, but also obliged to work exclusively or primarily for the community and its members; or they had to deliver a certain quantity of work as duties or at fixed prices. The uses of common property which were granted to them made handicraft possible and were regarded as compensation. They were a kind of payment. According to the way of thinking of the Gemeinschaft, that which we regard as the use of the common land for the payment of special services to the community, as such, is also regarded as a use of the common good for the immediate needs of everyone. Heads, officials, and servants, as well as employed artisans, are simply charged with a commission by the whole group, and useful to the community totally and individually. (O. Gierke, *op. cit.*, pp. 239 ff.)

They are comparable to organs of its body. The constitution of the group life is economic, which means that it is of the nature of Gemeinschaft (communal).

18. *The Town—Handicraft as Art—Art and Religion—Town and Trade*

According to the Aristotelian description and in conformity with the idea which underlies its natural phenomena, the town is a self-sufficient household, an organism with collective life. Whatever its empirical origin, the existing town must be regarded as a whole on which the individual fellowships and families constituting it are necessarily dependent. Thus, with its language, its customs, and its creed as well as with its land, its buildings, and its treasures, it represents something enduring which outlasts the sequence of generations and forever reproduces essentially the same intellectual attitude, partly from itself, partly through heredity and through the education of its burghers. It secures its foodstuffs and raw materials either from its own landed possessions, or from those of its citizens, or through regular purchases from the surrounding districts. In any case, it devotes its main strength to the more refined activities of the brain which, by giving to material objects a pleasing form in harmony with the collective spirit, represent the general essence of art. In its tendency and as determined by the style of the community and its estates (*Stände*), all urban handicraft is real art, although in some of its branches this tendency has only slight opportunity to materialize. As art, however, handicraft serves first of all the needs of the community: architecture for the town walls, towers, and gateways, for town halls and churches; sculpture and painting to decorate such buildings outside and inside, to retain and cultivate through images, statues, and portraits the memory of deities and eminent persons; in general, to bring the noble and eternal before the eyes of men. The especially close relationship between art and religion (as Goethe said, art is based on religious feeling) has its roots in the life of the house. Every original cult is bound up with the family and finds its most vigorous expression as a household cult, where in the beginning hearth and altar are one and the same. The cult itself is an art. What is done for the deceased and revered springs from a solemn and earnest mood and is performed in a thoughtful and measured manner fit to maintain or inspire this mood. Strict attention is given to pleasing and harmonious forms of speeches, performances and works, that is, to all that itself has rhythm and harmony or suits the quiet mood of those attending, as if they had created it themselves. All that is displeasing, without restraint, and contrary to tradition, is abhorred and rejected. It is true that what is honored by age or custom may very well hamper the striving for beauty in the cult, but that is only because for the pious mind and the tradition it is surrounded with a peculiar beauty and sanctity. In urban life, however, the attachment to tradition is diminished; the lust for creative work is predominant. In the same way the art of the spoken or written word recedes before the plastic arts, or it combines with and assimilates them.

Religion, which in its beginning is primarily given to a contemplation of death, attains a more cheerful relation to life as worship of the forces of nature. The joy over every renewed growth expresses itself in gigantic images or fantasies. The demons which, as ancestors, are only appeased subterraneous ghosts, are resurrected as gods and elevated to heaven. The town brings the gods nearer to its heart by creating their images for daily contemplation as was done with the laws of the household, which recede more and more into the background. At the same time the gods, brought down from heaven, as it were, and invested with a more spiritual significance, become examples of moral purity, excellence, and kindness; their priests become teachers and preachers of virtue. In this, the idea of religion finds its consummation. Such an element is all the more necessary the more varied and colorful urban life becomes, the more kinship and neighborhood as reasons for friendly feeling and action, and close friendship and mutual shame, lose their power or become limited to smaller groups. A much stronger stimulus is, in turn, given to art as a priestly practice. For what is good, noble, and, in that sense, holy, has to be sensually perceived in order to influence thought and conscience.

Handicraft and art are passed on by teaching and example, like a creed, as if they were a dogma and a religious mystery. They are, therefore, most easily preserved within the family, handed down to the sons, shared by the brothers. Thus, a fellowship may develop as a clan around the figure of an ancestor and inventor of their art. It upholds the common heritage and, as an integral part of the citizenry, represents an "office" of the urban community. The crafts, in their entirety constituting more and more the essential element of the town, in this way attain complete freedom and control of the community. The town is the protector of their collective peace and of the regulations in which such peace makes itself felt, within and without, as an organization of labor. These are sacred regulations of direct moral significance. The guild is a religious community, and such is the town itself. Accordingly, the economic existence of a perfect town, in either the Hellenic or the Germanic world, cannot be fully comprehended unless art as well as religion are taken as the highest and most important functions of the whole town and, consequently of its government, its estates, and its guilds. Art and religion exert influence and receive recognition as the meaning of the daily life in the functions of the town as standard and rule of thoughts and actions, order and law. The town (*polis*), says Plato (in *The Laws*), is like a real drama. To maintain itself in health and vigor is an art, just as the sensible and virtuous life of an individual is an art. For that reason, purchase and sale of commodities, together with the essential rights of storage and market, are for the town not the business of enterprising individuals but an undertaking of its own conducted either by itself or, in its name, by one of its offices. The town council sees to it that no goods which the town itself needs are exported, or harmful ones imported; the individual guild makes certain that the products sold by their masters are good and worthy of the guild. Church and clergy endeavor to avert the destructive effects of commerce and trade.

The indicated corporative character of the town is correctly considered by the economic historian from a purely commercial and political point of view. In this respect some striking statements of Schmoller *(Jahrbuch für Gesetzgebung,* etc. VIII, 1) confirm the theory as presented. In a significant manner he stresses "the dependence of the essential social-economic institutions at a given time on the most important political bodies." And in this connection he says, "The village is a closed economic and trade system in itself." (This could be extended to include the seigniorial estate and the convent in the Germanic culture area.) "Similar to the village-community and its organs, the town tends more to develop into an economic body with a strong life of its own, dominating everything individual . . . Each town, especially each larger town, attempts to isolate itself as an economic entity, but, at the same time, to extend its realm of economic and political domination as far as possible." And so on.

SECTION TWO: Theory of Gesellschaft

19. *The Fundamental Characteristic of the Gesellschaft,*
    a Negation—Equality of Value— the Objective Judgment

The theory of the Gesellschaft deals with the artificial construction of an aggregate of human beings which superficially resembles the Gemeinschaft insofar as the individuals live and dwell together peacefully. However, in the Gemeinschaft they remain essentially united in spite of all separating factors, whereas in the Gesellschaft they are essentially separated in spite of all uniting factors. In the Gesellschaft, as contrasted with the Gemeinschaft, we find no actions that can be derived from an a priori and necessarily existing unity; no actions, therefore, which manifest the will and the spirit of the unity even if performed by the individual; no actions which, insofar as they are performed by the individual, take place on behalf of those united with him. In the Gesellschaft such actions do not exist. On the contrary, here everybody is by himself and isolated, and there exists a condition of tension against all others. Their spheres of activity and power are sharply separated, so that everybody refuses to everyone else contact with and admittance to his sphere; i. e., intrusions are regarded as hostile acts. Such a negative attitude toward one another becomes the normal and always underlying relation of these power-endowed individuals, and it characterizes the Gesellschaft in the condition of rest; nobody wants to grant and produce anything for another individual, nor will he be inclined to give ungrudgingly to another individual, if it be not in exchange for a gift or labor equivalent that he considers at least equal to what he has given. It is even necessary that it be more desirable to him than what he could have kept himself; because he will be moved to give away a good only for the sake of receiving something that seems better to him. Inasmuch as each and every one is possessed of such will it is self-evident that for the individual "B" the object "a" may possibly be better than the object "b," and correspondingly, for the individual "A" the object "b" better than the object "a"; it is, however, only with reference to these relations that "a" is better than "b" and at the same time "b" is better than "a." This leads us to the question: with what meaning may one speak of the worth or of the value of things, independently of such relationships?

The answer runs as follows: in the concept presented here, all goods are conceived to be separate, as also are their owners. What somebody has and enjoys, he has and enjoys to the exclusion of all others. So, in reality, something that has a common value does not exist. Its existence may, however, be brought about through fiction on the part of the individuals, which means that they have to invent a common personality and his will, to whom this common value has to bear reference. Now, a manipulation of this kind must be warranted by a sufficient occasion. Such an occasion is given when we consider the simple action of the delivery of an object by one individual and its acceptance by another one. For then a contact takes place and there is brought into existence a common sphere which is desired by both individuals and lasts through the same length of time as does the "transaction." This period of time may be so small as to be negligible, but, on the other hand, it may also be extended indefinitely. At any rate, during this period the piece which is getting separated from the sphere of, for example, individual "A" has ceased to be under the exclusive dominion of "A" and has not yet begun to be entirely under the dominion of "B": It is still under the partial dominion of "A" and already under the partial dominion of "B." It is still dependent upon both individuals, provided that their wills with reference to it are in accord. This is, however, the case as long as the act of giving and receiving continues. During this time it is a common good and represents a social value. Now the will that is directed to this common good is combined and mutual and *can* also be regarded as homogeneous in that it keeps demanding from either individual the execution of the twofold act until it is entirely completed. This will *must*, however, be regarded as a unity inasmuch as it is conceived as a personality or inasmuch as a personality is assigned to it; for to conceive something as existing or as a thing is the same as conceiving it as a unity. There, however, we must be careful to discern whether and to what extent such an artificial being *(ens fictivum)* exists only in the theory, i.e., in scientific thinking, or whether and under which conditions it is also implanted in the thinking of the individuals who are its thinking agents. This last-mentioned possibility presupposes, of course, that the individuals are already capable of common willing and acting. For, again, it is quite a different proposition if they are imagined to be only participants in the authorship of something that is conceived as objective in the scientific sense because it is that which under given conditions "each and every one" is compelled to think.

Now, it is to be admitted that each act of giving and receiving implicitly includes a social will, in the way just indicated. These acts are, furthermore, not conceivable except in connection with their purpose or end, i.e., the receipt of the compensating gift. As, however, this latter act is conditioned in like manner, neither act can precede the other; they must concur. Or, expressing the same thought in other words, the acceptance equals the delivery of an accepted compensation. Thus, the exchange itself, considered as a united and single act, represents the content of the assumed social will. With regard to this will the exchanged goods are of equal value. This equality is the judgment of the will and is valid for both individuals, since they have passed it when their wills were in concord; hence it is binding only for the moment in which the act of exchange takes place or for the space of time during which it continues. In order that the judgment may even with this qualification become objective and universally valid, it must appear as a judgment passed by "each and every one." Hence, each and every one must have this single will; in other words, the will of the exchange becomes universal, i.e., each and every one becomes a participant in the single act and he confirms it; thus it becomes an absolute and public act. On the contrary, the Gesellschaft may deny this act and declare "a" is not equal to "b", but smaller than "b" or greater than "b", i.e., the objects are not being exchanged according to their true values. The true value is explained as that value which each and every one attributes to a thing that we thus regard as a general Gesellschaft-conditioned good. Hence, the true value is ascertained if there is nobody who estimates either object as higher or lower in terms of the other. Now, a general consensus of each and every one that is not accidental, but necessary, will be effected only with reference to what is sensible, right, and true. Since all individuals are thus of one mind we may imagine them as concentrated in the person of a measuring, weighing, and knowing judge who passes the objective judgment. This judgment must be recognizable by each and every one, and each and every one must conform to it inasmuch as they themselves are endowed with judgment and objective thinking, or, figuratively speaking, as they use the same yardstick or weigh with the same scales.

20. *Value as an Objective Quality—Quantities of Necessary Labor*

We are now confronted with the following question: What shall we consider to be the yardstick or balances in this procedure of deliberative comparing? We know the "quality" which is to be determined quantitatively by means of this constant tester, and we call it "value." Value must not, however, be identified with "worth," since worth is a quality which is perceived by the real individual. Moreover, the very difference of worth as it is sensed by real individuals, in relation to the same object, is the basis of a reasonable exchange. We, however, are concerned to find equality of value in objective judgment of different objects. In natural and naïve evaluation one takes things of the same category in order to compare them. The evaluation takes the form of a question, the answer to which consists of an affirmation or negation, in a stronger or lesser degree, according as the objects submit to the idea of such a comparison. In this sense we may establish a general category of serviceable things. Some may be considered as necessary, some as superfluous, some may be given prominence as very useful, and others rejected as very harmful. In this connection humanity would have to be pictured as a whole, or at least as a Gemeinschaft of human beings which—like the real individual—lives and therefore has needs; it has to be regarded as uniform in its will, so that it shares profit and loss (since the judgment is at the same time considered as a subjective one).

Now, if one asserts the equality of value of two exchanged objects, this does not at all mean that they are equally useful and necessary for an aggregate being. Otherwise the possibility of someone buying absolutely harmful things would have to be set up. But that would be monstrous and Utopian. One may assert on good grounds that a judgment is wrong when conditioned by desire, so that many a one acquires through exchange an object that is harmful to himself. But it is self-evident that the same liquor which is harmful to the workman is positively useful to the owner of the distillery, since he does not drink it but sells it. For a thing to be of any value in the Gesellschaft, it is only necessary that it be possessed by one party to the exclusion of another and that it be desired by one or another individual. Apart from this requirement all its other characteristics are insignificant. Saying that a thing has a certain value does not mean that it is endowed with an equal amount of usefulness. Value is an objective quality; as length is an objective quality for the senses of vision and of touch, and as weight for the muscular sense and the sense of touch, so value is an objective quality for the understanding that examines and comprehends social facts. This understanding takes note of and examines the objects as to whether they can be manufactured quickly, or whether they require much time;

as to whether they can be easily provided, or whether they require toil and drudgery. In other words, understanding analyzes the actuality of the objects by examining the possibility of their existence, and it then determines their probability. For determining value, the probability of existence is the only test, being subjective in regard to the sensible exchanging individual, and objective in regard to the Gesellschaft. This dictum in the first place carries only the following purport: if a sensible individual is confronted with objects being offered for sale, the thought comes (must come) to him that those objects naturally have a cost in order to be there at all, and particularly to be at that special place at that special time, be this cost represented by other objects against which they have been exchanged, or by labor, or by both items. However, the Gesellschaft, as it is an artificial being *(ens fictivum)* does not exchange anything, unless it be conceived of as an individual person, which here is quite out of the question. Therefore, since the exchange takes place only between human individuals, there is no being that could confront the Gesellschaft. From the viewpoint of the Gesellschaft the cost of the objects is, therefore, represented only by toil and labor. Robbery, as well as exchange, when considered as a means of acquiring objects, is based upon the assumption that goods already exist. Only producing, nurturing, creating, and fashioning labor is to be considered in this connection as the cause of the existence of things at a particular time. To this inherent labor can be added the extraneous labor of movement in space, as the cause of the existence of a given good at a particular place.

Things are considered as equal in so far as each object or each quantity of objects stands merely for a certain quantity of necessary labor. Thus, the Gesellschaft disregards the fact that some producers work faster or more productively than others, so that with greater skill or better tools the same objects can be produced with less labor. All such individual differences can be reduced to a common denominator. This process becomes all the more complete in the degree that the exchange of commodities becomes general or Gesellschaft-like. That is to say: each individual offers his commodity to everyone else, and all are capable of producing the same commodities, but everyone, through his own insight and free choice, confines himself to that commodity which presents the least difficulties to him. Thus, we exclude here the case of a work which is essentially Gemeinschaft-like but which is divided or divides itself up so that special arts are developed, inherited, and taught. But here we rather have in mind that each individual takes that piece of work which most closely approaches the price that the Gesellschaft attributes to it; that is to say, a piece of work which requires as little extra labor as possible. Thus, the Gesellschaft can be imagined to be in reality composed of such separate individuals all of whom are busy for the general Gesellschaft inasmuch as they seem to be active in their own interests and who are working for their own interests while they seem to be working for the Gesellschaft. As a consequence of repeated separate labor inputs and of indefinite exercise of free choice, the contribution of each may be reckoned in atomlike units which form an integrating part of the total labor of the Gesellschaft. By means of exchange each individual disposes of value not useful to him in order to acquire an equal value that he can use. The present investigation will show what relationship the real structure of the Gesellschaft bears to the concept presented here.

21. *The Commodity as Representing a Value— Value as Represented by a Commodity—Money —Paper Money*

If we now suppose that merely the exchange of commodities for commodities takes place in a continuous fashion, then we find that each individual manufacturer of commodities is entirely conditioned by and dependent upon all other manufacturers of commodities, since each individual's contribution would be a means of securing him a share of all other useful goods and also the replacement of his necessary means of production. (We take for granted here a different, not an equal, need of each individual for these goods.) This condition represents the dependence of the individual on the Gesellschaft; however, contained in it is also an element of superiority and control over the Gesellschaft. Accordingly, the individual faces the Gesellschaft either with a petition or with a command: The person with a petition is offering a commodity for exchange; the person with a command possesses something of value which can be used to purchase a commodity or commodities offered for exchange. To illustrate this, we suppose the existence of a commodity which by approval of each and every one, or, in other words, by the will of the Gesellschaft, is hallmarked as a general commodity. It is evident that this commodity will be desired unconditionally and thereby exercise a power over any other commodity which it, or rather its owner, may try to obtain in exchange for it. This commodity represents the abstract concept of value. By no means does this exclude its having value in itself, provided only that it is manageable and easily divisible and that the value is easily ascertainable. These and other well-known properties apply to the so-called precious metals. They are used to ascertain values and to fix them in relation to each other as current prices, and for this purpose they are as necessary as, for example, in physics a standard substance is necessary in terms of which weight and specific gravities of different bodies can be expressed. In their quality of being money, gold and silver do not belong to any individual but to the Gesellschaft *(I'argent n'a pas de maitre)*. In terms of quantities of these metals, it is the Gesellschaft, therefore, that fixes the market prices of the commodities, which can be moved upward and downward only within narrow limits by the individual desire of buyer and seller and by their bartering and bargaining. However, in a more abstract way than by any kind of "coinage," the conception of money may be manifested by a commodity without intrinsic value. A piece of paper, for example, marked with certain symbols, is such a commodity, to which not only its meaning but also its value is assigned solely by the Gesellschaft, and which is not to be used in any other way but for exchange in the Gesellschaft. Therefore, such money is desired by nobody for the sake of keeping it but by everybody with a view to getting rid of it. All the other things are good as long as and to the degree that they are useful and afford pleasure to their owner. However, this abstract thing, money, is good only as long as and in the measure to which it is attractive to those who do not possess it, by reason of their belief that by possessing it they will in their turn exercise the same attraction upon others. It must be admitted, though, that everything when considered as a commodity contains an element of this absence of worth and value, which we found to be characteristic of money; to a certain extent each commodity is money. The more it is like money, i. e., the more current it is, the better a commodity it is.

In the form of paper money, the Gesellschaft reproduces its own idea and circulates it by fixing a rate of exchange for it. This statement is valid inasmuch as the conception of value is inherent in the Gesellschaft and constitutes the necessary content of its will. For the Gesellschaft is merely abstract reason in which every reasonable being takes part in his idea—inasmuch as this abstract reason is conceived to be willing and acting. Abstract reason in a special investigation is scientific reason, and endowed with it is man who discerns objective relationships, i.e., who thinks abstractly. Scientific concepts are, with regard to their usual origin and to their objective quality, judgments by which complexes of perceptions are given a name. Consequently, scientific concepts assume the same position in a scientific system as commodities do in the Gesellschaft. In the scientific system they come together in much the same way as commodities do on the market. A supreme scientific concept that no longer denotes something real, e.g., the concept of the atom or the concept of energy, is similar to the concept of money.

22. Contract—Debt and Claim—Division of Ownership

The concord of will at each exchange, inasmuch as the exchange is regarded as taking place in the Gesellschaft, we call a contract. The contract is the resultant of two divergent individual wills, intersecting in one point. The contract lasts until the exchange has been completed, and it wills and demands the execution of the two acts of which it consists, each of which acts may be subdivided into a number of partial acts. Since the contract always deals with possible actions, it becomes meaningless and ceases to exist when such transactions either have been realized, or, on the other hand, have become impossible. We speak of the fulfillment or of a breach of the contract according to which of these two contingencies takes place. The individual will which enters into the contract refers either to a present and actual transaction, as, for example, the delivery of commodity or money, or to a future and possible transaction. This future transaction may appear in the form of a remaining part of a transaction which is regarded as present in its totality and which thus may consist in the delivery of the remainder of commodities or money. As a further alternative, the future transaction, inclusive of its beginning date, may be conceived as falling entirely within a period previous to a distant date (the due-date).

Under these conditions, the mere will *(der blosse Wille)* is being given and accepted either for the whole or for a part of the content of the contract. The mere will, it is true, may become evident also in other ways, but really perceptible only when transformed into the word. Thus, the word instead of an object is being given. For the recipient the word has the value of an object inasmuch as the connection of the word and the object is a necessary one, so that he is certain to obtain the object. The word is of no value as a "security," for it cannot be consumed nor can it be sold as a thing in itself. But it is equivalent to the surrender of the thing itself; i.e., the recipient has acquired the absolute right to the object, and this is all he can have by means of his own will, the actual power of which would form the natural basis of actual property. At the same time the recipient's right to the object is an outgrowth of the general will, i.e., of the will of the Gesellschaft. For the Gesellschaft is incapable of examining each case separately and, therefore, presumes that the delivery of a thing is a result of an exchange and in particular an exchange of equivalents. And this means that in the Gesellschaft, as rightly conceived, apart from the *de facto* condition of each individual, any exchange and any promise therewith is considered to be valid, that is, valid according to the will of each and every one. This means that any such promise is considered as rightful and therefore binding. However, the promise requires the consent of the receiver, for an object that belongs to him as a result of an exchange, an exchange being the only conceivable cause for this state of affairs, may only with his consent remain in the hands of the other individual. His consent may be interpreted as a promise not to tear away the object from the other, but to leave it to him until the day agreed upon.

The future delivery of an exchanged thing may be generally assumed to be the purport of every promise, but actually the promise results also in the present delivery of the object to the former owner to be his property for a limited time.

The will of the contract alone modifies this ownership, making the property a "debt" of the owner with regard to his "creditor" or a negative property because of the necessity to surrender the thing which is owed on a stipulated day. On the other hand, positive property in the conception of the Gesellschaft would be the absolute and unrestricted liberty to dispose of one's property over an unlimited period of time, and with no limit in regard to any other person. The debit also represents real property with regard to a third person even after the term expires. The abstract protection of property in legal systems of the Gesellschaft is herein founded. Until the due-day arrives, the holder keeps the thing as real property, even with reference to the creditor. That means that the only limitation, or rather negation, of his proprietorial right arises with reference to the creditor and from the necessity of "payment." Likewise, the proprietorial right of the creditor on the same object is until then denied, with all consequences, by cession to the debtor, and only after the due-day is it absolute with reference to anyone else. With only this modification it is called "outstanding debt" with reference to the debtor, and is connected with the right or liberty which may demand him to deliver after date of expiration. In the meantime, therefore, it is common and shared property in that the total right of ownership appertains to the creditor, with exception of the temporary right of use which belongs to the debtor.

23. Credit—Money Substitute—Private Money—
Obligation—Paradox of Society

In such a special contract, it is obvious that the receiver who "gives the credit" is as active as the promisee who "takes the credit." The sale of commodities for credit (given), a transaction which developed from exchange of commodity for commodity and the sale of commodities for money is, however, the normal case. Through the factor of credit this transaction is like lending, which, in its developed form, exists in the sale of money for credit. Credit is the postponed payment which is often abolished by counterclaims and is a great facilitation in settling payments. The promise fulfills, temporarily or permanently, the function of money. It is a money substitute. Therefore, the more it is supported by solvency or by counterclaims of the debtor and the more it can serve the receiver as does money, as means of buying and as means of payment, the more perfect it is. For giver as well as receiver it possesses the money value, for which it is accepted. Therefore, through such fictitious or imaginative value, which is based on joined rational will, it corresponds sufficiently to the idea of money. Absolute paper money is accepted by everyone for every commodity at the same value (because everyone is certain to receive in return an equal value of a chosen commodity). A "bill of exchange" or similar paper is, by way of comparison, valid only because and as long as the receiver is certain to be able to pass it on to another individual or return it to the giver (issuer) for the value of a particular good, for instance, gold. It is private money, which the Gesellschaft guarantees inasmuch as it supports the holder in his demands against the debtor or his "guarantors." The actual paper money, being issued by a person who in a limited territory represents Gesellschaft itself (as, for instance, the state or its bank), takes an intermediary position between such private paper money and the theoretical absolute public money, for which nobody would be responsible because all desire and want it, as is true in reality for money as general means of payment (in whatever form it may take).

More clearly than ever, the true nature of the Gesellschaft manifests itself when money is sold for credit, since both parties desire only money and have no other need. The "obligation" as it is given in return for a received loan becomes a special kind of commodity itself, which at varying prices can pass from hand to hand. He who acquires the obligation in order to keep and use it does not want anything from it except to receive the periodically due payments, the "interest" to which he has a legal claim. This is true even if the return of the "principal" has not been promised at a particular date. In this latter case the repayment is not really his aim, as he wants to preserve his claim as a constant source of renewed payments by the contracting party. Thus, his demand is merely an idea represented by a scrap of paper, as is also the case with absolute money; it is the absolute commodity, a commodity in perfection. It does not become timeworn or antiquated like a defunct tool or even like a useless piece of art designed for eternity; on the contrary, it remains in reality always young and a living source, as it were, of regularly repeated equal quantities of enjoyment.

An ancient philosopher has made the statement, which has been for a long time authoritative, that money does not beget. The statement is correct. Money is power, but never power of its own immediate reproduction. Whatsoever is given for it requires that it must leave the hand of its owner in order that this something be obtained. It grants nobody a right. In relation to money everyone is free and independent. The obligation, on the other hand, is absolutely legal power. For it is impossible in the world of facts to have in hand the future payment of someone else. It is only legally possible. The exchange of money for a good is a real process, even if it can be explained only through Gesellschaft. But to receive money payments because of the possession of a commodity (for this is the nature of obligation) without delivering it, is a transcendental condition in the Gesellschaft. For, in contradistinction to the concept of Gesellschaft, a bond has been created, uniting not objects but persons. This relation already appeared as a momentary one in the simple act of exchange, whereas here it is conceived as of indefinite duration. In the act of exchange the reaction was that of mutual balance; here it appears as a one-sided dependence.

24. *Activity as Object of a Promise—Power to Enforce it*
    —Relation—Natural Law— Convention

In every exchange, the place of a perceivable object can be taken by an activity. The activity itself is given and received. It must be useful or agreeable to the receiver as a commodity. This activity is thought of as a commodity, the production and consumption of which coincide in time. Although the performance which is not given but only promised may be contrasted with the thing which is not given and only promised, the result in both cases is similar. It belongs to the receiver legally; after the term expires he can force the promising party legally to perform the activity promised, just as he could legally force the debtor to give that which is owed or have it taken with force. A performance which is owed can be acquired only by force. The promise of a performance can as well be mutual as one-sided; therefore, resulting rights to coercion can also be mutual or one-sided, as the case may be. In this respect, several people can bind themselves for a certain equal activity in such a manner that everyone uses the performance of the other as an aid to himself. Finally, several people can agree to regard their association as an existing and independent being of the same individual nature as they are themselves, and to grant this fictitious person a special will and the capacity to act and therefore to make contracts and to incur obligations. Like all other things related to contracts, this so-called person is to be conceived as objective and real only insofar as the Gesellschaft seems to co-operate with it and to confirm its existence. Only in this way is this so-called person a thinking agent of the legal order of the Gesellschaft, and it is called a society, an association or special-interest group, a corporation, or any such name. The natural content of such an order can be comprised in the one formula: *"Pacta esse observanda"*—contracts must be executed. This includes the presupposition of a condition of separate realms or spheres of will so that an accepted and consequently legal change of each sphere can take place by contract in favor or in disfavor of spheres which are outside the system, or within the system. This means that the agreement of all is involved. Such concurrence of wills is according to its nature momentarily punctual so that the change, as creation of a new situation, does not have to have a duration in time. This necessitates no modification of the most important rule, that everyone can do legally within his realm that which he wishes, but nothing outside. If, however, a common realm originates, as might be the case in a lasting obligation and in an organization, freedom itself, as the total of rights to act freely, must be divided and altered or a new artificial or fictitious form of freedom created. The simple form of the general will of the Gesellschaft, insofar as it postulates this law of nature, I call *convention*. Positive definitions and regulations of all kinds, which according to their origin are of a very different style, can be recognized as conventional, so that convention is often understood as a synonym for tradition and custom. But what springs from tradition and custom or the folkways and mores is conventional only insofar as it is wanted and maintained for its general use, and insofar as the general use is maintained by the individual for his use. Convention is not, as in the case of tradition, kept as sacred inheritance of the ancestors. Consequently, the words tradition, customs, or folkways and mores are not adequate to convey the meaning of "convention."

25. *Bourgeois Society (bürgerliche Gesellschaft)—*
    Everyone a Merchant—Universal Competition
    —Gesellschaft in a Moral Sense

Gesellschaft, an aggregate by convention and law of nature, is to be understood as a multitude of natural and artificial individuals, the wills, and spheres of whom are in many relations with and to one another, and remain nevertheless independent of one another and devoid of mutual familiar relationships. This gives us the general description of "bourgeois society" or "exchange Gesellschaft," the nature and movements of which legislative economy attempts to understand; a condition in which, according to the expression of Adam Smith, "Every man ... becomes in some measure a merchant, ..." Where merchants, companies, or firms or associations deal with one another in international or national markets and exchanges, the nature of the Gesellschaft is erected as in a concave mirror or as in an extract.

The generality of this situation is by no means, as the famous Scotchman imagined, the immediate or even probable result of the innovation that labor is divided and products exchanged. It is more a remote goal with respect to which the development of the Gesellschaft must be understood. To the extent that this goal is realized, the existence of a Gesellschaft in the sense that it is used here is real at a given time. It is something in the process of becoming, something which should be conceived here as personality of the general will or the general reason, and at the same time (as we know) it is fictitious and nominal. It is like an emanation, as if it had emerged from the heads of the persons in whom it rests, who join hands eagerly to exchange across all distances, limits, and scruples, and establish this speculative Utopia as the only country, the only city, in which all fortune seekers and all merchant adventurers have a really common interest. As the fiction of money is represented by metal or paper, it is represented by the entire globe, or by a circumscribed territory.

In the conception of Gesellschaft, the original or natural relations of human beings to each other must be excluded. The possibility of a relation in the Gesellschaft assumes no more than a multitude of mere persons who are capable of delivering something, and consequently of promising something. Gesellschaft as a totality to which a system of conventional rules applies is limitless; it constantly breaks through its chance and real boundaries. In Gesellschaft every person strives for that which is to his own advantage and he affirms the actions of others only insofar as and as long as they can further his interest. Before and outside of convention and also before and outside of each special contract, the relation of all to all may therefore be conceived as potential hostility or latent war. Against this condition, all agreements of the will stand out as so many treaties and peace pacts. This conception is the only one which does justice to all facts of business and trade where all rights and duties can be reduced to mere value and definitions of ability to deliver. Every theory of pure private law or law of nature understood as pertaining to the Gesellschaft has to be considered as being based upon this conception. Buyer and seller in their manifold types stand in relation one to the other in such a manner that each one, for as little of his own wealth as possible, desires and attempts to obtain as much of the wealth of others as possible. The real commercial and business people race with each other on many sprinting tracks, as it were, trying each to get the better of the other and to be the first to reach the goal: the sale of their goods and of as large a quantity as possible. Thus, they are forced to crowd each other out or to trip each other up. The loss of one is the profit of the other, and this is the case in every individual exchange, unless owners exchange goods of actually equal value. This constitutes general competition which takes place in so many other spheres, but is nowhere so evident and so much in the consciousness of people as in trade, to which, consequently, the conception is limited in its common use. Competition has been described by many pessimists as an illustration of the war of all against all, which a famous thinker has conceived as the natural state of mankind.

However, even competition carries within it, as do all forms of such war, the possibility of being ended. Even enemies like these— although among these it may be the least likely—recognize that under certain conditions it is to their advantage to agree and to spare each other. They may even unite themselves together for a common purpose (or also—and this is the most likely—against a common enemy). Thus, competition is limited and abolished by coalition.

In analogy to this situation, based upon the exchange of material goods, all conventional society life, in the narrower sense of the word, can be understood. Its supreme rule is politeness. It consists of an exchange of words and courtesies in which everyone seems to be present for the good of everyone else and everyone seems to consider everyone else as his equal, whereas in reality everyone is thinking of himself and trying to bring to the fore his importance and advantages in competition with the others. For everything pleasant which someone does for someone else, he expects, even demands, at least an equivalent. He weighs exactly his services, flatteries, presents, and so on, to determine whether they will bring about the desired result. Formless contracts are made continuously, as it were, and constantly many are pushed aside in the race by the few fortunate and powerful ones.

Since all relations in the Gesellschaft are based upon comparison of possible and offered services, it is evident that the relations with visible, material matters have preference, and that mere activities and words form the foundation for such relationships only in an unreal way. In contrast to this, Gemeinschaft as a bond of "blood" is in the first place a physical relation, therefore expressing itself in deeds and words. Here, the common relation to the material objects is of a secondary nature, and such objects are not exchanged as often as they are used and possessed in common. Furthermore, Gesellschaft, in the sense which we may call moral, is also entirely dependent upon its relations with the state, which has not entered our theory so far because the economic Gesellschaft must be considered prior to it.

26. *Advance of the Gesellschaft—World Market— Capital*

If, confining our attention to the economic sphere, we consider the advance of the Gesellschaft which takes place as the final culmination of the developed Gemeinschaft-like folk life, there stands out the transition from general home (or household) economy to general trade economy, or the transition from the predominance of agriculture to the predominance of industry. This development can be conceived as if it had been planfully carried out in such a way that, with increasing success within every nation, the traders as capitalists and the capitalists as traders force themselves to the front and seem to unite for a common purpose. This purpose can be expressed best through the word "trade" *(Verkehr)*.

The head of a household, a peasant or burgher, turns his attention inwardly toward the center of the locality, the Gemeinschaft, to which he belongs; whereas the trading class lends its attention to the outside world; it is concerned only with the roads which connect towns and with the means of transit. This class seems to reside in the center of every such locality, which it tends to penetrate and revolutionize. The whole country is nothing but a market in which to purchase and sell. In the case of domestic trade, it functions alternatingly through absorption and contraction as systole, and through expulsion and expansion as diastole. With foreign trade, this process permits the discharging of superfluous goods and the acceptance of goods which are needed. Each country can develop into such a trading area. The more extensive the area, the more completely it becomes an area of the Gesellschaft, for the more widespread and freer trade becomes. Also, the more extensive the trade area, the more probable it is that the pure laws of exchange trade prevail and that those other noncommercial qualities which relate men and things may be ignored. Trade tends, finally, to concentrate in one main market, the world market, upon which all other markets become dependent. The larger the area, the more evident the truth becomes that the leaders and creators of trade do everything that they do for the sake of their own profit. They put themselves into the center of this area, and from their point of view the land and labor of the country, like those of all other countries with which they deal, are actual or possible objects for investment and circulation of their capital, which is for them a means for augmenting their capital. In addition, the more the directors of actual work and production, as owners of the soil and other material factors and also as owners of laborers or purchased labor, conduct their business solely with a view to profit or increased value, the nearer they themselves come to being a mere group of traders. Their activities resemble, and are on the same level with, those characteristics of the sphere of commerce, sharing many of its interests but standing opposed to some of them. Both groups, producers and tradesmen, are the amassers of liquid, movable wealth, which, increasing constantly through its use for productive or commercial purposes, is called capital. Capital demonstrates its nature, however, in the first place as the trader plays the game of taking the risk and making the sacrifice necessary for investment by buying in a cheap market in an effort to sell in a higher one.

Each seller who offers products of his own labor for sale can be considered as a trader in so far as he conducts himself as such and calculates the relation between the price he obtains and the disbursements. However, he will regard the difference as the equivalent of his activity which, in reality, produced new value. Inasmuch as this equivalent is real and valid, he did not take more from the same market than he gave. If mutual exchange would take place only between such sellers (as is supposed in the concept of a developed Gemeinschaft), it could in reality be regarded as Gesellschaft-like trade in so far as each one might strive for a limitless domain, to obtain the highest possible prices. The final result of such effort, however, is its elimination through other tendencies, notwithstanding the fact that some individual seller may actually get the better of another. (The more everyone learns to act as a trader the less one is apt to get the advantage of another. In this sense it has been said that bourgeois Gesellschaft society requires everyone to have an encyclopedic knowledge of goods.—K. Marx, *Kapital I*, Ch. 1, footnote.)

27. *Position of the Merchant—Credit and*
    Commerce—Organic Concept

All creative, formative, and contributive activity of man is akin to art and, as it were, an organic process by which human will flows into the alien matter and gives form to it. Where such activity serves to maintain, further, or give joy to a Gemeinschaft, as is the case in natural and original relationships, it can be conceived of as a function of this Gemeinschaft; it is as if the Gemeinschaft itself through the agency of the individual producer (or an individual group of producers) would want to afford itself this enjoyment. Commerce, as the skill to make profits, is the opposite of all such art. Profit is not value; it means only a change in the proportions of wealth, and the gain of one is the loss of the other. *("Le proufict de l'un c'est le dommage d'aultruy."*—Montaigne.) The appropriation is merely an act of occupation; in so far as damage is thereby inflicted on others, it is predatory. It is not labor which transforms into goods (or objects of use) that which existed previously only as natural matter or which at least did not have such good quality. The activities which commerce performs on these objects are essentially nothing but demand, appropriation, supply, and delivery—that is, merely activities which leave the nature of the things unchanged. This is true even though some labor may be added by the same agency, namely, commerce.

On the other hand, the merchant, by seeing a tangible and neverthe-less abstract advantage as the real and rational purpose of his activity apart from this activity itself, is, in this sense, the first thinking and free human being to appear in the normal development of social life. He is, as much as possible, isolated from all necessary relationships, duties, and prejudices. ("A merchant, it has been said very properly, is not necessarily the citizen of any particular country,"—Adam Smith, *Wealth of Nations*, Bk. Ill, Ch. 4; a statement which should be compared with the aforementioned remark of the same author to the effect that exchange and barter tend to make every human being a merchant.) He is free from the ties of the life of the Gemeinschaft; the freer he is from them, the better for him. Before him, with him and his like, is, in the first place, the creditor. The difference between them is evident: The creditor deals with one and the same contracting party to whom he gives something to receive more in return. He himself acquires nothing but a claim, that is, a right which is given to him through the promise of the debtor. With this he obtains a possible right of coercion against the debtor or (at least) the right to keep or take a thing as his own which the debtor by way of reinforcement of the claim gave as security, either in reality or symbolically.

This has already been represented as the typical case of a contract which creates an obligation effective in time. The condition that actu-ally is more promised than given does not constitute an essential ele-ment of the concept of obligation. It is, however, essential to the barter underlying the obligation, inasmuch as there is a party to it who is inter-ested in the expiration of the obligation as the ultimate purpose of the barter. This party has deliberately given present goods in exchange for more at a future date. And therein the creditor resembles the merchant: as long as a loan is only a kind of assistance and interest is asked only as a compensation (for *lucrum cessans* or *damnum emergens*—loss of gain or damage suffered) profit is not thought of as the decisive motive. The merchant, on the contrary, is by definition acting deliberately and rationally, and profit is the necessary and exclusive motive of his ac-tions. He acts, however, without recourse to coercion and without any of the ruthlessness which may bring the creditor into disrepute as a usurer. The merchant uses peaceful agreement; he deals as buyer with one person, as seller with another and perhaps distant one. Obligations are not necessary, although they are possible and probable. They make the merchant himself a debtor or creditor, or both at the same time. The creditor, however, develops into a kind of merchant as soon as he conducts his business systematically and for profit. The obligation, in the form of the draft, becomes itself a transferable commodity which can be brought up for the purpose of sale, and the consumption of which takes place through its final sale as its realization. In this way the credit system develops as a side line of regular commerce.

If the merchants are intermediaries of exchange, the bankers are intermediaries of intermediation. In reality, however, it is an essential characteristic of both types (whatever services they may render each other as well as third parties) that they do not act on behalf and under the instructions of anybody, but entirely of their own free will and on their own risk, as free and independent powers whose every action is a calculated means to their own rationally defined ends. Nevertheless, in so far as these activities may directly or indirectly aid a need already existing at two (or more) different points, they can indeed be considered secondary functions of an organism encompassing both of them, provided such organisms can be conceived of as actually existing. Consequently, the whole trade, the merchant class (estate) if not the individual merchant, can be thought of as such an organism which has been created from the Gemeinschaft-like will and life. But where there is no Gemeinschaft, there is no organ of intermediation. However, if considered only from one side, such an organ may present itself as an organ of favorable sales; or it can, on the other side, be used and assimilated as an organ of supply. Both these functions are legitimate only on condition that the turnover in reality benefits such totality through the transformation of less useful into more useful value. A further condition is that the remuneration of such organ (although derived in the form of a regular profit) be adequate for that value which its activities can be justly estimated to have for the whole (thereby a higher profit is not precluded, if made at the expense of outsiders).

28. A Contradiction—the Lords of the Gesellschaft— Slavery—Slaves as Subjects?

In reality, however, there remains a contradiction which calls for a reversal of all these relationships: While the seller, in general, offers the product of his own labor as a real commodity, finally seeking other real commodities as its equivalent, it is characteristic of both the merchant and the moneylender to hold a commodity which they have not produced themselves, i.e., money, which is by definition a purely abstract commodity although, as a rule, representing the real commodity of coined metal. Money embodies only the abstract quality of all commodities to buy other commodities, the power of a lever or a weight which cannot be produced but only collected. And thus to collect money is the merchant's sole aim. He buys money with money, although through the medium of commodities; the moneylender does so even without this intermediary. That is in contradistinction to the characteristic of noncommercial loans given for the sake of kindness and friendship or of sales at purchase price which become sometimes necessary in the interest of a negative profit, i.e., to avoid losses. But the merchant and the usurers, both of whom are proficient in their trade, want regularly to obtain a larger quantity by the transfer of a smaller one. They want to make a profit. The degree to which they succeed is dependent upon the extent to which they benefit from the existing differences in time and place. They are thus able to increase their money holdings or their wealth beyond measure, especially by shrewdly exploiting these and other favorable circumstances. This is in contrast to the producers who market the returns of their own labor to change them into a more dura-ble or agreeable form, i.e., one better suited to consumption or storage, although the monetary form is often preferred, where possible, as em-bodying complete freedom of choice and of allocation for future use. As a matter of fact, there is, then, always a possibility of such utilization of these funds as will allow money to increase by itself. If such an in-crease is conceived and stipulated as an absolute end, the choice can be only between usury and commerce, as the simplest and easiest methods of attaining this goal. But even though there be no lack of desires and attempts, nevertheless, opportunity for, and means of participating in, such activities are bound up with many special conditions.

In contradistinction, the increase of money as the return from labor is limited by material and instruments as well as the skill and profi-ciency of the worker. Such return, even in the form of money, can justly be considered as the natural wage and price which the "people" *(Volk)* (or whatever name is given to this concept of Gemeinschaft) pay their workers for the support of their present and future life. In reality it consists of food, shelter, clothing, and a variety of useful and pleasant things. But the people, thought of in this sense, i.e., as a *Volk,* would be out of their senses if they gave a servant, however valuable and exceptional, a large sum of money for buying commodities from them which they in turn had to repurchase from him for a larger sum. For this reason those observations about the specific reality called "Gesellschaft" are inadequate. The merchants or capitalists (the owners of money which can be increased by double exchange) are the natural masters and rulers of the Gesellschaft. The Gesellschaft exists for their sake. It is their tool. All noncapitalists within the Gesellschaft are either them-selves like inanimate tools—that is, the perfect concept of slavery—or they are legally nonentities, i.e., they are considered incapable of free will and consequently incapable of action under the existing system of contracts. Hereby the concept of hierarchy of control as the opposite principle of this slavery would find its clearest expression. But at the same time it would mean a denial of the concept of (general, human) Gesellschaft. Between master and slaves no relationship of Gesellschaft and, consequently, no relationship at all, would exist.

The other alternative is the assumption that the slaves are persons, personalities of free will and as such capable of transacting barter and entering into contracts. They are, therefore, individuals of Gesellschaft itself and of its conventions. According to the conception of natural law characteristic of Gesellschaft all human beings as rational persons and free agents are, a priori, equal. Everybody represents and possesses a certain power and freedom and his sphere of rational will. Everybody can kill his fellow men, if he deems it wise. Everybody can appropriate and use derelicts and defend them against attack. Everyone can, if he has material and tools, produce new things and acquire ownership in them by his own labor. And, thus, everybody can transform his activity into a commodity to sell. He can also make the object of a promise, i.e., a contract. The recognition of these general and necessary qualities as inherent in every adult human being makes legal slavery an absurdity and abolishes it.

29. *Labor—Purchase and Resale*

To the extent that the free workers, as we may call the entire group, become deprived of property—as the possession of working tools and consumption goods—the natural rule of free merchants and capitalists over workers in the Gesellschaft is realized and becomes actual domination, in spite of the latter's freedom. They become mere possessors of working power ("hands") who are forced by circumstances (i.e., the impossibility of living otherwise) and, are, therefore, waiting to sell their labor for money. This selling for money makes them nominally a kind of merchant; they offer their specific commodity and, like all other sellers, exchange it for the general commodity. This commodity may be disposed of at will, which may entail spending and saving. This also includes the logical possibility of increasing the commodity through usury and commerce. This temporary property in money makes workers potential capitalists. To what extent they may really become capitalists is beyond the scope of this discussion. In any case, it is only a secondary characteristic which has nothing to do with the concept of a worker. But the possibility of becoming temporary money-owners is essential for this concept. The necessity of transforming money into consumption goods, however, limits that trade to the exchange of labor for (by presupposition) the needed consumption goods. Such trade is, therefore, no real trade, but merely exchange, although carried out in two successive stages. It is contrasted with the nature of real trade, i.e., trade for profit. In the latter case, labor is a commodity purchased for the sole purpose of resale. Such resale can take place directly by simple transfer. Then such trade is like all the other types, however specific the type of commodity may be. For the commodity labor is distinguished from all others by the fact that it can be consumed only by application to and in co-ordination with given implements of production (materials and tools), through which they are transformed into pleasant or useful things, consumption and production goods, i.e., generally speaking, into objects of use. The specific trade in the commodity labor is therefore determined by its consumption and requires its resale in the form of consumption goods which, besides labor, also contain parts of the implements of production or of their forces. The sale of finished consumption goods is essentially the same as the sale of labor. Although in the first case the money obtained may have a different significance, it means primarily nothing but the possibility of retransformation into other consumption goods. In contrast to the purchase, the sale is never conceived as being carried out for the sake of future profitable resale (of the money). The sources of commercial profits in general are not to be discussed here. Its condition is the preservation of the commodity. Divided up or increased or changed in character or appearance, the commodity must never be consumed, never be used up. The commodity labor has to be consumed; it must, so to speak, perish that it may be resurrected in the forms of goods.

30. *Other Economic Enterprises Compared with Commerce*

Usury, the first act of which is to advance money for any arbitrary use, is clearly distinguished from commerce. In the case of usury, the passive contracting party—insofar as he, in spite of his formal freedom, is compelled to buy goods for his consumption or the tools for his work with "alien brass"—can be brought into material dependence as debtor. Thus, his possession of these goods is counterbalanced by what might be called a negative wealth of principal and interest for which he is indebted. But, in its effects, usury comes close to the renting of land, houses, and apartments if done on a business basis. Here, too, the tenant can, by virtue of his obligation to transfer the goods after the expiration of the contract and to pay rent, be considered a negative owner of these things. But, in contradistinction, the principal element, i.e., the capital, is preserved in its reality and cannot in any way be substituted. For this reason, in this aspect, landlordism, is not, like usury, akin to commerce. In both usury and commerce, capital is risked, although the former receives a promise on a claim (obligation, draft, and perhaps in addition a security or a lien, i.e., property rights in an object that would cover the loss of capital), while the latter acquires commodities with it. Money disappears in circulation, land does not disappear—the peasant can always tread upon it with his feet and feel it with his hands. In this respect, landlordism is a very unreal kind of trade. Land must first by a mental process be transformed into money or money equivalent; it is then considered nothing but a means, and the rent becomes an end in itself, just as capital is only the means of the moneylender and the merchant, interest or profit their ultimate purpose. However, in this case it should be said that money is treated according to its nature—because as money it is chiefly means by which consumption goods are obtained, rather than a means of obtaining money again in an increased quantity. Land that is not to be used as money, might be used. Land is of substantial reality, playing an important conditioning role in man's life. It marks great progress in thinking, however, when the individual and society begin to handle land as a special kind of property and capital.

The painful effect of the rule of commerce is surpassed by the direct personal pressure which a creditor can exert upon the debtor. However, well-known historical facts show that, possibly, the landlord and his agent are no less hostile to the tenant, ruthlessly collecting rent and mercilessly driving him from home and land. The merchant can as buyer or seller, cheat his customers; as a professional profit maker he is often strongly tempted and has ample opportunity to do so, and he very often possesses an acquired or inherited cleverness, an inclination and the necessary unscrupulousness for such action. But there are single, unrelated acts against the repetition of which a person aware and warned may well protect himself and which, moreover, calculating cleverness (especially in dealings of merchants among themselves) will itself prohibit.

No dependence, no claim, no right or coercion, which would make the merchant master of other persons' activities, will, in fact, result from such actions. But the creditor and the landlord possess such claims and rights and therewith the opportunity to have their debtors work directly for them and to exploit them. And the same is true of the merchant who advances an artisan materials or tools or both. Inasmuch as these represent the basis of any labor, the merchant is comparable to the landlord. But he decidedly differs from him in that he does not leave the worker to himself to draw a rent from his money returns. He himself wants to acquire the products of labor in kind. This acquisition takes the form of a purchase, but it is better called an appropriation because the merchant fixes the price, the artisan being his debtor and therefore dependent on him. It is not a new contract of exchange but the results of the former one, which, for that reason, amounts, in reality, to a sale of the commodity to be produced, i.e., to a sale of labor. Thereby the merchant must appear as the owner of such labor and consequently as the formal producer of the goods. That is also the case with the landlord (unless he is a capitalist entrepreneur) in a system that forces his tenants by contract to work in the fields of his demesne and thus to make him the owner of salable products. Insofar as the tenants work for themselves, the landlord can only, in the worst case, be an overlord who extracts from them not goods but money. This looks like an exchange of roles. Money rent is in its origin always rent in kind and does not result from a contractual relationship. The landlord (unless he is a real capitalist on the side), too, is concerned with sums of money primarily because they represent for him a number of goods and satisfactions. For the merchant, the goods which he produces represent a sum of money and this, in turn, means for him primarily an opportunity and a means for its own increase.

31. *Trade Developed from the Workshop—Machinery— the Phases of Industry—Agriculture or Industry*

The concept of the merchant turning industrialist reveals the first method by which commerce lodges itself in the process of production. But side by side with it runs another process through which the principle of trade grows out of the workshop of the independent artisan. If such a workshop works to the order of and for the actual needs of its customers who, living in the neighborhood, can dispense with any intermediary, it can, nevertheless, begin to produce for stock and to look for sale in distant markets. The greater the success of such enterprise, the greater the temptation for the master to gather in his house, instead of a naturally or legally limited number of apprentices and helpers, as large a labor force as possible and to have it work for his profit, while he restricts himself to the direction of the work, the responsibility, and the business transactions. On the other hand, the poorer and weaker the independent artisan, the better he is suited for the purpose of the merchant entering his field from the outside. This difference is exemplified by the rural and the town worker. The town worker, as we may at first assume, is a master of his craft or has the intention and the chance of becoming one. He may have inherited or can acquire a home workshop and the necessary tools. The same is true of the required skill and the customers. He has his regular work the year round or at least during the seasons of demand. In all these respects he enjoys the protection of his cooperative or guild, which inhibits the tendencies toward capitalist differentiation within the workshop. Under these conditions it is more difficult to lay hands on him from the outside.

The rural worker, who is free from most of these protective ties, therefore, is the real prey for the merchant. Insofar as urban crafts do not decay under the impact of a growing population, changing techniques, and increased traffic, the industry erected by commerce is in its first stage a rural one, although in contradiction to its origin and inherent tendencies. This predominantly rural industry is mainly home industry. Although the peasant or day laborer is dependent on his master, obliged to do forced labor, and engaged in caring for his own land, he has ample time to spare during the winter months. Together with his wife and children, he makes use of this spare time to practice the traditional homecrafts, such as weaving and spinning or carpentering and wood carving. He produces for his own demand, but occasionally also works for the town market or the peddling merchant. The latter, well acquainted with the market and able to reach even distant trade centers, finds those homecrafts the richest source of accruing value. The merchant furnishes the homeworker with materials, tools, and patterns and even has to provide him with foodstuffs. In the end, the worker, besides his hands and possibly his skill, has nothing left but the workshop in his home to contribute as his own to the production. But the unity of home and workshop is purely accidental here. In the independent crafts, such unity is natural, if not necessary; it means a useful and pleasant independence which the artisan endeavors to achieve and to retain wherever the character of the craft will permit it. With the rural worker, such unity may still be desirable; however, it no longer depends on his own free will but to an increasing degree on the direction of the merchant. The merchant will tolerate it, troublesome though it may be, until the advantages of concentrating the individual workers or groups of them in large buildings will outweigh the costs involved. The general advantages are: easier and more effective supervision; quicker, better-planned co-ordination of separate or separable processes within the same unit of production; better facilities for bringing production nearer to the most important market. But it is the development of technology which decides this change and makes a centralized workshop necessary. This development proceeds partly through the breaking up of the artistic working processes into their elements by simplifying individual operations and allocating the performance of these related but purposely separated functions to trained specialists, and partly, and this is of special importance, through the introduction of tools which a single worker and his family are no longer able to cope with and the dimensions of which far outgrow the space of the home workshop—that is to say, through the introduction of machinery. The result is the same when the independent master himself enlarges his

home workshop to a factory, and tools take the place of the human instruments of production. In the total development of industry, i.e., of
the domination of commerce over labor, three types and phases are to
be distinguished (according to the masterly analysis of Karl Marx, with
a slight modification of interpretation), of which the last two are more
closely related to each other than to the first. The three phases are: (1)
simple co-operation, (2) manufacture, (3) industry based on machinery
(real "large-scale" industry). The concept of the factory *(manufacture
réunie)* can cover the last two types and thus be justly contrasted with
the home industry *(manufacture séparée).*

The rule of commerce or of capital has industrial production as its
specific and natural sphere. There are many reasons for this, the most
important of which are rather self-evident and do not need discussion.
It has, nevertheless, a parallel in agriculture, which is degraded from
the rank of mother of all regular work to a branch of national or world
industry. Even if the rule of the landlord, mentioned above, is not directly aimed at the production of commodities, it nevertheless furthers
the latter because the money rent forces the producers to sell in the
highest market. Besides the landlord, the peasant is confronted with
the grain dealer and the usurer, both bent on appropriating the largest
possible amount of the money into which the sweat of his brow will be
transformed. With independent production of commodities, the estate
gains ascendancy over the small holding. First, the manor house is the
central point of service of the peasants as found in serfdom; finally,
there develops a free independent estate which has its own implements
and machines and works the land with free, mobile day laborers. Land
and labor are deliberately exploited for the sake of the greatest net
returns. The axiom "profit is the sole end of trade" thus finds its application, and to this oldest and most real "economy."

32. *Merchant and Master Craftsman—Separable*
Management—the Entrepreneur—Variety—
Capitalistic Production—Contrast to Commerce

Wherever these tendencies materialize, productive human labor becomes a means to the end of a profitable resale of this unique commodity.
The merchant or capitalist disguises himself in this process as a worker
or creator of work, a peasant or an artisan; he becomes an entrepreneur
of working processes. This process can be reversed in historical development: The owner of an estate or the master of a craft can become manufacturer and thereby merchant. That is irrelevant for the concept as such.
Commerce is presupposed as existent. The problem is: How does it attain
its dominating position? The master who has turned manufacturer is,

no less than the merchant who manufactures, essentially a capitalist or, so to speak, an abstract person of wealth (this is at the same time the general concept of the merchant himself). He has, as it were, covered up his nakedness a posteriori with the cloak of apparent mastership. The manufacturer or entrepreneur may, in reality, add some labor of his own, or at least some activity and service to the process of production, so that he co-operates in achieving the result and contributes to the production of actual value. All activities such as management, guidance, allocations of productive factors, and ultimate supervision—in short, the direction of a complex system of movements and activities—fall into this category, as clearly distinguished from actual labor. Although this combination of functions is easily maintained in theory and practice, it exists, nevertheless, only by accident and can, therefore, like all real labor, be separated from the entrepreneurial functions. It has to be separated from them if there is to be the concept of entrepreneurial activity. For the merchant to exist, there is no necessity for such an evolution, or only in very unusual cases, because he has, by nature, nothing to do with productive labor. But it is all the more necessary for the master craftsman, or whatever we call the productive worker. He has, as it were, to withdraw from the inner workings of the productive process in order to regard labor as an extraneous means and nothing else. The merchant, on the contrary, needs only to establish a (causal) relationship with labor; it is not probable that this would assume any emotional character. Thus, both types meet halfway on their road. The concept of the capitalist entrepreneur encompasses them both, and in addition there is the concept of the capitalist leader, according to the original distinction of commerce and usury. But, like these occupations, the two functions can be united in one and the same person. A mutation developed from both types and taking a place beside them is the gambling, risking, and betting capitalist. For commerce is by nature akin to gambling *(le commerce est un jeu)*, the purchase being risked for profitable sale which, although probable, is not altogether certain. In the same way usury is a gamble, for it is not certain that the capital loaned will be returned, let alone a profit—the interest— realized. Business rests primarily on hope, secondarily on calculation and a combination of probabilities. If bad cases are balanced by good ones and if the good cases are in the majority, the purpose is achieved. If in a game the unpredictable (chance) elements (the business cycle) are given free play and the probability of a loss is fully taken into account, there is, nevertheless, a very natural intention to eliminate the element of insecurity and to insure a certain regular profit. Of the many methods which those lending capital can make use of for this purpose, the taking of security is the most important one.

Of the methods used by commerce, we are concerned only with those by which it gains control of production and makes its profit an inherent element of the process of production. The sale of manufactured commodities can be as uncertain and as subject to failure as the sale of purchased commodities. True. But this is only a temporary situation. It results from the painful separation from a system of Gemeinschaften which produce goods for their own use and distribute them among the people themselves. In a fully developed Gesellschaft, however, every commodity would be produced in adequate quantities and sold for its value by a single capitalistic person possessed of a perfect knowledge of existing normal demand. Such a concept cannot be realized. It is in the approximating of this goal that the respectability of capitalist production distinguishes itself from that of common trade.

33. *Finished Commodities—Commodities to Be Produced* *—Working and Having Work Done— Quantity*

Here we shall pursue the following line of argument: the objects of sale and purchase as such are called commodities. In this sense, all that belongs to the sphere of rational will of one person, and can consequently be transferred to the sphere of another, can take the form of a commodity, as, for example, plots of land, rare books or paintings, and other noninterchangeable things. Thus, one's own activities—labor or service—also take the form of commodities. For the merchant who endeavors to sell the commodities purchased, all commodities are of this type and, therefore, are alike insofar as he does not attempt to influence production. He can, for example, as agent for domestic help or as a theatrical agent, deal in labor power or voices, just as well as in old clothes. The same holds for the grain dealer who trades with the peasantry of a specific region. Every harvest makes a certain amount of grain available for trade. If the producers thereof are conceived of as one single person, it becomes evident that such a person can manipulate that object for the benefit of or to the detriment of the rest of society. He can burn part of the grain to raise the value of the remainder above the former value of the total. Or, what seems more public-spirited, he can store a part of the grain to offer it for sale at a later date; in short, he can do whatever promises the highest profit.

Now commodities can also be especially produced for sale. This is possible only by working and having others work. This tenet does not need to be proved, as the proof is contained in the premise. It is assumed that to produce goods or increase their number, in short, to "provide" goods, is a matter of human free will. Now it is true that for a given region the merchant can import any work on his part or others, furnish any kind of commodities by buying and transporting it in from another region. But if such a region is extended as far as possible or, what amounts to the same thing for a smaller region, if no such extension is possible, the alternative becomes evident. However, it is important to note that the concept of rational will in providing things is less in keeping with work of one's own than with work done by others. The person who hires others attains his aim not only by appearing as the producer of all the goods of which he is the natural owner, but also by limiting the amount of goods produced solely at his discretion and through the means at his disposal. That is to say, he will attain this if he is able to extend his production at will by providing the necessary implements and employing purchased labor.

34. Profits from Trade—Profits from Productions— Value of Labor Force—Value of Labor

The profit made at all other trade is unnatural if one reasons as follows: In a general social system it is to be considered as profit to the class engaged in trade regardless of how this profit may be divided among the individual persons. This profit will be equal to the value which the services rendered through the transfer of the goods have, and in the general development of Gesellschaft this profit is reduced. This tendency holds true not only for the services performed but also for all goods in general, as the equations of price, varying according to time and place, oscillate in diminishing fluctuations about the ideal equations of value, which vary only according to time. On the other hand, trade which engages in manufacturing is in a safer position. It adds value to a given value through labor similar to that of the homeworker, peasant, or artisan who brings his products to the market or works and sells on order. Such labor, in a system of exchange and value, must be paid for in proportion to the contribution which it has made to the product. In the same manner the capitalist should be paid for his contribution. He buys this labor by hiring workers. This raises the problem: how is it possible to obtain a regular profit through the differentiation between labor as purchased goods and the value of labor contained in the sold goods (supposing that the goods are bought on the market according to their value)?

35. Value and Price of Labor—Purchase and Consumption of Commodities

Labor and services as commodities are offered for sale and purchased. They have their prices, as do a loaf of bread and a needle. But they differ from these commodities which consist of raw materials and labor. They are raw materials, not products of labor. In this, they resemble the land. The supply of land cannot, in a given area, be artificially or arbitrarily increased. The supply of labor can, it is true, be increased by import, which, however, presupposes that labor has already become an object of trade. If this is not the case, but every man offers "his own hide," the number of workers is limited in the same way as the quantity of land. Neither of these types of commodity can be made or fabricated. Their value and price are, therefore, determined solely by their existing actual supply, not a possible future one, and the relation of this supply to the effective demand. In reality, however, not only general undefined labor and services, but also specific, definite ones are asked for and offered. This makes the limitation on supply all the more obvious, and, other conditions being equal, this is to the advantage of those offering the commodities. Those supplying labor are disadvantaged by their urgent need for the commodity to be received in exchange for it (money or consumption goods). For the higher the (subjective) value of the commodity in demand, the lower necessarily the (subjective) value of the commodity offered in exchange, and the more violent and stronger the desire to sell it. On the one hand, the wish to obtain money or foodstuffs is unlimited with every individual who does not have them or is not provided with them from his own Gemeinschaft (which is not to be discussed here). He is left only the choice of appropriating what he desires by violence (which is against the natural law of Gesellschaft) or of acquiring it by the way of exchange, i.e., by selling his labor power.

On the other hand, it makes a great difference whether a commodity is asked for and purchased by somebody who wants to use it, i.e., for whom it represents an end, a material thing, and a use-value, or if it is bought by somebody who intends to resell it. In the first case the commodity is taken possession of as an object of one's own will and a supplement to one's own forces. It is as much needed as it is desired. Where there is no actual need, there will at least exist a certain liking, even a passion for it, at any rate a desire of some real strength. This counts also in favor of those offering services. In such cases, especially with regard to services as commodities of a specific kind, as mentioned above, it is evident that the character of such barter is not of the Gesellschaft. This is especially true if the seller's greed is not absolute or is nonexistent, for even if the urgent desire for the other person's commodity as such is noncommercial, the ardent wish to sell one's own wares is doubtless of a commercial nature. A decrease in the intensity of the desire for a commodity does not make such demand commercial, but with it the desire to sell diminishes, too. The conditions for other than a Gesellschaft-like exchange are most favorable where on both sides there is only a moderate desire to exchange goods, prompted by a liking or need for the object in question or any quality the other party may possess. In fact, barter, then, represents only the form in which a principle of distribution according to the principles of Gemeinschaft manifests itself.

36. *Purchase and Will to Sell—Price of Labor*

The case is different if a commodity is demanded and bought by somebody who wants to have it only in order to sell it again. He has no personal relation to the object of his purchase and is completely indifferent to it. He is in no way tempted, by tenderness or benevolence or pleasure in the work, to reward the artist or worker according to his own discretion and in the manner of a gift. On the contrary, it is the sole task of the trader to give as little as possible in order to make the margin to the future price as wide as possible. For this margin is the aim and purpose of his intention. In his hands the commodity represents nothing but an exchange value, a means and an instrument through which other people's goods may be acquired. It is the same as money in anyone's hands. Whereas everybody buys things, foodstuffs and pleasures—natural use-values—with money at the natural exchange value, the merchant, on the contrary, wants to buy, with foodstuffs and so forth, the use of money. This artificial use-value of money lies in the purchase of commodities not for use but for sale. As a buyer, the merchant is not driven by need, for it is assumed that he has his own money, which he is at liberty to use also for the purchase of consumption goods. He is absolutely free and superior, and in no hurry to get rid of his money. That is his position toward the sellers of labor.

These circumstances make it highly probable that the price of labor will be equal to that quantity of foodstuffs which, in the opinion of the worker, represents the minimum necessary for the worker's support during the period of his employment. This is the negative limit which the seller of labor is himself forced to establish, though he may try to set a higher price. It is at the same time the positive limit which the buyer has to acknowledge as necessary but to go beyond which to his own detriment he will be strongly disinclined. That limit may, however, specify a great variety of magnitude. The lower limit is the maintenance of mere existence (in the mental outline which the will of the individual might allow to be given to this concept). Dire need reduces the limit to its minimum. This is the natural cost price of labor per se; conditions and material of its reproduction, which in this respect may indeed be compared to a production and would, therefore, represent the real value determined in the Gesellschaft. The concept is directly concerned only with the individual labor which a worker, to keep himself alive, is in a position to offer anew at, say, the beginning of another week. If, however, the concept of a minimum of existence includes also the support of wife and child, it is subject to a reduction, as women and children beyond their teens can also sell labor.

37. Necessary Labor-Time in Gesellschaft—Monopolists

The concept of an average necessary labor-time in Gesellschaft, which is as profound in meaning as it is difficult to apply (as are all true concepts of political economy), must be confined to the production of goods in commercial enterprises. For then the competing firms can produce a practically unlimited amount of commodities, and the producer, enjoying the most favorable conditions of production, can—at least so it seems—satisfy the whole demand for that particular commodity. To retain their thus endangered market, the other producers will then be forced to adjust their prices to his or to make them equal. In consequence they will try to establish equally favorable conditions for their production in order not to suffer a permanent reduction of their profits. Therein lies the real principle of commercial competition; the merchant (or businessman) who buys commodities at the lower price can also sell them more cheaply, and, through the quantity of his commodities and the continuance of his buying opportunities, he becomes a competitor for the others. But there exists another counteracting tendency: The commodities actually offered for sale have, insofar as they are of the same type, equal chance for sale (and will try to command a price equivalent to their specific value) quite independent of the productive capacity of the respective enterprises. At the same time it is impossible, or at least very difficult, deliberately and arbitrarily to improve unfavorable conditions of production.

In studying the exchange of commodities, the agency of commerce has to be left out of consideration. Each category of commodities appears on the market in a certain quantity of, let us say, equivalent specimens and endeavors to obtain the largest possible quantity of other commodities in the market. In this respect, all inside competition within the category ceases to exist. The natural differences are dissolved as if the total quantity of commodities were in the hands of one and the same person who, representing a united power, determines the price of each individual type or kind of the commodity in question. In this way price competition among monopolists would take place. Each category would fight against each other with equal effort and equivalent methods of attack. It then will result that each quantity of a certain category of commodities commands those quantities of commodities of other categories which in reality are equal to it in respect to the only quality valued in the market, i.e., their exchange value. The process can be observed in nature where, according to the theory of mechanics, each quantity of energy is transformed into another equal one and also replaced by another equal one.

In this way all fortuitous and abstract gains within the market are excluded. In reality only an exchange of concrete use-values in accordance with the standard of an abstract exchange value takes place. The possibility of the realization of this rests upon the equality of the conditions of production for all categories of commodities (however different they may be for the types and species within the category). This implies an equal distribution of the most favorable conditions of production for each category of commodities.

The most favorable conditions exist when (1) natural forces do not have an exchange value as their natural price, (2) the co-operation of human beings with each other is most effective, (3) an equally effective co-operation exists between men and the most suitable instruments (tools, machines). If these conditions are fulfilled and all differences in human labor have been reduced to their common denominator, labor-time (which calculation is facilitated by their actual relationship to each other), the value of each category of commodities and consequently of every possible quantity thereof is determined by the average labor power required in the Gesellschaft for their production. The development of Gesellschaft and its center, the world market, is directed toward this point of relative equilibrium, which is constantly approximated.

The law of value has at first only a purely conceptual significance and can be reduced through logic to the rules of calculation, which permits synthesis or the construction of identical statements. Such a law has its basis in the consideration that a certain amount of human labor has been added to the natural forces and those things presupposed as existing, and that this has produced the present forms of objects.

Natural forces have, according to our assumption, no exchange value. The exchange value of other things necessary for production (raw materials and instruments) is itself dissoluble into quantities of labor. Consequently, the raw exchange value can be dissolved into parts of the exchange value and added labor, thus into labor altogether. Labor has become embodied in these objects; it is, as it were, coagulated in the fixed surplus which they represent over and against the free natural forces. The commodity and its owner are by no means compelled to demand more exchange value from the market than they offer, and the value received in exchange under normal conditions must comprise only

(a) the value of the materials used for the commodity sold and those parts of the value which the instruments have contributed, and (b) the value of the labor added in the production of the commodity. The real meaning of the value, which is obscured by the intervention of money, becomes the more evident when money ceases to be bound up with commodities and, as credit, reveals more and more its abstract nature as a mere representation of commodities in a form of scrip.

38. *Commodity Market and Labor Market*

Profit, or surplus value, is the difference between the purchase price of labor and the sales price, not of the labor's product, but of the exchange value of the labor embodied in the product. In the real or commodity market, labor appears only in this changed form which results from its application to raw materials and instruments; that is, it appears as the property not of the workers but of the capitalists. But labor comes to the market also in the form of services to be exchanged for goods, i.e., labor which, not being embodied in any product, has, as it were, retained its liquidity. It is consumed and effaced in the very act of giving and receiving. As immaterial commodities, services may demand a value, although they do not possess any value measurable by the labor-time embodied in them. Their value, like that of many goods, is better defined as a normal or standard price. It is proportionate to the quality of services in relation to the average intensity of the demand. That means: the value of the services can be expressed only as a price, i.e., in a certain quantity of other goods. It is, therefore, always a fraction and never a whole. The labor which produces commodities is, however, not to be found on this market. It is not a commodity in the same sense as things by nature are, or as services can be. It does not meet the other commodities on an equal footing, that is to say, as if the exchange effected meant the end of a cycle after which the goods exchanged would be put in channels leading to consumption, or consumed immediately.

As a principle of production, labor is conceivable only in respect to, previous and subordinate to, production. As the connection of labor with the other factors of production is possible only through its purchase, this takes place prior to the sale of finished goods. The labor market is definitely separated from the commodity market and subordinate to the latter. It can also be called a secret market, the preexistence of which has left no trace in the open commodity market. There, labor is bought and paid for as if it represented merely future services to be consumed in the performance itself. The fiction underlying this is that the manufacturer (some capitalist, let us say the joint-stock company) is the real author and producer and hires workers only as helpers. This fiction gains in verisimilitude the more the conditions of co-operation and later the implements of production—all of which are the property of the manufacturers—become, as it were, alive and set in motion and capable of carrying out automatic imitation of human craft and skill through their cleverly planned construction. If these factors serve the purpose of the owner, it is his initiative, his thought, and his will that govern them and direct their motions.

The workers have no will of their own; their tasks are assigned to them. Such tasks are determined through the configuration of the whole and through a well-defined plan and method for the working of given materials. The result is the division of labor within industry or industrialized agriculture. Furthermore, the tools, organized as machines in systems of production, are served in their work by, and dominate, the toiling human beings. Thus, these toilers are no longer directly dependent so much upon an alien human will which gives them orders as upon the given qualities of a "dead monster" against which they react as a collective whole. In consequence, the workers are also more inclined to take a collective stand against their employer. Real and objective opinion, however, will always and necessarily consider human labor done as the source of human works, regardless of how powerful are the instruments it uses; i.e., individual labor is the source of individual work, collective labor the source of collective work. Not the joint-stock company, but the workers' company, produces goods and values. As only works have natural value, the statement that labor is the source of all values is valid also from this point of view. In manufacturing establishments of the older or premachine type, labor is united only by a common goal and the use of common methods of work, which (because they represent brain products of men), however, can be conceived of as products, and, therefore, genuine property of the directing entrepreneur. In a real factory the labor force is essentially united by this common necessary relationship to the machinery which forms the visible body of the factory. In both cases it is clearly evident that only the unity of labor, welded together by the intelligent use of materials, plans, and instruments, constitutes the real productive principle.

In the labor market, workers can unite as sellers of labor and by excluding competition compel a higher price. But as proprietor of all agencies in which labor is incorporated as a subordinate part, the manufacturing person remains, in a natural and logically determined way, creator and thus owner of all human work produced by outside human labor and sold on the market in order to retain this value. However, empirical evidence refutes this idea of the importance of the proprietor as creator.

39. *Retail Market—Counter Movement—Services*

The labor market does not presuppose a commodity market. The manner in which the capitalist has acquired his money, with which he pays his workers, or where the products come from which this money represents, are absolutely irrelevant for the present consideration. Part of them may derive from previous production—perhaps from the labor of the capitalist himself; another part depends on present or future production. The transformation of money into consumption goods has no direct connection with either the commodity market or the labor market. It belongs to a third market which we call the retail market, and which represents the normal agency of distribution. It presupposes production and can be conceived as depending, by way of a regular circulation, on the commodity market. Then the retail market is the last link which is coupled with the first one and springs from the second. It moves from the center to the periphery. The retail market gives commodities to all those in possession of money; it even forces the goods on those with money, as if itself craving money which, soaked up in innumerable small portions, is thus absorbed in large quantities by the commodity market. The commodity market moves in an opposite direction, from the periphery to the center. It is a mere assemblage of products—as systole, or contraction, which must be followed by the diastole, or expansion. The origin of these products is irrelevant so far as this commodity market is concerned. The labor market is a point of communication within the periphery. Exchange on the commodity as well as on the labor market has been conceived of without the intervention of trade. In contradistinction, the retail market and the ultimate distribution are quite naturally a business of buying and selling, thus the real sphere of merchants. In the fully developed system of production of Gesellschaft and capitalist, retail distribution can be considered a service in Gesellschaft which must demand and take its value and be recompensed from the commodity market. Thereby it is postulated that all other services which are classed as quasi-production and parts of the total production of Gesellschaft appear on the commodity market and there realize their value.

Furthermore, all services can be considered as produced and used in a capitalistic manner insofar as their performance is dependent upon agencies (institutions), materials, and tools. That, again, presupposes a special division of labor market where such services can be purchased as a crude potentiality for performance.

40. *The Classes—Conditions Determining the Whole Construction*

If the retail market is considered only as the necessary consequence of the existence of a commodity market, the essential structure of

Gesellschaft is then described by three acts, all performed by the capitalist class. As the performer of the acts, this class is conceived as equipped with the implements of production (which are thus not acquired in the market, but already existing in their place). The three acts are: (1) the purchase of labor, (2) the employment of labor, (3) the sale of labor in the form of value elements of the products. The working class actively participates in the first act chiefly by getting rid of the superfluous for the sake of the necessary. The laboring class seemingly has its share only as an object; in reality all material which is apparently the causation of the second act lies with this laboring class, and only the formal causation lies with the capitalist class. The third act is performed solely by the capitalist class; the working class is present only in the form of the value which is, as it were, squeezed out of it. Where the working class takes an active part, it is free; its labor is only the realization of its contract, i.e., of an exchange which it undertakes from well-known necessity. All exchange (i.e., sale) is the form of an act of rational will itself, whereas commerce is its material perfection. From this it follows that the working class is semifree—namely, up to the middle of the three acts—and formally capable of deliberate action, as distinct from a class of slaves, which would take part in the process only as would a tool and material. In contradistinction, the capitalist class is completely free and materially capable of deliberate action. Its members are, therefore, to be considered voluntary, enthusiastic, and material elements of Gesellschaft; opposite them is the mass of partially voluntary and only formal operators. Interest and participation in these three acts and their interrelations are equivalent to the complete orientation of Gesellschaft and the acceptance of its existence and its underlying conventions.

The question of whether this dualistic construction of the concept of Gesellschaft is the only one possible does not concern us here. It is, at any rate, the construction which necessarily follows from the premise of commerce. That holds, however, only on condition that commerce is limited to that purely fictitious, unnatural commodity created by human will, which is labor power. Labor, done apart from or including the service function of commerce, can free profit (which is the ultimate aim and essential principle of commerce) from all chance elements and secure it by its very essence as the necessary and regular result of the activities of commerce. Thus, all these concepts are classified and differentiated in the theory of the individual human will to which we are, therefore, irresistibly led by this whole study.

Addition (1911). When this treatise was written (1880-1887), the completion of the Marxian system which has, among others, influenced its contents, was not yet made known. The author, however, in subsequent years has not found that Marx's solution of the enigma of the average rate of profit has been subjected to valid criticism on the part of the Austrian and German scholars. They argue that the law of value becomes meaningless by its application to the total value of all commodities because such total value is not an object of exchange and is, in reality, only another name for the total product or, better, for its newly produced components. Such objection is, in the opinion of the author, absolutely unfounded. It is reasonable to argue that the annual product of labor is equivalent to the socially necessary labor-time spent in its production, and that this standard of value which makes it similar to and commensurable with all previous and future annual products originally determines also the exchange value of the individual commodity in comparison with others (i.e., the exchanged parts of the total product). But it is then stated that the capitalistic character of production destroys this relationship so that the surplus value, transformed into profit, is distributed to the commodities in proportion to the capital involved and the prices of production. Such a line of reasoning is possible, although somewhat forced and artificial. I have never accepted the theory of value of Ricardo, Rodbertus, and Marx in the form in which it was presented, but I fully agree with its principal arguments. In this treatise the modification and directions which I deem necessary have been pointed out. Today, as ever, I stand for the maxim that only labor creates new values. But I add the further statement, that labor does not create equal value in equal periods of socially necessary labor-time. Furthermore, not only does skilled labor produce many times the value of general labor (Marx has pointed this out himself) but it also creates very different values in the same time according to its effective co-operation either with other labor or with the most appropriate material means of production. This correction saves the statement that in a free market commodity prices oscillate around their value. But labor power itself has no more a natural value than land. Its price varies with its quality, with size and intensity of supply and demand, and with the strength of the association of its sellers, the workers themselves. The upper limit is fixed by its utility, as it is purchased for the sake of profit to be made by the entrepreneur; the lower limit is fixed by the mere food requirements of the isolated worker.

PART TWO

Natural Will and Rational Will

SECTION ONE: The Forms of Human Will

1. *Definition of the Concepts*

The concept of human will, the correct interpretation of which is essential to the subject of this treatise, implies a twofold meaning. Since all mental action involves thinking, I distinguish between the will which includes the thinking and the thinking which encompasses the will. Each represents an inherent whole which unites in itself a multiplicity of feelings, instincts, and desires. This unity should in the first case be understood as a real or natural one; in the second case as a conceptual or artificial one. The will of the human being in the first form I call natural will *(Wesenwille)*; in the second form, rational will (*Kürwille*).

2. *Relations to Thinking*

Natural will is the psychological equivalent of the human body, or the principle of the unity of life, supposing that life is conceived under that form of reality to which thinking itself belongs *(quatenus sub attributo cogitationis concipitur)*. Natural will involves thinking in the same way as the organism contains those cells of the cerebrum which, if stimulated, cause the psychological activities which are to be regarded as equivalent to thinking (and in which the center of speech is undoubtedly a participator).

Rational will is a product of thinking itself and consequently possesses reality only with reference to its author, the thinking individual, although this reality can be recognized and acknowledged as such by others. These two different concepts of will have in common the fact that they are conceived as the causes for or tendencies toward action. Their very existence and nature allow, therefore, an inference from them as to whether certain behavior of the individual is probable, or, under specific conditions, is necessary. Natural will derives from and can be explained only in terms of the past, just as the future in turn evolves from the past. Rational will can be understood only from the future developments with which it is concerned. Natural will contains the future in embryo or emergent form; rational will contains it as an image.

3. *Relations with Activity*

In the same way as a force is related to the work which it performs, natural will is related to the activity to which it refers. Therefore, in any activity performed by an individual human organism, natural will is necessarily involved in some form or other, and it appears as the constituting element in individuality in the psychic sense. Natural will is immanent in activity. In order to comprehend fully the concept of natural will, it is necessary to see beyond the independent existence of outward objects and to conceive the experience thereof only as a subjective reality. Thus, only psychic reality and psychic causality obtain; that is to say, only a coexistence and succession of sensations of existence, instinct, and activities, which develop in their totality and interrelation from the original embryonal disposition of this individual being, may be considered. This is true even though the specific development may be conditioned and thus modified by the substance of these emotions (which is equivalent to what is generally called the outside world). In the same way, the body, requiring food and other things for its support, is influenced and changed by these very requirements.

Rational will is prior to the activity to which it refers and maintains its separate identity. It has only an imaginary existence, while activity is its realization. The ego of both forms of will sets the body (otherwise conceived as motionless) into action by external stimulus. This ego is an abstraction. It is the human "I" in so far as it is conceived as stripped of all other qualities and as essentially thinking. Thinking in this connection means imagining the results (probable or certain) of possible actions undertaken by one and measuring such actions by a final result, the idea of which is taken as a standard, then sorting out and arraying such actions for future realization. In such a way, according to this conception, thinking works, as it were, with mechanical pressure, on nerves and muscles and through them on the limbs of the body. Since this concept is valid only in a physical or physiological sense, it is necessary to conceive of thinking itself as a movement, i.e., as a function of the brain. The brain, then, must be understood as a reality, an object in space.

4. *Organic Life—Development of Natural Will*

The problem of will as natural will, according to this view, is manifold, like the problem of organic life itself. Specific natural will is inborn in the human being in the same way as in any species a specific form of body and soul is natural. Every individual natural will arrives at its complete and mature existence in the same way as the organism which it represents, by gradual growth developing from an embryo or tender bud which contains the (psychic as well as physical) form as it has been predetermined and originated by the union of cells derived from the procreators. According to this origin, natural will has to be understood as inborn and inherited. Through the mixture of paternal and maternal elements and through the particular nature of surrounding conditions, it obtains the principles from which it develops into a new and different form or at least into a form with certain modifications. Its development corresponds with every phase of physical development; the same amount of strength and unity that is found in the organism is also found in the natural will. The development of natural will is self-generative to the same extent as is the development of the organism.

To our knowledge this growth appears as movement speeded up to an indescribable degree by forces which have continually increased and become more diversified through all successions of generations, which may connect this single being with the original forms of organic matter. Through these forces the real activity of the physical will becomes the more negligible the closer it still is to its origin, although such activity is nevertheless existent and takes place under conditions furnished by the environment.

More and more, however, these conditions become evident as different from the inner tendencies, and only then does it become possible to observe changes which, in relative independence from the potentialities of the ancestors, are brought about by the natural will itself. Such changes are almost nonexistent in the embryo; they become important in the child and increase, generally speaking, with age. Although will is thus different at any given moment, just as is the case with the body, its individual growth can, in this way, be considered as a succession of acts of will, each of which presupposes those which preceded; i.e., the already existing organic force, as well as exterior stimuli of a certain character. All the preceding acts of will include also the original will, the original disposition which comprises them all not as logical but as real possibilities or even probabilities which under given conditions become necessities and develop as such into reality. Potentialities or tendencies during this process become faculties, in which they are active as instincts in constant connection with the original will as well as with its further developments and ramifications. Will, therefore, if its development is conceived as completed at a given point, confronts the objects of the outer world as a clearly determined entity influenced by, and itself causing, actions. Each of these actions could be considered, in a deeper sense, as its act (act of this will) inasmuch as this will in its totality is subject to a change which it effects itself. However, all those forces which bring about the "miracle" of development continue to work on and on. Therefore, the origin of such volition can be conceived as a species of higher order from which these forces, as well as the individual himself, derive. If we understand the development of the individual as his volition, although admitting that an unknown and endless force is active in this process, we still must learn to consider also volition, which is outside this development, equally as a process of creation and growth. The volition should be recognized in this case as merely representative, i.e., it does not itself cause these processes but rather is the object of them. The processes, however, which cause a total change should perhaps be distinguished in this manner; namely, as caused by the individual himself, because they are known to his consciousness through a feeling of activity which is, strictly speaking, identical with one's general situation if understood in a subjective way (and this general subjective situation is really what comprises everything, first and last, all that one has and knows).

5. *Vegetative and Animal Will—Mental Will*

The most general division of bodily organs and functions distinguishes between those of vegetative (inner) and those of animal (outer) life. In the same way there is sufficient reason to postulate a vegetative and an animal will both of which, like the physical structures of the body, are united and interdependent in the will of an animal. This connection, however, assumes such special significance in the specific characteristics and activities of the human being that it becomes necessary, from a psychological point of view, to distinguish the human or mental will (and this species of life) from the animal and vegetative will in the same manner as these are distinguished from each other, and to conceive the three elements as united in the human being in the same way as the two other ones are united in the general constitution of an animal. The activities of the vegetative or organic will are conditioned by general stimuli received or experienced (material stimuli); those of the animal will by perceptions or visible impressions (sensory or motor stimuli), those of mental will by thoughts or verbal sensations (intellectual or mental stimuli which are not measurable as far as their material—or motion—value is concerned).

Vegetative life consists entirely in maintenance, accumulation, and reproduction of its own adequate energies and forms. It is the foundation of all other kinds of life and postulates itself as constant in substance, all specific activities being conceived as its modifications and expressions. It is being and effect in itself: assimilation of nutritious elements, maintenance and renewal of organs. Animal life is mainly the exterior movement necessary for this, under the forms of energy spent on other objects or beings, stimulation and contraction of muscular tissues for locomotive change of the entire body or its parts. Mental life manifests itself through communication, i.e., through the effect on kindred beings through signs, especially words pronounced by the use of vocal organs. From this develops thinking, i.e., the communication of thoughts to oneself through audible or inaudible speech. As communication finds its preparation and origin already in animal life, all capacities and activities which belong to this are increased, intensified, and strengthened through speech and thinking.

The entire third category should be understood as retroactive modification of the second category; and this second one has the same relation toward the first. Natural will of human beings should be conceived of as including all those categories, which form a unity. It is the organic will, defined by the animal-mental will; it is the animal will, expressed by the organic and mental will together; it is the mental will itself in its dependence upon the organic-animal will. All its motives rest in organic life; they receive their direction and guidance, as well as their special form, from mental life; in animal life all its most important and most ordinary expressions become most evident.

In accordance with this, I define several groups of psychological concepts as the forms of human natural will, in which this will demonstrates its existence through affirmation or negation of other things. The names will designate only the positive meaning. This positive sense indicates at the same time its negation: will, ill-will or aversion. In each form the psychic values of real or productive and motor activities are connected in such a manner with those of the receptive, sensitive, or intellectual activities that they represent their order and connection as do the central organs of the animal nerve system considered in a physiological sense. Thus, a certain reception is always the beginning or tendency (*conatus*) toward a certain effort which attempts to follow and has to take the direction of least resistance or strongest impulse. With the impressions (or ideas) of certain objects, the tendencies (or ideas) toward certain reactions are necessarily connected as the expressions of our own being. Will can be understood as being related to those objects—that is, related to their perception and consequently to such activity—or as being related to this activity from the inside toward the outside. In both relations, insofar as they are positive or affirmative, will is defined by its own nature and norm, connecting with the objects, inclined toward and prepared for corresponding activities.

6. Liking—Development and Growth—Sensory Organs

The inborn pleasure derived from certain objects and the propensity for certain activities which are apparent in the human being may be called "liking," which is the human form of the general animal instinct. This concept explains everything that cannot be explained otherwise than by the development and normal growth of a psychical constitution as determined by the genetic inheritance. This is the complex of organic instincts which permeate and dominate the life, thought, and energy of man. All individual ideas or sensations are derived from such original unity and retain their necessary interrelationship. This unity is characterized by three different attributes: (a) as a will to life per se, that is, a will to affirm all those activities and emotions which further life, and to negate the actions of those obstructing it; (b) as a will to nourishment and to the activities and sensations connected therewith; (c) as a will to procreation. It is this last characteristic which gives to the conception its full meaning, for reproduction is life itself. It becomes the object of a special will only when and inasmuch as specific emotions and activities are required for it.

These needs and desires which correspond to functions common to all organisms strike the keynote in the chords of human feelings. All those differences in sympathies and antipathies which, as moods and physical conditions, result in permanent or temporary individual characteristics, depend on the fitness of these organs and the degree of satisfaction derived. They are usually considered mere physical conditions. In reality, it can be positively proven that all that is pleasing to the spirit, i.e., the mind of men, depends, too, on these conditions and in turn reacts upon them. But the original and real intermediaries between the inner and the outer world which are common, at least to some degree, to all animal beings, are the sensory organs, i.e., the nervous system. The senses, like the rest of the body, partly derive satisfaction from themselves; in this they are directly conditioned by the quality and physical conditions of the vital organs as well as by their own quality and conditions. But the senses also derive pleasure from their environment, the outer world, of which they are aware in peculiar and varied ways. They find it pleasant or repulsive. The positive feelings, or liking, and the negative ones, or displeasure, do not cause corresponding reactions, but are themselves these reactions; they become real manifestations of will in the form of movements which contract the muscles through the efferent neurons.

There are, then, two possibilities of further research. The first one is a study of the causes of movements as movements. This presupposes an explanation of the phenomenon of life itself and makes it necessary to find the connecting link between the development of the individual life and life in general. That must, then, lead further to a theory of nerve excitations as caused by such movements. It would have to explain how these excitations result from interaction with outside forces and how they are partly transmitted to the outside again, partly pass into a state of tension or relative rest after the molecules reach a new equilibrium.

The other possibility is to present the history and interrelationship of emotions which are in reality only the subjective aspect of those objective biological phenomena. Every cell, tissue, or organ is a complex of homogeneous will in relation to itself and to the outer world. That holds also for the organism as a whole. Those of its changes which are efferent movements (from the nerve center) necessary to perpetuate life are always determined also by simultaneous sensory impressions received from the outside. If the expressions are conceived as originating from the centers which regulate organic life, such impressions are for the human being only of the animal-mental kind. Such are the instinctive movements or expressions of will by which an emotion is accepted or rejected. It is as if the general will puts questions to things by means of the senses and tries to examine their qualities. Will itself, however, decides and judges whether they correspond to its liking, whether they are good or bad. The animal and mental centers (of the spinal column and the brain) and organs are only considered to take part in this insofar as they themselves are expressions of vegetative life (are dependent upon the expressions of the sympathetic nervous system). The sensory organs, inasmuch as their individual character rests in the development of an original disposition, represent just as many varieties of liking or preference as does positive (or negative) will. The actual subjective senses such as touch, smell, and taste best illustrate this quality. They are the organs which most directly enjoy.

7. *Habit—Experience and Development—*
    the Substance of Human (and Animal) Mind

To be distinguished from this is habit, as the other, the animal form of natural will. This is will or lust resulting from experience. Originally indifferent or unpleasant ideas become more pleasant themselves, through association with original pleasant ones, until they finally enter the circulation of life. Experience is practice. Practice is the formative element of habit as mere development is that of pleasure. Practice comes first through development. How it later becomes detached therefrom and maintains itself as a separate and specific factor outside of and along with this development must be explained. This results from a more decisive influence of the conditions of individual life which are dealt with through a more variegated co-ordination of the impressions received. In their normal course, development and growth represent an easy and safe process of a general nature (encompassing the whole organism); practice, though difficult in the beginning, becomes easier with repetition, makes indefinite and uncertain movements definite and certain, and develops special organs and energies. Countless minute effects produce such results. As the repulsive or hostile phenomena cause pain, so the alien or unwanted ones arouse fear (instinctive fear), which decreases with repetition if the danger passes without inflicting pain. Thus, what has been dreaded and abhorred becomes first tolerable and finally even pleasant. The reverse process can also be brought on through experience and denotes a kind of retrogression and gradual detachment. The obstacles which obstruct a calm and easy perception or assimilation of an object are overcome by the individual's own force strengthened by practice. But such an increase in strength has definite limits set up by the laws of nature. Over practice is overexertion and either is undertaken at the cost of, and detriment to, other organs or results in immediate fatigue of the muscles used and in indirect strain on the whole organism, i.e., an exhaustion of existing forces without a sufficient regeneration. This explains why an activity which originally is easy and natural may become difficult and finally impossible to perform and, further, why pleasant sensations and activities may become indifferent or even painful, why hunger and thirst through overindulgence may turn into oversaturation, sexual desire into repugnance—in general, likes into dislikes.

But in the first place, where genuine inclination comes into play, habits are formed, and what has been originally pleasant is all the more cherished. Thus, special types of activities based on liking or preference become more easily habitual and acquire a more specific prominence; a certain mode of living (hence the natural environment) becomes, as a habit, pleasant to the animal and finally indispensable; and the same is true for certain types of diet and of companionship with its kind. In this respect, man is fully an animal, although in his own peculiar way. It is a common saying that man is an animal of habit, a slave to his habits, and so on, wherein a general and correct understanding of human nature expresses itself. To man as an animal species as opposed to the other large category of organic beings, habit is an essential and substantial element of his mind. All practice, and thus also habit, presupposes some perceptions; human habits therefore presuppose the understanding of word symbols.

An animal first becomes accustomed to objects, and to pleasures derived therefrom, which are directly connected with the activities of life; then he habituates himself to certain necessary movements induced by special perceptions, i.e., functions which he must practice. Finally, he becomes used to processes and interrelationships of perceptions and images which are simultaneous with these movements and interact with them. This is the basis for reasoning as the interpretation of given facts through their associations with past experiences. Reasoning processes are common to all higher species of animals, and reasoning power, as distinguished therefrom, is termed intelligence. In human nature these types of habits are only specialized and modified so that we can distinguish human habits of living, working, and imagination, which are also connected with one another through many cross lines. It is quite evident that, as everybody knows, everything that one knows and is capable of doing coincides with what one likes and feels inclined to. For ability itself, that feeling of strength, is an urge and will for action (achievement) as the imperative need of the organism to live in this way in order at least to maintain itself in its given state of perfection. For an organ in disuse, as well as unused strength, degenerates by atrophy, but activity of an organ is the very element and condition of its growth. That explains why habit, as the real principle of ability, is at the same time active will. One is ready and willing to do what one knows and is capable of doing; but the stranger a task, the more painfully and reluctantly it is undertaken. The terms used in the two classical languages are highly indicative in this respect: The Greek word *philein* means "one likes," i.e., one is accustomed to do such and such. Furthermore, there is the special term of *ethelein* which significantly denotes "volition" and "readiness," and also "habitude." It is well to remember, too, the Roman word *consuetudo*, which signifies all that the mind has created and assimilated as its own; whereas the *suum* (root, *sva-*) denotes blood and breath as inherited possessions, *consuetudo* stands for this newly-acquired property which, however, has become similar to the other two. Finally, the meaning of habit *(Gewohnheit)* itself should be studied, like that of the corresponding Greek term *(ethos)*. Both point, as it were, to settlements of ideas and impulses. These have won their proper location, the native soil to which their Gemeinschaft-like activity refers and to which they have adapted and accustomed themselves, and thus have become the more closely connected with each other.

Intelligence as the specially developed *sensus communis* has the same relation to habit as the different sense organs and their functions have to liking or preference.

8. Memory—Learning of Interrelationships— Speech—Imagination—Reason

The third form of natural will I call memory. It is only a special development of the second one and has the same meaning with regard to the upper cerebral centers, which are well developed in man, as has the more general concept with regard to the spinal cord. Memory is conceived of here as the principle of mental life and, therefore, as the specific characteristic of human natural will. As the latter is originally equal to all organic life, it may well be said that the real nature of will per se most clearly manifests itself as memory or as the association of ideas (for it is as such that the sensations or experiences attain to a comparatively separate existence). In fact, memory has often been defined as a general quality and capacity of organic matter (Hering, Haeckel, S. Butler, and recently especially Semon), and animal instincts have been conceived of as inherited memories. But it is equally possible to think of them as habits, and they are indeed nothing else, if considered in relation to the species instead of the individual. For the primal organic instincts, which cannot be traced back any further, have assimilated such capacities and tendencies and tend to perpetuate them beyond the individual life as ever stronger and ever more closely related attributes.

Habit and memory have a similar relation to each other. The latter concept detaches itself from the former, but tends at the same time to fall back into it as an increasingly stronger power. In this sense English psychologists (Lewes, Romanes) have developed the theory of lapsing intellect. This theorem provides a formula for the well-known phenomenon of so-called voluntary acts becoming automatic or free from conscious direction. This refers to acts partaking of intellect or, in animals, induced by certain processes of perception and imagination, and implies that these acts will require stimuli of less and less intensity for their performance. This process signifies, in its general meaning, the permeation of intellectual activities with kinetic impulses. It has, however, to be kept in mind that all types of sensation as well as of reaction can be explained only by their common origin in the unity of the organism and that, therefore, their combination must be potentially included therein.

Memory, in the usual sense, denotes the ability to reproduce impressions received; in its scientific meaning, it is the ability to repeat acts appropriate to achieving desired ends. This would be meaningless if it were not known that impressions themselves are activities and that this dualism is implied, although undeveloped, in the conception of organic life, of which all specific life represents only a modification, as a unity of nutrition and reproduced activities.

This unity is partly maintained in the development of organic life, and it is partly further developed by practice. It is, finally, a special combination which has to be learned in order to be preserved. It is present in all activities which are, in their essence, determined by specific human abilities. Such learning is acquired partly by experience and partly by imitation, and especially by guidance and teaching as to how something has to be done in order to be right and good and as to which things and beings are wholesome and valuable. This, then, is truly the treasure of memory: to know what is right and good in order to cherish it and to do it. For to recognize it as such and to stand for it is one and the same thing, just as it is one and the same thing to be accustomed to something and to approve it or to like something and to believe in it. However, none of these positive attitudes will by itself necessarily lead to the corresponding activities, and even a combination of all of them will do so only in case it can overcome an opposition which is always considerable.

The general expression of mental life is speech, the communication of one's own feelings, desires, and intellectual experiences to others or, in quiet thinking, to oneself. The language itself, as the knowledge of the meaning and value of word symbols and as the ability to combine and use these, has to be learned, which is in the main achieved by practice and habit. But with this art mastered, the spoken word depends very little on thinking and as a rule only on momentary likings or sudden ideas, the meaning of which is evident from the condition of the speaker, given circumstances of the occasion, and especially from the way in which the speaker is addressed, asked, and questioned. Liking or preference can always be interpreted as subconscious judgment; in the German language it is also synonymous with arbitrary judgment. Thus, liking rules all life by arbitrary selection, and this applies also to the life of imagination, that form of memory which is not determined by word symbols but which, once they exist, constantly reproduces them in varied groups like other ideas. In the same way, however, familiar ideas make themselves most strongly felt as functions of imagination and memory. Finally, there are ideas concerning which the relation itself is based on memory; this means that memory or some special idea and thought is needed as a standard of measurement, so to speak, in order to distinguish and evaluate them before they are accepted as one's own. Similar to speech are all other human activities which are primarily determined by imagination, memory, or reason, and which, as creative and artistic, are clearly distinguished from those of most animals, especially those nearest to man.

The same relationship as exists between intelligence and habit or between sensuality and liking exists between reason as the power of speech, thinking, and rational action on one side and memory on the other. If memory is mental liking or preference and habit in one, then habit is a lower (animal) form of memory, and liking is the elemental (general organic) form of memory.

Note. Spinoza has recognized memory as an element of human will. See the passage at the end of the *Ethics*, III, prop. 2, which begins as follows: "There is another fact to which I particularly wish to draw attention, namely, that we cannot do anything by free decision of our will if we do not remember it. For instance, we cannot use a word if it does not come to our mind. But it is not in the power of the mind to remember or forget a thing." After discussing an objection to his statements, he concludes his argument: "It must, therefore, necessarily be admitted that this decision of the mind, which is considered a free and independent one, cannot be distinguished from imagination itself or from memory. It is nothing else but that approval which involves the idea inasmuch as it is an idea. Furthermore, these decisions of the mind come to existence in the mind with the same necessity as the ideas of things existing in reality. Those who believe that they speak or are silent or act by free decision of their own will are dreaming with their eyes wide open."

We believe, however, that we shall be able to formulate this truth with still greater precision when we shall discuss the forms of rational will.

9. *Feeling—Faculties and Circumstances—Faculties and Practice—
    the Process of Learning —Human Nature—Second and Third
    Nature—Passion—Courage—Genius—Qualities of Will*

In this section the ideas propounded so far will be summarized in a few generalizations and elaborated for the definition of other concepts.

(A) All specifically human activities, that is, the conscious activities usually termed arbitrary, are derived, insofar as they belong to the sphere of natural will, from its qualities and its prevailing state of excitation. The latter can be defined as mood, affection, or determined image, opinion, or delusion. Quite generally, it is termed feeling, which seems to indicate the direction or the kind of emotion involved: one does as one feels, as one is wont to, or as one sees fit. In each case there is existent in the brain a certain quantity of nervous energy which is transmitted to the muscles insofar as it cannot be discharged within the brain itself. This distribution of nervous energy is determined partly by given external stimuli, partly by the interrelation existing within the organism (nervous system), in which the established pathways are those requiring a minimum of energy. All these activities, in expending and using energy, depend thus on a specific previous or simultaneous intake of energy, which cannot be accomplished otherwise than by labor although performed, as it were, on inherited ground. This labor is the developing and training of the brain, its growth through the mental functions themselves, constantly nourished from the vegetative system. The energy which these functions consume and increase and which at the same time is received from the outside is intellectual experience. Such experience is provided partly by the activities, single and connected, of the sense organs, which are every time performed with the co-operation of the already existing brain power and involve parts of former experiences, and partly by the activities of all other organs, especially those controlled by the sense organs and the brain. Among these, speech has the most important effects; it is at the same time a practice of highly complex mental and muscular activities and perception with the aid of one's own auditory apparatus. Lastly, experience is provided by a threefold independent activity of the brain: (1) by preservation and reproduction of genuine ideas, i.e., the functions of memory per se; (2) by forming these ideas and combining them in independent images which have, so to speak, a life of their own and seem to be perceived by a sort of "inner eye"; this involves a very subjective activity based on a specific energy of memory, namely, that of imagination; (3) by differentiating and combining images through the definition, acceptance, and rejection of them; this is conscious memory, from which comparative thinking or calculating based on definite concepts is derived.

(B) The development of specific types of liking or preference as representing the main trends of will is most dependent on internal conditions, i.e., natural tendencies, and least on external circumstances. Both may have an equal share in the developing of habits, but the external circumstances predominate in the development of the modifications of memory. In this sense, they are also meant to include the results of practice and training, which was distinguished as a specific type of practice called learning. There is no doubt that the possibility of practice, as everybody knows, depends on the given natural tendencies and that the ensuing results may differ greatly. But a weak natural ability can, through sustained practice, become at least equal to a strong but poorly developed ability. This refers to the abilities for specific acts and activities as well as to the tendencies toward certain types of behavior, action, or thought in general. It has been the custom—and here traditional opinion coincides with Schopenhauer's theorem—to distinguish between intellectual and moral psychic qualities and tendencies (apart from the physical qualities). Thereby intellectual qualities are clearly defined as natural abilities, whereas the moral qualities are conceived only as likes or dislikes. For the purpose of the present study there exist only types of will which, on the one hand, derive their objective reality from the total bodily constitution and, on the other hand, represent at the same time abilities which under every condition attain some perfection. They are most clearly recognizable through the objects and activities which the individual likes, through those to which he becomes easily accustomed, and finally through those for which he displays a good memory.

(C) All that is connected with the liking (i.e., the human instinct), the habits, and the memory of an individual can be conceived as being absorbed by and assimilated to his specific character so that the two form a whole. Or, liking or preference is assumed to be so fully identical with the original qualities of a person's nature that under favorable conditions it develops through the sheer growth of the whole organism. Then habit (as developed by practice) is the second nature, and memory (through imitation and learning) is the third. But the nature of every animal invariably represents itself in acceptance and rejection, attack and defense, approach or flight; or to express it in a psychological and at the same time intellectual way, in lust and pain, desire and aversion, hope and fear; or to use neutral and logical terms, in affirmation and negation. All life and all volition are self-assertion, hence assertion or negation of another being according to the relation it may have to the self or ego (as the unity of body and soul); i.e., it depends on whether or to what degree the other being is considered good or evil (i.e., desired or abhorred), friendly or hostile.

The whole meaning of our specific nature or our individual self can be defined as what we can do or are capable of doing, as our real power, i.e., as what we have willed and possess, including our whole system of our instincts, habits, and memories. These become evident in the individual acts of volition: (a) through the immediate (instinctive, vegetative) expression of feelings, which, like contraction or expansion of the body size, allows least for an expression of individuality; (b) through the communication of feelings by gestures, movements and sounds; (c) through their sublimation into judgments as spoken or reflected statements, wherein individuality finds its most important expression. Furthermore, power and nature of a human being are revealed in his objective achievements, in the realities of which his existence and his actions are considered the cause, i.e., his influence, his deeds, and his works. The more difficult some of these tasks are to accomplish, the more man depends upon the imitation of his fellows and his masters in order to learn these arts; like the higher animals, he is endowed for such accomplishment with a special faculty and tendency as a hereditary characteristic.

(D) From all such manifestations one tries to gain a knowledge of the essential character of the human being. If the necessary actions of such character reveal nothing but blind impulse and urge, the manifestations of this impulse are, nevertheless, different in vegetative as compared with animal and mental life. If an impulse is deep and important, it is called passion, as the urge to pleasure, a general "urge to live" which shows its greatest strength as the urge to procreation or sexual lust. As "urge to action," it can be called animal power or courage. Finally the "urge to creation" or the desire to organize, form, and communicate what is alive in memory and imagination is defined as genius. Every human being possesses a certain measure of passion and courage, as well as a certain measure and manner of genius. But all these faculties must always be thought of in relation to definite achievements, which makes the first the least variable and the last the most variable. It also becomes evident that these are only specified terms for the simple forms of natural will and that passion is based on liking, courage on habit, and genius on memory. Insofar as the natural will finds its expression in these mixed or complex forms which involve and influence the elements of rational will, it may be defined as natural disposition. In the natural disposition of a human being the tendencies and forces of passion, courage, and genius are mixed in different proportions. But passion and vivacity are the original characteristics and, as it were, the basis of this concept.

When manifested as positive or negative behavior of a human being toward others, passion is defined as sentiment, namely, love or hatred. Courage, as the will to friendly or hostile manifestation of such sentiment and, therefore, as the essence of moral qualities, is called soul or mind. Finally, the specific genius of an individual can take the form of memory and rational will in weighing and judging one's own or other people's friendly or hostile behavior. It then represents the concept which stands for moral tendencies and opinions and is by general consensus defined as conscience.

(E) These phenomena show the qualities of will which are admired, praised, and honored, or despised, blamed, and scorned. In general, good will, with the emphasis on "will," is the intensive exertion of all given forces, which has as its object some activity or the completion of some specific work, in contrast to ability and perfect achievement. Here force—i.e., the complex of qualities as potentiality of action—and will as the reality of action, which heretofore were encompassed by one and the same concept, are differentiated: force as a congealed and firm substance of will; will as a function, i.e., a dissolving, fluid energy. The relation between the two is comparable to that between potential and kinetic energy. In general, forces and faculties appear as gifts received from fate or from the gods, but man himself in his permanent unity and individuality is conceived as the author of all work achieved, of its results as well as of the activities leading thereto. This is not in the specific sense to be considered as occurring later than he has beforehand willed or chosen them in his mind, which might be considered as free to do otherwise. It is rather with the understanding that the specific will seems to originate within the total and general will, even if an identity of action and will is assumed.

According to the definitions given here, the distinction made is essentially that between mere development and actual practice (together with training and practical use) of given faculties (or tendencies). In practice, the whole, fully developed human being participates as well as do his specific qualities of intelligence and reason, that is, in physiological terms, certain centers of his cerebrum. For this reason, any judgment with regard to the activity or the will of the individual applies also to his whole being as the pertinent cause or the totality thereof. The natural will is thus characterized by permanent qualities which explain it not so much in terms of substance and power as in the indicated sense of volition and action. If great and important, the latter represent its specific merits, excellences, and virtues. The general virtue is energy, power of action, and will power. In the realm of action it expresses itself as valor, in the realm of work as industry (or earnestness, diligence, and care). These are the concepts correlative to passion, courage, and genius. Since these can be limited to a meaning denoting will as a natural force or faculty (although in many different applications), the former are defined especially as rational will, i.e., as the principles of human endeavor, practice, and labor.

But in these virtues and their manifold variations the real moral goodness of will, that is, human goodness, cannot be found. A person may, by virtue of his activities and skills, distinguish himself and render extraordinary and useful services; he may be a good artisan, soldier, or writer, but that does not necessarily make him a good human being. On the strength of these virtues, of a strong will to achievement in some field, one can be an efficient or important, but never a good (kind) human being. Human goodness (to use this term for the general concept) manifests itself only in the behavior of an individual toward his fellow beings, and relates, therefore, only to the second series of the phenomena (or manifestations) of natural will. It is a genuine, friendly, and benevolent tendency of will, considerateness ("flower of the noblest mind," as a poet said), ready sympathy with other people's joy and sorrow, devotion to, and grateful memory of, friendly companions in life. Thus, we may define the purity and beauty of "sentiment" as sincerity and truthfulness, the depth, as we say, and nobleness of the mind as kindness, and the goodness and integrity of conscience as faithfulness. From these three all natural moral values can be derived. Compared to them, those common achievements of will, however important they may be otherwise, appear indifferent in the moral field. Much confusion results from mixing up one category of judgments with the other in the discussion of moral issues.

However, these morally indifferent virtues acquire moral importance insofar as they please, further the well-being of others, and represent in general useful qualities or forces or seem to be practiced with such intention. The lack of these virtues, or their opposite, is not only despised and censured, but may even appear as offensive ill-will (which arouses indignation, just as good will evokes sympathy). Virtues are admired, vices are despised, even in enemies, although there the latter can be as terrible as the former pleasant and useful.

Note (1911). The distinction made here with regard to ethical values is also of great importance for the theory of social life, that is, for the antithesis of Gemeinschaft and Gesellschaft, and is usually ignored by writers who are not able to think in terms of concepts. In contrast, Hobbes (*De Homine,* Ch. XIII, 9) has stressed their importance in his statement: "The three cardinal virtues, courage, cleverness, and temperance, are not virtues of the citizens, they are general virtues of man, because they are useful not alone to the commonwealth, but also to such individuals as possess them. Just as the commonwealth can maintain itself only through the courage, cleverness, and temperance of its citizens, it may also be destroyed by the courage, cleverness, and temperance of its enemies."

10. *Rational Will—Unity*

It is an entirely different theory which deals with the will as product of thinking, as rational will, for the theory presupposes a fully developed will inherent in the human organism. The innumerable potentialities which exist as images of future activity in every memory, can be realized and formed only through consistent, renewed, and extended thinking. The various tendencies or forces, as intellectual concepts, evolve or are developed into systems in which each one has its own place and performs a certain function in regard to the others. Such unity, however, as it is imagined (that is, exists only as a product of thinking) always represents an expression or action of the whole human being. An imagined end, that is to say, an object to be obtained or an occurrence to be brought about, always establishes a standard according to which the future activities are planned and determined. In the ideal case, the end itself—i.e., the thought of it—dominates all other thoughts and considerations and, therefore, all deliberate actions. They must serve the end or purpose, conduct *(conducere)* toward it, or at least not impede it. Therefore, many ends or purposes become subservient to one single end, and many thoughts are amalgamated into one leading idea, the realization of which seems to serve their own ends. These secondary ends are thus themselves degraded to mere means, viz., in regard to the ulterior purpose. The perfect domination of thinking over volition would establish a hierarchy, every end and purpose would finally lead to a higher and more general end or purpose. But also according to our conception, these final ends derive their forces from thinking insofar as this gives them recognition and approval, thereby proving the supreme position of thinking. Under these conditions, it must be possible to derive or explain all phenomena of volition from ulterior thoughts.

The tendency toward such domination is evident in every act of the intellect (understood as existing separately), for every actual observation also serves for the guidance and direction of impulses caused by natural will. Observation does not create motives but furnishes direction for the existing ones. Images and thoughts can even serve as the necessary conditions or accidental causes to awaken dormant potentialities of will. Nevertheless, these potentialities of will are in reality not dependent upon them, just as a force of nature is not dependent upon the laws of motion. Thinking, however, establishes itself as the ruling power; it becomes the deity which gives motion to inert substance. Thus, it should be conceived as separate and free from the original will (from which it nevertheless originated), containing and manifesting will and wishes instead of being contained by them and manifest in them. A rational will can exist because the results of thinking with regard to future action can persist and acquire a seemingly independent existence, although they do not possess any reality except through the creating and conserving thought. Thinking, as a mode of volition and motion, precedes other modes of volition and motion and is therefore considered their cause. For this reason only its psychic aspects are taken into consideration, while it is the physical aspects which are observed in the other modes. Thus, the conclusion is drawn that the soul (or the will) influences the body. This is impossible, as both are identical. The truth in this case is as follows: Insofar as reality is attributed to these products of thought (which is absolutely permissible, if properly understood), something ideally real acts on something physically real, ideal will on real will (as also the possibility of being moved must be interpreted in a psychological sense), ideal matter on real matter. Thus is explained the very complicated physiological process by which a quantity of brain energy is transmitted, by means of nerves and muscles, to the members of the body.

11. *Forms of Rational Will*

Three simple forms of the concept of rational will can be distinguished according as it refers (a) to free behavior in general or to the choice of a specific object, i.e., an activity in relation thereto. This latter form is called deliberation. In this case, it is assumed that two inherently hostile ideas meet each other, viz., one of pleasure and one of displeasure. In the mind, the former represents the reason for one kind of volition, while the other provides a reason against it and for another kind of volition. In thought, they are compatible with each other and mutually serve each other. Deliberation as will is directed toward that which is painful, that which is not wanted per se, but only thereby to get that pleasure which results from it and which is actually and primarily desired. At first, however, the idea of pleasure is submerged and must remain an ulterior motive without immediate manifestation. Thus, the idea of aversion or displeasure is subjugated to the will and the idea of will to the aversion. They reach an agreement. Their common end, viz., a surplus of pleasure, which is unconditionally desired, becomes evident. The same relation exists if a pleasure is renounced for another pleasure or if pains are borne to avoid future displeasure. The antithesis is the essential point, for through thinking in relation to action the sharp division between ends and means is achieved. This division is completed and becomes evident through its antithetical character, where one is the negative of the other, viz., the end something good or pleasant, the means something bad or painful. Neither of the two is felt as such, because they are but objects of thinking; but they are conceived as contrasting concepts which have nothing in common but the scale in which they have been brought together. The one, by postulating itself as the cause of the other, is at the same time postulated as necessary and, therefore, to be desired, as soon as the desired pleasure seems to compensate for such a sacrifice. Cause and effect, therefore, are compared according to their values. They must be commensurable, i.e., they must be dissolved into their elements and reduced to common units of measurement. All specific qualities of pleasure and displeasure disappear, therefore, as unreal and imaginary; they are transformed into quantitative differences so that, in the normal case, one quantity of pleasure and one quantity of displeasure are opposed to each other as equal.

Another form of rational will which is directed (b) toward certain definite actions, is called discrimination. It presupposes a fully developed thinking "ego" which in regard to a definite end has a permanent existence, although this end may exist only for the sake of many other ends which postulate the first one as their central point. Within its sphere, all these ends are subordinated to this dominant one; but all the original ends are derived from a common quantity of intellectual experience, viz., as memories and knowledge of pleasant sensations and things, whereas for the dominant aim such relations no longer exist. It has at its disposition only a homogeneous and indifferent quantity of possibilities and decides, in every given instance, to realize as much of it as is necessary to bring about an imagined result. A number of different possible actions which appear to the mind as real objects are, so to speak, combined to be called no longer the possible, but the real will of the thinking subject. This real will, as "decision," stands between the ego and the objects; however, it has no binding force for the ego, who, as its author, may easily dissolve and destroy it. As long as it is in existence, he may approach and treat beings and things in accordance with it through his will. Insofar as conceived as in immediate reaction to things or insofar as the individual is thought of as a direct causality (in a physical sense) he has to follow his will as a model or prescription which contains the general features of that form which, through individual action, receives its specific characteristics.

The same relation exists between discrimination and decision on one side and action on the other as exists (c) between thinking and concept, viz., a binding judgment about the use of words in a certain meaning according to which the thinking person can form his speech. At the same time, he is able to use such terms as a standard, or measure for comparing and defining the real objects and relationships. For the concept itself, for example, of a circle, is mainly a product of thought, and plane figures, either existent or constructed, are defined and treated as circles according to their resemblance to this concept. Here the real achievement of thinking becomes evident; it develops, out of the complexity and variability of experience, simple and constant categories to which the various phenomena can be related, thus creating a common denominator for their interpretation. This also holds true of the concepts of the right, the useful, and the efficient which the thinking mind has formed or at least confirmed for itself in order to conform to them in judgment and action. With their help he measures the values of things and decides what has to be done to achieve the desired end. Such concepts are, therefore, either implicitly included in his decision or applied to it as general maxims.

In deliberation, action and idea are one. Discrimination is related thereto as a general principle to which many special purposes are subordinated. Finally, conception itself does not determine the realization by action, and conceives of it only as a consequence of its realization in thought itself. To understand deliberation, it is essential to study the end, aim, or purpose; to understand discrimination, where end or purpose is presupposed, it is essential to investigate the reasons; to understand conception, we have to find the principles according to which it is constructed.

12. *Mixed or Complex Forms*

The mixed or complex forms of rational will—which contain the elements of natural will—should (according to the foregoing) be understood as systems of thoughts, viz., intentions, ends, and means, which, like an apparatus, a human being carries in his mind as an instrument to comprehend and to deal with reality. From these systems of thoughts the main tendencies of his rational actions can be derived, insofar as they do not evolve from the mixed or complex forms of his natural will. Such a system is called, in general, intention.

This is what dominates the rational will, although its agent may have built up himself this total of his desires and aims and perhaps considers them as his free choice. His friendly or hostile behavior toward his fellow beings results from it; because of the idea that it serves his intention, one thing or the other may become easy; where his sentiment is uncertain, things become more difficult, because a prejudice must be overcome. The climber must have no scruples to put on a semblance of what, in its results, may amount to its real counterpart. What the truth could spoil can often be saved by a lie. To control feelings which are ugly or horrid is taught by conscience. To hide them where the expression could be detrimental is a rule of low cunning. To take on or leave their manifestations according to circumstances, yes, often even to show emotions contrary to the real ones, but, above all, to conceal one's ends, or, at least, to leave them in the dark: all this is characteristic of a way of acting which is motivated by calculations. It constitutes another aspect of the concept of the apparatus or system of thought. The climber does not want to do anything for nothing; everything he does is intended to be profitable; what he spends should return in another form; he thinks always about his advantage; he always has an ax to grind. The calculating person aims at a final result, its value; he does many things apparently for nothing, but they are part and parcel of his calculations and evaluated as such. The final account of his actions must not only recover his losses but also yield a profit which is not counterbalanced by any part of his original outlay. This profit is the ultimate aim and should not require any special expense, but must be obtained through skillful disposal of existing means, through calculation, and through well-planned and well-timed use. Calculation is thus more evident in the configuration of comprehensive actions than in single minor features, gestures and speech. The climber seeks his way, of which he sees only a short stretch; he is aware of his dependence upon chance incidents, and trusts his luck. The calculating person feels superior and free, certain of his aims and master of his resources, which he controls in his mind and directs according to his decisions, however much they may seem to follow their own path. The totality of utilized knowledge and opinions which one may possess about the regular or probable trend of things, whether this trend be determined by him or not, and, consequently, the knowledge of his own power and of alien forces, which may oppose him (therefore to be conquered) or be of a friendly nature (therefore to be won), is called his consciousness. Such consciousness must be at the root of all moves and estimates if the calculation is to prove correct. It means the available knowledge fit for planned use; theory and method of control over nature and man. The conscious individual scorns all dark feelings, premonitions, prejudices, as they are of doubtful or negligible value in this respect. He desires only to arrange his plans, his way of living, his philosophy of life, according to his own clear and definite conceptions. Consciousness implies self-criticism; and this self-criticism turns as much against one's own (practical) blunders as conscience against one's own imagined wickedness. Self-criticism is the highest or most intellectual form of rational will, conscience the highest or most intellectual form of natural will.

13. *The Supreme End*

The supreme end which dominates the thought system of a human being is an object of will as thought only insofar as volition is intense wishing. The end is thus imagined as pleasure which is to come. It is not a matter of freedom, something that one could at will do or omit, take and use, or keep to oneself unused. It is something akin, possibly belonging to, an alien will and an alien freedom, and necessarily different from one's own actions. Happiness, which everybody longs for and desires, is first of all simply the favorable and agreeable circumstances which make life and work easier, ensure the success of any undertaking, and safely guide one through all danger. These are circumstances which, like fair weather, can perhaps be foreseen and foretold but cannot possibly be brought about. And little of what we desire are we able and inclined to establish as an end to be realized or attained. But happiness is also that after which innumerable people strive, which they pursue and chase as if it were a goal that had to be attained and attained quickly because the desire is so urgent. This haste to attain the goal exists because of fear lest it might escape or others might take the lead and get hold of it, or lest the goal elude us before overtaken and grasped or brought down from a distance with arrow or bullet.

According to this conception, happiness is like an external object of which one may take possession by using one's power if one has luck, i.e., if chance circumstances are favorable. But one can also hope for it and even, calculating the probabilities, undertake something at the risk of failure or loss, like a gambler. And such persistent or often repeated attempts are similar to striving and struggling, as if one wanted to master chance itself. And, indeed, a correct foresight of future events amounts to a kind of domination over them; although they cannot be changed, one can at least take them into account in order to enjoy the favorable and avoid the evil ones. Foresight thus discourages vain attempts and encourages others more promising. But such foresight is possible only within limited spheres; as purely factual knowledge is highly uncertain, as knowledge based on casual relationships it is highly imperfect. If such foresight were certain and at the same time perfect, it would eliminate the concept of chance. Actually, however, for chance the widest range remains in all fields of events as the effect of unusual or unknown circumstances. The greater the distance is and the less success depends on our own strength and the quality of a constant will determining it, the more important the element of chance.

In this striving for and pursuing of happiness, a future event through thinking becomes similar to an object the reality of which is determined by its causes and the causes of which seem to offer themselves as possible modes of action. In defining his rational will as disposal of means, man transforms a piece of his imaginary freedom into its very opposite, which at first is itself only imaginary but becomes real in the process. His own master otherwise, man becomes, in thus pledging himself, his own debtor and servant. But the full meaning of this whole concept can be comprehended only if such rational action is considered a sacrifice, i.e., performed unwillingly and with aversion. Then only the thought of the (solely desired) end, i.e., of pleasure, advantage, happiness, can bring this sacrificing about as a voluntary act. This element of free will is itself the absence of freedom in relation to one's self, or self-compulsion, for alien compulsion and need would destroy it. All rational will contains something false and unnatural. This corresponds with the reaction of the neutral observer, often terming such actions

"affected," "forced," "tendentious," or "deliberate." It is a feeling of aes-
thetic-moral displeasure, as is often energetically voiced in life and art.

14. *The Desire for Power and Money*

People strive for pleasure, advantage, happiness in various ways, as is
well known; the highest good is believed to be hidden in many different
things. Such objects, however, can be distinguished according to their
relation to the three types of life. Within each category a dichotomy
may be set up; thus, the ends take on one aspect when the mind reserves
for itself the pleasure to be derived therefrom and when its enjoyment
rests essentially in its own activity. This aspect changes if the impulses
and desires are encompassed and controlled by the mind. But no less
intense are the pleasures of the lower "parts of the soul" of the great
mass of people; the pleasures of the mind are those of the upper parts,
of the few, the select, the distinguished. A person can be very much
the subject of rational will even in his intellectual characteristics and
still know only of vulgar happiness and nothing of the pleasures of the
mind. Thus, it can never occur to him to strive for any-thing like them,
except for the sake of other ends more congenial to him. On the other
hand, there are those who disdain any of the happiness of the multitude, but, in order to obtain what seems desirable to them, will resort
to all possible means. However, all are alike in one respect: they want
the means or the power which guarantees them, through their very
use, as much of the pleasures as they desire. Hobbes is, therefore, right
in describing "a general inclination of all mankind, a perpetual and
restless desire of power after power, that ceaseth only in death. And
the cause of this is not always that a man hopes for a more intensive
delight than he has already attained to, or that he cannot be content
with a moderate power, but that he cannot preserve the power and
means to live well, which he hath present without the acquisition of
more." (*Leviathan*, Ch. XI, Part I, p. 71, following translation, James
Thornton, Oxford 1881.)

For the reasons given, such desire is well-nigh identical with the desire for money, because in a certain social system money means power
over all goods and pleasures which can be reduced to this denominator;
i.e., money is the general commodity, pleasure is the abstract.

But the actual aims as defined by the types of intention are different.
In general and in the first place I mention side by side: (a) self-interest,
(aa) vanity. Self-interest passes from general crude and material objects,
which themselves undergo a manifold development, to specific refined
and intellectual manifestations. The intellectual motive, which, besides
the organic-animal stimuli, is at the root of it, is strikingly defined by

the statement of the aforementioned author that for man ". . . joy consisteth in comparing himself with other men," and "can relish nothing but what is eminent." (Hobbes, *De Cive*. I, 5). That is the essence of vanity, the endeavor to make pretenses and to shine, to be admired, to have influence, and to make a favorable impression. If these pleasures of power and of its effects on others become the very end of one's intention, the lust for pleasure is the general character which it has in common with self-interest, for what is useful is also sought only for the sake of ultimate pleasures. However, the self-interested person finds himself able to forego pleasures; being rational, he thinks of the future by preferring something useful to what is merely pleasant. Self-interest and vanity are the motives for sociability. Vanity needs the other people as a mirror, self-interest as a tool.

As already hinted, self-interest takes on a specific form wherein it envisages as its end the means for all possible pleasures, and in this form it appears as (b) greed for money. Vanity is thus transformed into a specific type of desire for pleasure with regard to material goods, i.e., (bb) greed for profits, a refined type of greed. It is more a desire for the increase of wealth than for an absolute quantity thereof and, therefore, not limited by such, but increasing in importance to it, that is, to the degree in which the greed as such is satisfied and leaves the field to the thoughts related to greed for profits. What is common to them both is best expressed as greediness.

If self-interest uses other people as tools, it can be defined as (c) ambition, striving for such immaterial and purely intellectual means, i.e., the control of available human wills. The most perfect control of matters and men, in a certain sense, results from "science." It is that superiority which comes from a knowledge of the interrelationship of things and of the general conditions of the course of events and results in a foresight and forecast of the future. Thus, (cc) thirst for knowledge can be at the service of all these other ends or purposes, but it may also detach itself and be completely self-contained. Even in its purest form it is a development and a type of vanity. Nevertheless, the scholar and scientist will be happy and content with the opinion he has of himself and in the knowledge of the depth and meaning of his insight (which is expressed in the famous line, *Felix qui potuit rerum cognoscere causas)*, so that a noble thirst for knowledge rises high over vulgar vanity. On the other side, ambition and lust for power imperceptibly merge into each other. The ruler wants to be honored; he wants to see and receive the outward tokens of his power, to know that he is recognized, feared, or loved. The ambitious person wants to rule, even if only to be free of the domination of others and of their competition.

15. *Desires — Enlightenment*

All such motives are, according to this theory, nothing but empty wishes of the imagination or the subconscious impulses and types of liking, insofar as their objects have been made the objects and ends of thought. The individual acts of rational will which are in systematic connection with them conform thereto. They are not, as they would be if representing qualities of natural will, genuine lust for and urge to, and, to a certain extent, ability in certain tasks, deeds, or works by the value and quality of which their own value could be measured. Nothing follows from them but that this individual will use many already existing means at his disposal which seem to be capable of producing the desired results. This will not result in a creative action which expresses the individuality of the subject, but the means are more adequate the more they resemble what an abstract ego would want or do when this ego has at his disposal means suited to all ends and in unlimited quantity and when the sole task of this ego is to adapt the quantity of outlay to the result desired. Thereupon follows as fulfillment the simple and easy act of "getting rid" of these means and "applying" them in the right place.

For these reasons the will cannot in this case be praised as "good will" with respect to its task, to a work to be completed; it expresses itself in attempts and intentions which will always have to be added to make even the perfect talent creative. Rational will is not linked to perfection or even ability, but only to attainment. It is thereby expressed in action or work which may be praised or blamed, but such praise or blame will never refer to the will behind it, neither in a morally indifferent nor in a moral sense. The first case is excluded because rational will is no reality which belongs to the essence of the human being; and the second case, because rational will does not encompass a positive attitude toward fellow beings which is rooted in sentiment, mind, and conscience. For abstract and free thinking must forever ask the reasons for, or end of, such attitude and can discover reasons or end only in relation to its own well-being. Only in this relationship can the well-being of another person have any meaning; it has, therefore, to be subjugated to and made dependent on one's own well-being. Cleverness will be recognized and admired only as the specific virtue and skill of thinking itself, on the strength of which it chooses the means suited to given ends, gauges the results of its activities, and in general makes the best possible use of all known circumstances. Intellect is the virtue of the mind, just as speed is the virtue of the legs and sharpness that of the eyes or ears. It is not a virtue of the human being because it does not express his whole will. The intelligent person contemplates and reasons concerning his tasks and intentions; he is clever if in his calculations he knows how to find unusual means and to base complex plans thereon. He is enlightened, clear, and concise in his concepts if he has correct abstract knowledge of the external relationships of human affairs and is not led astray by feelings or prejudices. From the combination and unity of these qualities results the consistency of the rational will and its manifestations, which are admired and sometimes feared as a power and a rare and important quality.

16. *Criticism—Opposition*

It is different if these types of intention and the rational will itself are judged from the point of view of the natural will, where they appear only as its highly developed modifications. From the viewpoint of natural will, everything that directly and actually belongs to it can be taken as good and friendly insofar as it expresses the totality and the unity of the human being. Such unity is, indeed, defined by the form of the body as well as by that of the mind and the will which is given at birth to every human being as the substance of his species. In contradistinction, the "egotist" mind, which enhances the principle of "individuality" to the highest point, will appear as hostile and evil. In the meaning of this consideration, which is not altogether correct but nevertheless well founded, mind or heart as well as sentiment and conscience are linked and even identified with kindness, as if it were their necessary corollary. The calculating and scheming person, however, is considered bad and evil because "heartless" and "unconscientious," and "egotism" is equivalent to spiteful and hostile sentiment. In reality, the more perfectly egotistic one is, the more indifferent he is toward the weal and woe of other people. He is not immediately concerned with either their ill fortune or their well-being. But he can instigate ill fortune as well as he can further well-being if it seems to serve his ends.

Pure general malignancy, however, is just as rare and well-nigh impossible as pure kindness of heart. By nature, every human being is good and friendly toward his friends and those he considers such (as far as they are kind toward him), but he is wicked and hostile toward his enemies (who maltreat, attack, and threaten him). Our abstract or artificial human being is neither the one nor the other in his relations with other people. He knows only allies or opponents with regard to the ends he pursues. Both are only forces or powers to him, and feelings of hatred or ire toward the one are as improper as feelings of love or pity for the others. If such feelings should ever rise in him, his thinking will consider them as something alien, disturbing, and irrational, which it is his task to suppress and even to extirpate rather than to cultivate and foster. For they involve a positive or negative attitude which is not

caused by and bound to his own interest and plans and they may, therefore, lead him to rash acts. He may, while acting in a hostile manner
in treating human beings like inanimate objects and tools, appear bad
to his own mind and conscience; but this at best presupposes that such
forces are still alive in him and that they demand a contrary behavior,
as they usually do with regard to relatives and friends. He will appear
in the same light to the mind and conscience of others who put themselves in his place. And people, as we know them, will only reluctantly
give up this notion and conceive of those who do evil as still having a
mind that holds them back, as being gifted with natural kindness of
heart, and having a voice of conscience which is not yet silenced and
dead. For that reason, a "guilty" conscience is always considered a guarantee of at least a modicum of good and right sentiment because it has
necessarily to disapprove of the evil deeds and plans against friends,
although nonetheless also of the good deeds and the lack of the proper
degree of malice toward enemies. For it is the friends who judge this
and approve of mind and conscience. Insofar as they hold hostile conduct against foes desirable and honorable, the mind is good except when
it goes astray and shows ill will toward friends and good will toward
enemies. Conscience is simply good in the same sense because it judges
one's acts by these standards. From this point of view all those very
rational intentions (by their form) to attain happiness and the means
thereto are, if not outright evil, at least intemperate passions which
are outside the sphere of virtue, whatever meaning may be given for
that term. Furthermore, conscious egotistic action can be considered
hostile and insulting insofar as it is deliberate acting of roles, as in all
cases where it is used to create, in another person, an opinion which
the actor (the person acting) knows to be wrong. Out of nothing he
fabricates fictitious things and gives them the semblance of reality.
But whoever accepts them, under the assumption that he is receiving
something, will react accordingly, i.e., give something in return. This
something, then, is taken away and stolen from him by such trickery.
The same relation as between this type of conscious (arbitrary) action
and its general concept exists between deception and barter, between
fraud and selling. A false coin or an adulterated commodity and, in
general, lies and make-believe, have, if they produce the same results
(either in a single case or in the average of cases), the same value as the
genuine article or the true word or the natural conduct. There is also
the case in which such deceptions, if they produce greater results, have
even higher value; if the results are smaller, their value is correspondingly lower. In relation to the general category of available power (or
force) the existing and also that which is nonexistent but assumed by

the deceived party to be existent (or the real thing and what is imitated, fabricated, or fictitious) are of equal quality.

17. *Brain and Heart*

In our language, we make a distinction between what springs from the mere cold intellect, i.e., the brain, and the warm impulses of the heart. The contrast in question is generally recognized if feeling as an impulse and directive influence is distinguished from intellect, but the differentiation is made most vivid and impressive if the distinction is illustrated by the difference between heart and brain. Antiquated theories conceived such feeling as confused. The acts of intellect, however, were conceived as clear and distinct imagination, and until this day attempts are still being made to derive the former from the latter, which are supposed to be simple and therefore original phenomena. In reality, thinking—however rational and self-evident it may appear—is the most complex of all psychical activities and requires, especially if it is to function independently of the impulses of organic life, much training and practice even if only to be applied to such simple categories as the relation between ends and means. Definition and differentiation of these concepts and, following that, the establishing of a relationship between them, can be achieved only through word images as real and discursive thinking. The same is true of the creation of a form of rational will, if undertaken only for well-considered reasons that command to oneself: "I must and I will." But all animals, and to a large extent also man himself, in their movements and utterances, follow much more their "feelings" and their "hearts," i.e., a disposition and inclination which is in embryo contained in the individual character and has developed along with it. If conceived as an intellectual possession, this is in the original state related to the psychical constitution the same as what later becomes dependent on the organ of thought and thereby is brought into a new system. This system is simpler because it is composed, if possible, of like or (in the geometrical sense) similar elements, i.e., self-made ones. In a human being who remembers the past and retains innumerable usual sensations which recur in the order of their inherent relationship and under the influence of given stimuli, that "priority of will" can be inferred only if the dependence of such activity of the memory and the imagination upon the complicated system of sympathies and antipathies is taken into account. We are easily misled because all intellectual processes seem to cause the feelings, desires, and so forth. In reality, however, the processes of differentiation and combination of given tendencies and the transition from a state of equilibrium into one of motion are repeated here, motion being attracted to or repulsed from a perceived or imagined object (or simply place). In contrast, the tension and attention and, therefore, the acuteness of the senses are essentially conditioned by the given impulses and their intensity as expressed in activities, and the same holds of ideas and thought. According to the underlying relation to our desires, sympathies, and displeasures, our hopes and fears, in short, to all conditions of pleasure or pain, we dream one thing often, easily, and with liking or pleasure, and another seldom and with dislike or displeasure. With regard thereto, one should not raise the objection that sad and unpleasant ideas take up the same space in our consciousness as the happy and pleasant ones. For such ideas can themselves be considered as sensations of pain, and insofar as they are such the organism or the will fights them and tries to get rid of them. That does not, however, preclude the possibility that in these ideas there are parts which are felt with pleasure, even those in which "the soul delights."

18. *Sense of Duty*

As is well known, the laws governing the associations of ideas are manifold because the possible connections and interrelations are innumerable. But too little emphasis is given to the fact that the individual disposition and ability to pass from one thing to another and to produce one thing out of another are very different and bound up with the physical and mental constitution as developed through all experiences of life, because they derive therefrom. On the whole, everybody thinks of his own affairs; his thinking is concerned with his own cares or hopes, or at least with his doubts or considerations as to what to do and how to do it in the right manner. That is, the center of his mental activity is formed by his usual occupation, consequently by his tasks and duties, his past, present, or future functions, his work and his art. And for that very reason, memory can be defined as a form of natural will; for it is sense of duty or the voice of reason which indicates what is necessary and right in such work, and it is the recalling of all one has learned, experienced, and thought, and it is kept as a treasure in oneself; it is really a practical reason, *opinio necessitatis*, a categorical imperative. In its most perfect form it is, therefore, identical with what is conceived of as conscience or genius. There is nothing mysterious about that except insofar as organic volition is itself dark, irrational, and, so to speak, the cause of itself. For these special faculties, although inborn on one side and developed on the other, are fixed associations and, if developing into activities, they only prove the strength of their tendency or their *conatus*. For many such "beginnings" struggle and vie with one another. In merely thinking of something feasible, one is already tempted and prompted to do it, but even a mere perception may be sufficient to excite the nerves and muscles, and all the more so the more strongly we are attracted to or repulsed by it from liking or habit. In that case, the intellectual conception of the object can counteract and influence it in another direction. Where feeling and also that which has been thought of as feeling is active or even dominates, there our conduct, our behavior, our speech are only specific expressions of our life, our strength, and our nature. In a way similar to that which makes us feel and conceive of ourselves as thinking agents of these organic functions of our growth and decay, we also feel as if we were thinking agents of our actions and of other sentiments to which "the spirit" incites us—a state of mind and an urge together with a rational interpretation of given conditions as to what is required or what is under all conditions the right thing, the beautiful, good, and noble.

The relation changes to the degree in which the activity of the intellect becomes independent and seems to deal unrestrictedly with its material by separating and combining what should be done. Heretofore conditioned by the work and supported by its idea, thinking frees itself therefrom, rises above it as the ultimate purpose, allowing the work as if separated and different from it, to become means and useful cause in successful attainment of ends. But as such it is no longer essential and necessary, because, insofar as many roads lead to the same end or many causes may have the same effect, the attempt is now made to find the best possible means, i.e., to balance the relations between means and ends as much as possible in favor of the end. Insofar, however, as the result seems actually dependent on some means, whether or not this be the sole or the best one, these means are also the necessary cause and have to be used.

Addition (1911). The association of ideas is analogous to the association of people. The associations of thought which form the natural will correspond with the Gemeinschaft, those which indicate rational will correspond to Gesellschaft. The individuality of a human being is as fictitious as the individual and isolated existence of a purpose and its corresponding means. This idea was not explicitly expressed in the first edition of this book, but it necessarily follows from the whole line of reasoning because it is contained therein. The author has, therefore, on several occasions (for example, treatise on pure sociology in the *Annales de I'Institut international,* Tom. VI, Paris, 1900) taken the opportunity to point it out. He has especially stressed the fundamental problem as to whether the ideas of means and ends are mutually inclusive, belong to each other by nature and confirm each other, or whether they are, like Hobbes' human beings and their descendants in my "Gesellschaft," enemies by nature, mutually exclusive and negating each other. Without knowledge and recognition of this psychological contrast, a sociological understanding of the concepts described here is impossible. Special emphasis must be laid on the fact that the forms of will such as liking, habit, and memory are as essential for and characteristic of Gemeinschaft-like associations as those of deliberation, decision, and concept are of Gesellschaft-like associations. In both cases they represent the existing bonds.

SECTION TWO: Explanation of the Distinction

19. *Analogies of Forms*

An aggregate or form of the rational will is related to an aggregate of the natural will in the same manner as an artificial tool or machine built for definite ends or purposes compares with the organic systems and the various organs of the animal body. If considered as discernible objects, the phenomena compared can be more easily observed, and such observation will make it possible to understand the contrasting variations of the given psychological concepts. Tools and organs have this in common that they both contain and represent accumulated labor or energy which gives definiteness as well as augmentation to the total energy of their respective owners. Furthermore, both possess their specific energy only in relation to and dependent on this total energy. The two, however, differ in their origin and in their qualities.

An organ comes into existence by itself, through repetition of the same activity by the whole organism or by an already existing organ; this additional and specific energy is developed to a greater or lesser degree of perfection. A tool is made by the human hand which takes an extraneous substance and gives it unity and form according to the idea of the end or purpose which it is expected to serve in accordance with the will of its creator. Thus, the tool, after its completion, will be capable of performing special tasks.

Tools and organs differ, further, in their characteristics; an organ exists as a unity only in relation to the unity of the organism and cannot be separated from it without losing its specific qualities and powers. Its individuality is, therefore, only derivative and secondary. It represents only a specific manifestation and differentiation of the total organism. The total organism, and with it the individual organ, attain uniqueness through their very substance. They are, therefore, so our experience tells us, really individual, or at least constantly tending to individuality.

In contradistinction, a tool is, in substance, like all other substances and represents only a certain quantity thereof, which can be reduced to imaginary atomical units and conceived as an arrangement of such.

Its own unity exists only in its form and is apprehended only through consideration of the use or the end to which it is to be put. As such it can change from the control of one human being to another, and can be employed by everyone who knows the rules of its use. Its individual and separate existence is to a certain degree perfect, but it is dead because it does not maintain or reproduce itself; it wears out and another one can be produced only by the same alien and extraneous labor, the same spirit which created the first one, i.e., produced it in its own image or in the image which existed before it.

20. *Freedom and Choice*

The psychic substance from which the forms of human natural will originate is human will itself, or freedom. Freedom is nothing but the real possibility of individual life and action as it is felt or known, a general and indefinite tendency (activity, force) which becomes special and definite in those forms—the possibility develops into a determinate probability. The thinking agent of natural will, insofar as it is identical with this substance, is related to its forms as the mass of an organism, if conceived under abstraction of its form, is related to the form itself and to the individual organs. It is nothing aside and apart from them; it is their entity and substance. Its forms grow and differentiate through its own action and practice. This process evolves, however, only to a very small degree through the specific labor of the individual. Modifications which the individual has developed are transmitted to his progeny as potentialities (thus the substance of forms of will). The progeny develop these potentialities and practice them if conditions are favorable. Thus, the modifications become intensified through training and use or again specialized through particular application; all such labor of his ancestors is repeated by the individual in his growth and development in a peculiar, abbreviated and easier way.

The substance of rational will is freedom insofar as it is present in the individual's mind as the total of possibilities or forces of volition or nonvolition, action and nonaction. The mind encompasses a large quantity of such substance; it chooses from it and gives it form and formal unity. This thing, the formed rational will, is also under the control of its creator, who by acting holds it and uses it as his power. Through action he diminishes the number of his possibilities or consumes his power. Until that moment, he could still (according to his own thinking) leave the action undone; by his acting, this possibility disappears from his sphere at the same time as the opposite one, viz., of the action. For an imaginary possibility is annihilated by becoming either reality or impossibility. The previous volition of a possible action can be regarded as a preparation for this double annihilation. It increases one and diminishes the other possibility, and more so the more probable the execution and consequence of the action may be to his thought and the more clearly this thought, by its very existence, presents itself as the necessary and absolute cause of such action. The action, however, is only a tool, an instrument, and is in reality dependent upon the individual who is the creator of both the thought and the action.

21. *Consumption of Means*

On the other hand, action in reality (as considered from the subjective viewpoint) implies that it is willed in its entirety in the anticipatory idea, viz., that it includes the consumption of means which to be conceived as such are entirely dependent upon the mind. The (imagined) rational will itself is, therefore, nothing but the existence of these means, insofar as a certain quantity of them has been brought to unity and form as required by the end or purpose sought. These imagined possibilities are not equivalent any longer if they are conceived as means for attaining pleasure, but become elements of pleasure; they become more definite if the mind visualizes them as things and thus, so to speak, dissects freedom. Thus calculated it then may seem that in acting the individual is giving up, if not real things, at least part of his freedom. In this sense, each action becomes a purchase, viz., acquisition of something alien in exchange for something of one's own. This conception corresponds more or less adequately to reality. What we receive are pleasures or goods (that is to say objects as possibilities of pleasure); what we pay are elements of pleasure, means, parts of freedom, or again goods. If, however, such materialization is, so to speak, relinquished by returning to the status previous to the action and the purely subjective concept of freedom is re-established, the absolute, self-affirmation of the mind is demonstrated. In contradistinction, the idea of rational will is itself negative; for the rational will postulates, with regard to existing relationships in nature, a certain action as cause and therefore required by one's own wish and will (of an end, result, or purpose). "I will" means in this case as much as "you shall" or "you must." One owes it to one's end or purpose, which means to himself. By carrying out this command one is absolved from the obligation. Thus, in thought and in action, the pleasure or positive elements and the displeasure or negative elements are mutually exclusive and cancel each other out.

22. *Ability and Obligation*

In the realm of reality and natural will there is no dual possibility, no power of volition or nonvolition; possibility and probability are like forces signifying the action itself which represents in an imperfect manner their content and realization. What can be separated as a single element is only the form and expression of something permanent and stable which not only maintains itself through such a function but even, under certain conditions, is strengthened and increased by it. This is true to the extent that it is fed from a reserve which nourishes and maintains itself through its contacts and interaction with the surrounding objects, which can be understood as psychic as well as physical. It is a present thing which was extant as a thing of the past, whereas, in contrast, the possibility which is contained in the rational will means existence as something of the future, something unreal. The first form can be experienced and known by all kinds of feeling, as thinking agent and object are the same and both equally real. The future thing is known and understood only by the mind. It is an object like something formed or fictitious, but in a minor and more general sense than the creations which are produced from such imaginary material by thought. What, in the case of natural will, is meant by production can be defined as a movement of organized matter itself, although with the creative co-operation of the thinking agent. The completion of such movement is already contained in its very beginning so that always the same forms develop from the same, more indefinite ones.

Thus, the following characteristics are relevant to the concept of natural will. All ability involves an obligation which is not imaginary but real and also implies action which coincides with the obligation. It is an entelechy, a predetermined process, similar to the development of the fruit from the blossom, or the animal from the egg. It is the same matter in a modified form. Living matter is assimilated to the forces of the individual being, and, in turn, these forces are transmitted to the matter, a process comparable to that of procreation and of all artistic creation. Such a process stands in sharp contrast to one in which the thing given and the thing received have nothing in common except that one is the price of the other. The conception of the former process is based on an important general law: All organic differentiation develops and grows by action, and through this process increases the force of action itself. Inertia of the organs means regress and death, the cell-substance and the tissues no longer being renewed.

By analogy, this law applies also to the will. It can be generalized into the statement that also through activity as related to something foreign, that is to say through directing one's will toward something, or through application of one's energy for its cultivation and development, a special organ, or in other words a special will, and (through practice) a special capacity must develop. For instance, sight is such a (general

animal) activity in regard to light and lighted objects, and the eye is
the result of this activity. The eye again is only an organ which is most
perfectly connected to the central organ, from which it springs, and
with the center of life, the heart, which nourishes it. This nourishment
itself depends again upon its specific function. Thus, through affection,
protection, and care *(amplecti)* for beings and things, we can develop
organs of a psychologically real existence or develop our organic force
through specialization.

Furthermore, through love, through communication of the energy
of my being, in accordance with the degree of its intensity and duration
and the vicinity of its object, the activity becomes and remains alive
through my being, like an organ which is not temporary but is a lasting
emanation of my being and substance. This holds true for everything
which lives and works as my creation—that which I have created or
borne, that which through cultivation and care, nourishment and protection, is dependent upon me or derived from me, and, finally, that
which I have created or gained, shaped or formed, by my mind and art.
In a way I belong as much to all this as it belongs to me. Thus, there exists between the individual and his creations a mutual interdependence.
In the same way as the eye belongs to the body, the body belongs to the
eye, although to a lesser degree because the body can exist without the
eye but the eye cannot exist without the body.

23. *Whole and Part*

And thus the organic whole should always be considered and conceived
in relation to its parts, insofar as they have a distinct and separate
existence as such. The whole and general will or life, as well as the
special one, is neither pleasure nor pain, but, insofar as it is unified,
it is a constant tendency toward pleasure, for pleasure is, according
to Spinoza, development toward greater perfection, and pain toward
lesser perfection. Both are only excesses or disturbances in the unstable
balance which is the expression of will or life. This results in a necessary consensus, which means that pleasure or pain for the whole must
be pleasure or pain for the parts, inasmuch as they express a totality;
thus, the same holds for one part as well as for another if the parts all
belong to and partake of the same source. The forms of will themselves
stand in such an organic relation to one another that there always exists
before and beyond them a totality which expresses itself in them and
has a relation to them; the relation between the whole and the parts is
primary, the one from which all others must be derived. All authority
and distinction between parts is only a representation of the power of
the whole over all parts. Within the parts there can develop relatively

new wholes which have the same relation to their members or parts. This still holds true if the forms of will are created and substantiated as ideas, insofar as they develop from the inner life and remain a part of it.

Natural will is (objective) freedom itself, its product not an artifice but something created. Rational will is the negative of (subjective) freedom, and action based on it means diminution of individual power; the (extraneous) result, however, is compensation therefor. The same relationship exists between creation through work as contrasted with acquisition by exchange (purchase). And this holds also for creative work, which forms its image out of the depths of its own being, as compared with the mere synthesis of given material elements into a dead, lifeless whole which is only present to the extent that it can be conceived by the mind as means to an end.

24. *Forms of Rational Will—the Isolated Human Being*

The forms of rational will set the individual as giving and receiving against the whole of nature. Man tries to control nature and to receive from it more than he himself is giving. But within nature he is confronted with another rational will which aspires to the same, i.e., with another individual who is to gain by his losses. In order to exist together, they must either not come into contact with each other or come to an understanding, for if there should be coercion only one of the individuals would exert his will and carry out his actions. For the other one, under such conditions, action would no longer mean realization of his rational will. That is to say, the pure concept of an abstract personality creates its dialectic counterpart: person against person, merchant against merchant, competitors and contracting parties.

The same relationship as between the forms of will exist between human beings as such insofar as the behavior of each is determined by his natural will. Force and coercion destroy the freedom of the individual or self which is coerced, and without freedom there is no force. But all such relationships can be understood only in terms of a whole that is innate in all of them. These separate entities may, in the course of their development, become differentiated from one another and thus oblivious to their common origin. Each then will function and act for his own personal ends, which only accidentally may serve the general good of all the others. However, as long as they can still be considered as a unity, even exchange between them is only a manifestation of their functions, i.e., of their existence as organic modifications, and of their natural unity.

Addition (from the original manuscript). The forms of rational will mean a discord of the human being as thinking agent of rational will.

This discord exists even though the person who postulates the end or purpose and enjoys the pleasure of an action is really one actor. Each phase of the action can be personified, and as such they are antagonistic to each other. I give (according to our theory) parts of my freedom or elements of pleasure—but to myself; I receive pleasure—but from myself. The relation makes sense only if this *alter ego* is not *ego* but another person who really uses his means exclusive of and in contrast to mine. As such he trades with his means and it is his end or purpose to obtain something from me just as I need something of his. But if I take from him or force him, I act alone; in the opposite case he acts alone.

25. *Normal Concepts and Deviations Therefrom*

The concepts of the forms of will are nothing but products of thought, tools devised in order to facilitate the understanding of reality. The great qualitative variety of human willing is made comparable by relating it—under the dual aspect of real or imaginary will—to these normal concepts as common denominators.

As free and arbitrary products of thinking, these normal concepts are mutually exclusive; rational will and natural will are strictly separate entities. The same concepts, however, are conceived of as empirical concepts (in which case they are nothing more than names comprising and denoting a multiplicity of observations or ideas, in that the content will decrease with the range of phenomena covered). Observation and inference will easily show that no natural will can ever occur empirically without rational will by which it finds expression, and no rational will without natural will on which it is based. But the strict distinction between these normal concepts enables us to discern the existing empirical tendencies toward the one or the other. They can co-exist and mutually serve each other, but, on the other hand, to the extent that each aspires to power and control, they will necessarily contradict and oppose each other even though their separate components as expressed in norms and rules of behavior are comparable. If rational will desires to order and define everything according to end, purpose, or utility, it has to overcome the given, traditional, deeply rooted rules insofar as they cannot be applied to such purposes, or to subordinate them if possible. The more decisive rational will or purposeful thinking becomes and concentrates on the knowledge, acquisition, and application of means, the more the emotions and thoughts which form the individuality of natural will are in danger of withering away. And not only this, but there is also a direct antagonism, because the forms of natural will try to repress rational will and oppose its rule and domination, whereas rational will tries first to free itself from natural will and then to dissolve, destroy, or dominate it. These relations become evident most easily if we take neutral empirical concepts to investigate such tendencies, concepts of human nature and psychological disposition, which are conceived as corresponding to and underlying actual and, under certain conditions, regular behavior. Such general disposition may be more favorable either to the natural or to the rational will. Elements of both may blend together in such disposition, and one or the other may predominate in determining its character.

This general disposition has a different aspect if it appears in either organic, animal, or mental life, and this leads to the following well-known concepts:

1.   Temperament,
2.   Character,
3.   Intellectual Attitude.

These concepts have, however, to be divested of all connotations which give them a meaning identical with that of nature or natural will, and they must be reduced to the purely logical meaning of "dispositions" which are conceived as corresponding to and preceding average reality. But this relationship can also be presented in the following manner: in addition and also in opposition to the given as well as (with respect to the rational will) a priori qualities which are conceived as inherent in the natural will, the rational will can produce new and special qualities and thus bring about something like an artificial character which, however, has nothing but the name in common with the original character, i.e., that based on natural will. This common name is founded on the fact that both the changing phenomena are related to a permanent or substantial personality. Therefore, this concept of character, or character in the general sense, will, as a rule, have a twofold origin. Or, in other words, normal conduct, behavior, or judgment (speech) will derive partly from sentiment, mind and heart, and conscience, and partly, to a greater or lesser degree, from interest (intention), calculation, and consciousness. One should, however, recall in this connection how little the human being will, in general, be inclined or able to follow his own will and his own laws, especially in a direct way.

26. *Matter and Substance of Feelings*

Given intelligent observation, however, our feelings are stimulated by the behavior of human beings in much the same way as they are by external objects; not only is a positive or negative attitude brought out in us, but psychical conditions and events themselves are judged as if the feelings involved were similar to tactile and dermal sensations, i.e., the most general types of differentiating perceptions. For the opposites, fluid and dry, soft and hard, warm and cold, are colloquially applied (although not to the same degree) to the differences of human character and behavior. The fluid (flowing) soft and warm qualities are ascribed to the feelings; of such kind is matter, if it abounds in inner motion, i.e., individual, organized matter; thus life is often likened to a river and a flame, and plastic softness is the most general quality of the cell-substance. In contradistinction, the last particles of substance which are the carriers of mechanical effects must be conceived as firm, hard, cold, and void of inner motion. The same sensations are also evoked by pure thinking and the intellect, its substance as well as what it produces. From that it can be easily understood how a temperament, etc., in which the phenomena of natural will prevail can be characterized as fluid, soft, and warm; but if the phenomena of rational will predominate, the terms dry, hard, and cold are used. For what is contained in and springs from natural will must itself be like it, and imagined actions are the elements of which the rational will is composed. In natural will there is the concrete and original element (the originality) of the individuals, what has already been defined as nature or disposition. In rational will there is the abstract and the artificial, the cut and dried and patterned. And that is what we will call apparatus. Temperament, character, and intellectual attitude are themselves natural insofar as they correspond to nature or disposition, artificial insofar as they relate to apparatus. They then are nothing but an assumed (affected) way of being, a part which is acted.

27. *Calling and Business*

Human life or volition (and thus the entirety of human activities) may be regarded from two different viewpoints. In the first case it may be considered an essentially organic process which, as such, reaches into a wide variety of intellectual life and is the same for all people only insofar as their organic constitution and the conditions of their growth and their existence are alike. This organic process is different insofar as the people are differently constituted. Volition consequently cannot be taught, as is already pointed out in the old saying of Seneca's: *Velle non discitur.* Or it can be taught only in the same way as a fine art, the works of which cannot be produced according to rules but must spring from the specific physical and intellectual qualities and especially from the force and mood directed thereto, that is, from the creative imagination of the artist. To learn means nothing else here but to grow, to develop an inborn talent by practice and imitation. Artistic activity is part of the ways of living, speaking, and creating which are peculiar to the artist.

These activities express themselves in a genuine work just as the nature and the power of any organism is found to be expressed in some way in all its parts. The activities, as in the case of inheritance of traits, are most perfectly contained in their own products and transmitted to new beings of their own kind. This is life and way of living as a calling.

From the second point of view, life is conceived and conducted as a business, that is, with the definite end or view of attaining an imaginary happiness as its ultimate purpose. It is then, of course, possible to form concepts and set up rules which represent and prove the best method of arriving at such an end and result in such a way as to be understood and applied by any person capable of logical reasoning which, in reality, has to be carried out by everybody and in every activity. The nature of all such theory is most clearly evident in mechanics. Mechanics is nothing but applied mathematics. Mathematics is nothing but applied logic. The principle of applied mechanics can be formulated in general terms as follows: to obtain the greatest possible result with the least possible expense of energy or labor. The meaning of this principle, however, can, when considered as related to any undertaking directed to a definite end, be expressed in the following way: the end should be attained in the most perfect possible way with the easiest and simplest possible means. Or, if applied to a business carried on for money: highest possible profit with lowest possible costs, or highest possible net profit. And if this principle is applied to life as such a business: the greatest amount of pleasure or happiness with the least amount of pain, effort, or trouble, the smallest sacrifice of goods or vital energy (through labor).

For wherever an end is to be attained, it is necessary to concentrate quite definitely on such purpose. Just as the eye of the marksman is on the visible target, thinking must be focused on the end. It must be coolly and calmly deliberated as to which are the best, surest, and easiest means of carrying out the undertaking in the most perfect way. It is equally necessary that these means are, so to speak, grasped with a firm hand and applied in that manner considered to be correct. One has, therefore, (1) to aim correctly, (2) to judge correctly, and (3) to act or behave correctly. The third phase is decisive and closest to the end. Phases one and two are subordinated to it as means in relation to their end. But correct acting or behaving is itself only a means of producing or attaining the desired result, and thus we have three categories of such instrumental activities which are required by that end and which are co-ordinated with regard to it: (1) The exertion of the mind on the imagination of the desired object or the conscious or rational attention, i.e., attention linked to thought. This is a form which underlies all rational activities. One focuses, as it were, one's telescope on that object.

This is identical with one's conception of what is to be attained, with the full understanding of one's own interest. But anybody can become informed on that subject; an adviser will show him the advantages he does not see himself; he will "open his eyes" and "draw his attention" to it. (2) Correct judgment requires correct concepts of the relative values of things, of the certain or to some degree probable effects of human action. These, too, can be transmitted in finished form, as measuring instruments the use of which is in general self-evident. (3) Such use of correct acting and behaving as consists in the appropriate distribution of existing means and forces is least suited to being learned in a direct way, but has nevertheless its own specific method, which can be taught.

28. *Volition as a Trick*

The acquired knowledge of how a thing has to be done is thus the decisive condition, and it is presupposed that everybody can easily and automatically carry out the actions which are the application of such knowledge. The general human faculties are adequate: Nothing is required but what a human being can do provided he wants to. In this sense no art, no handiwork is ever taught; but techniques or tricks can be taught. And volition itself is such a trick insofar as it is conceived as rational will and therefore separated from and prior to action. But it is not something that one is able to do only if he wants to, but that one will (not only possibly or probably but) necessarily and certainly do as soon as he has recognized and knows that it is really "the best." The faculty of acting in this way is the general human faculty of thinking (just as that of perception is generally common with animals) insofar as thinking simultaneously brings about apprehension and volition. Action is, however, postulated as the necessary consequence of volition. This also means that a man will always do what he knows to be most useful in attaining his intended purpose or end. That must be acknowledged as correct to the degree in which man approaches the concept of a pure (abstract) ego of rational will. In contradistinction, the farther he is removed therefrom the more the judgment refers to his entire being and its total situation, of which present thoughts constitute only one striking characteristic, and from it his observed activities have to be explained in every instance. To these activities belongs thinking itself, which is able to create manifold and complex interrelationships of ideas according to the talents, habits, and moods of its author and to the stimuli affecting him at that particular time. Above all, thinking lays down the law for his future actions with regard to defined and determined ends. This work does not require so much knowledge of its own method as the most perfect possible knowledge of all available means,

of favorable and counteracting conditions, of the probability of good
or evil chance incidents. That is, it requires judgment and distinct and
clear knowledge or science which is, at least in general, applicable to
given cases and can be received from the outside as a finished product.
To the degree in which that takes place, one's own work consists only
in the application, i.e., partly in the drawing of conclusions, partly in
the consideration and appraisal of given factors; the former if maxims
or rules are involved, the latter if facts or events come into play which
are known or considered probable, expected or hoped for so that they
are taken "into account." For all this is like an account, a calculation
of the chances of an undertaking, and if it goes far, a mental preparation for different possible situations. It is, therefore, thoroughly
scientific thinking, which must be free of all subjective admixtures.
It is the combination (synthesis) and division (analysis) of arbitrarily
limited (defined) elements which, however, are conceived as real. It is
the method, technique, or theory of all such procedure which must be
taught under the name of logic, an organon of science, the theory of
how to work with conceptual objects *(entia rationis)* or of how to think
and calculate in order to achieve correct results. These rules are used
in the most deliberate manner in arithmetic proper and allied branches
of mathematics, but they can also be applied to all scientific thinking,
and consequently to every form of egotistic calculating. Calculating
is nothing but "mechanical" (external) combination and division of a
fictitious matter, the numbers or algebraic symbols.

29. *Organic and Mechanical Thinking*

A comparison of the thinking which creates the forms of rational will
with mechanical labor, and its perfection with cleverly applied labor,
will now be attempted. This is also reflected in the similes of our language which have created the following expressions: to mold plans, to
hatch up plots, to set a trap, a carefully worked-out enterprise, a fabri-
cation of lies, and so forth. In contrast, the creation and existence of the
forms of natural will have already been compared with organic activity,
and in their ideal perfection have been likened, quite unintentionally,
as we see, to the artistic activity of man. For, indeed, speaking and
thinking, through which human nature and the qualities of the individual soul are most clearly revealed in their characteristic form, are
the common art of man, just as nest-building and singing are the art of
the bird, and weaving its gossamer that of the spider. But the question
arises here: how is the human being enabled to do such things? And the
answer, a threefold answer, is always the same: by inborn talents and
their development, by repetition (of attempts) and practice, by learning

and imitating, i.e., by receiving knowledge from those who have mastered it and, with understanding and sympathy, pass it on.

Talents and teaching refer in different ways to an endless chain of causation. Talents are wholly transmitted by the progenitors in a purely organic act; only their development involves activity, and that essentially of an organic type, i.e., the activity of the human being so endowed. Circumstances must be favorable for such development, and it will be assisted by careful education, as the mental continuation or supplement of the procreative act. To learn is a typically individualistic and, in the human being, essentially mental activity, but it is furthered by the active efforts of the elders, the well-informed and the experienced, so that teaching and learning require and complement each other. In contradistinction, practice is an essentially animal activity and labor, however much it is influenced and ennobled by the human mind; it is in the highest degree individual and essentially conditioned by the will power of the human being. Although external coercion, command, and stimulus can also provide an incentive, ideals and examples are imitated and stimulate the zeal of the pupil. Consequently teaching and instruction make it easy to learn and to extend knowledge.

30. *Art in Toolmaking*

Human art, manifold and differentiated, is also concerned to a large extent with the production of tools and utensils so that finally each type, kind, and variety requires its own master and artist. Thus, they are more than mere objects of use, because something of the inner harmony, beauty, and perfection of the creative organism enters into their form. But a point might be reached in the development of one branch in a whole field of art when the influence of the tools used or (what leads to the same result) of the working method begins to predominate or is by nature the most essential element, leading to a condition in which nothing else is required but to understand and apply the tools or method. In that case, only mechanical or quasi-mechanical operations are involved, in the sense that therein the consumption of energy, even if directed or carried out by a human mind of average capacity, is the real and decisive function which has to be performed in order to transmit to the given machinery the amount of energy necessary to enable it to carry out certain tasks, to produce certain works. In these operations that quantity of human labor can, without any change in the ultimate result, be substituted for by an equal quantity of any other mechanical power.

This development is brought about the more easily the more a thing is produced solely for its utility, its application, and its consumption. There is, however, a limit beyond which that rational human labor, even without the mediation of working tools, becomes the only necessary and natural process.

That previously mentioned process in which the tools assume a productive role must be taken purely in a symbolical sense. But the analogy can be easily understood if concepts and methods are thought of as the tools used in intellectual work and especially in scientific thought. No special talents, training, or practice is required to create such work, but simply the average abstract quality of the animal rationale, because method makes everything much easier and does the actual work. But its use must be learned, and, for that reason, its nature must be fully understood. For this purpose, real mental production, the activity of memory or imagination, becomes entirely superfluous, even dangerous. Rational will must take their place, i.e., intention (attentiveness) and logical operations, the simple process of which stands in the same relation to mental production as the controlled exertion of muscular power stands in relation to the work of mind and hand which the sculptor or painter performs with loving care according to his taste.

31. *Artistic Spirit*

Natural will itself is artistic spirit. It develops itself by absorbing new contents, which it reproduces in new forms. In the same way it also forms combinations of imagination and thought, words and sentences which represent judgments, ideas, intentions. All this springs from imagination, from an entity of feelings. However, where this productive activity freezes, so to speak, into purely logical thinking, abstract and general mental labor takes the place of all special, concrete, and qualified labor. It is by nature of this type even without being made easier and reduced by the use of tools. Insofar, however, as these tools are directed entirely toward attaining its purpose, utility, and ends, they are products and elements of rational will, and instead of concrete-human products become abstract-human products. Thus, a free system of rational will develops, or higher forms of rational will as compared with lower ones are created, the latter appearing to be determined by and dependent on the former. And it is especially the concepts which are "made" like tools or instruments and pass from one hand to another like objects of the outer world. In receiving and applying these, all men are equal. For everybody to whom the correct method has been proved is able to understand and remember how something is done. Proof appeals to the general human power of reason (i.e., of logical thinking), which has to judge the proven statement as correct, i.e., the implied relationship of concepts as existing in reality. A "truth" is thus made as objective for the reason as an object is for the senses. And the same holds true, if, for a given end, a means is indicated and such "advice" accepted. No conclusion can be better founded than the following: he who has definitely chosen an end and fully knows the means to attain it will also seize upon and apply these means if they are within his power, or if not he will try to obtain them. A guide and teacher can achieve everything from without, and still he does nothing but give or point out a correct method or the ways and means to an end. To comprehend, to seize, and to use them is the disciple's own affair; it is presupposed that he has the general ability to do so. That it may have to be developed for that task does not concern the teacher as such. He, as teacher or adviser, has a definitely limited task and business. He can acquit himself of it and transmit his achievements to the other person so that he may use them as if they were his own. With regard to the effects of such knowledge as well as of the method comprehended and the advice taken (which is the decision and thus action itself) it remains irrelevant whether the person has created it and worked it out himself or whether he received and accepted it as a finished product. But the truth and correctness of this knowledge can be proved only by the actual success of the action which follows and uses it, for it is only as true and correct as it is useful and appropriate for its purpose. The same relation as between knowledge and the purposeful action which is implied in making a decision exists in all those cases where knowledge is concerned with the most correct and appropriate possible formation of the instruments of volition as such.

The teacher and adviser may conduct himself differently if it is not so much a case of transmitting truths as of creating and developing the ability to do certain things, especially insofar as mental power is involved. In that case the teacher himself must be a master or experienced and practiced in that art, or, if teachings and wisdom have to be transmitted, he must be able to inspire and evoke faith and confidence. He has to appeal to good will instead of to reason, for it is more necessary to try and to strive than to comprehend and understand.

32. *Motives and Norms*

The forms of natural will are always active, to a lesser or greater degree, because they belong to life itself. But they play a decisive role as motives on those occasions when the contents to which they refer come into question or are offered for choice. These contents consist especially of norms and laws which can develop from the general and undefined to the specific and defined.

The forms of rational will are applied by being realized. Such realization takes place through the individual who retains them in his thinking and by measured and determined action carries them from their imitation and transmission into reality. It is, however, the task and purpose of these forms of rational will to serve as the motive for action, either only once (after which their value of usefulness ceases), or regularly under certain conditions. Their contents develop progressively, by additions and accumulation, from individual to comprehensive and general norms.

The will is free and independent only to the degree in which, on the one hand, it follows and conforms to its own inner norms and laws, i.e., its natural liking or preference, its sense and taste (for or against something), its habits, its ideas (the combinations of which are in its memory), and, in general, its sentiment, mind, or conscience—or in which, on the other hand, it adheres to the external rules which it may have set up through its intentions, calculations, and consciousness. For those are the determinants of freedom in which it is itself retained as in its necessary forms (even if the forms of rational will are at the same time its negations). That is the relation of the crude and material freedom of possibility to the formed and determined freedom of reality. This follows because will and freedom are the same. But every volition, like every motion, is necessary in so far as it is contained in the nature of things, and it is free in so far as an individual body or the individual will of an organism is its author. In this sense the movement of the waterdrop which, falling on the stone, seems to seek its way downward and finds it in the line of least resistance or strongest pull, is at the same time both free and necessary: free since its position and direction are at all times determined by its own force and its own momentum, but necessary because it is determined by other alien forces and momenta. Thus, even the most intellectual and rational movements of human beings have to be explained partly from their own will, but partly from the pressure of circumstances. Insofar as the will is subject to such pressure, it is forced and without freedom. It is presupposed as logical a priori truth that nothing—neither an object and its constitution, thus no form of natural or rational will, nor a movement or act of will—could be called free in the sense that it is (because of the perfection of its inner and outer conditions) not at every moment completely conditioned and determined. The real freedom of will is extant in one's existence, as a psychological attribute which is a mode of the infinite, incomprehensible, uncaused substance. This attribute is not, however, to be thought of as a modality but as substance. Besides this, there exists an imaginary freedom for the mind of the human being insofar as he thinks of his actions or omissions as objects among which he can choose or insofar as he makes and constructs his will himself and thus stands as lord and creator over this creature of his thoughts.

SECTION THREE: Empirical Meaning

33. *Contrast of the Sexes*

When we endeavor to understand the recognizable characteristics of human beings through the use of these categories, the following observations are immediately forthcoming. In the first place we distinguish in general features the psychological contrast between the sexes. It is an old truth—but just for that reason important as the outcome of general experience—that women are usually led by feelings, men more by intellect. Men are more clever. They alone are capable of calculation, of calm (abstract) thinking, of consideration, combination, and logic. As a rule, women follow these pursuits ineffectively. They lack the necessary requirement of rational will. It is not true that the human being acquires individual activity, independence from nature, and domination over it only by abstract thinking and by rational will. The truth is that activity necessitates and develops rational will and indefinitely increases with its aid. Because the male must make provision for food, his life is more active. This holds true not only among human beings but also among other mammals and generally where the female has to devote a great part of her time and care to the offspring. The role of the male is attack and robbery, even in the form of killing of rivals in order to capture his desired mate. As hunter and robber, he is prompted to listen and explore into space. He trains these most active and independent senses and sharpens them for the observation of distant things. Thereby he makes their use more conscious, more dependent upon his own general condition and less upon directly received impressions (behavior which in common and psychological terminology is designated as rationally voluntary or controlled). (Sight is more capable of such improvement and close attention than hearing.) Therefore, a man is more capable of the active perception and apperception which masters and orders the substance of impressions and forms the given pieces and symbols synthetically into their entity. It is this ready attention through which, as was stated previously, intellect and animalistic memory grow and develop. Thus, an organ in which these qualities are centered becomes potentially more perfect with every generation and tends to be inherited also by the feminine sex. Although activity of the intellect by no means signifies thinking, it is nevertheless a preparation thereto insofar as it is an intellectual activity which can be performed independent of the direct stimuli of life and independent of directly received impressions. (Actually this independence is what intellect adds to the active impulses received. This is in line with the statement of Greek philosophy to the effect that it is the intellect which sees and hears, everything else being deaf and blind.) Real (or abstract) thinking consists of active attention resulting in comparisons of data which could not be conceived if it were not for memory of word symbols. Also, the analysis and recombination of such data is real thinking and is rational will if the data consist of voluntary acts and their probable or certain results. In the case of rational will, the idea of a definite volition is chosen (conceived) or formed as pure consequence of thinking about a desired result (totally different) from existing conditions. The more such a result is hidden in the future, the more it requires mental farsightedness, projection into time instead of space, to measure and direct the conceived aim.

The man has to practice this farsightedness because to him falls the guidance and leadership, at least in all activities concerned with the outside world. This is natural for him as the stronger and more pugnacious being, also more mobile and nimble than the woman, who is relatively more immobile and slow. But a traveler, especially a scout, needs farsightedness, prudence, and caution in every respect; he also has to learn to make judgments, to decide what is the best thing to do under given circumstances. The premonition of approaching evil develops suspicion, signs furnish conviction, knowledge of dangers determines plans. The leader also has to decide how to keep order within his group of followers. Decisions rendered in case of quarrels foster and create the qualities which distinguish the judge: the balance scale is the symbol of justice which represents the objective, true, and real relations of acting and suffering, indebtedness and credit, rights and duties. Especially where it becomes necessary to give everyone his proper share to endure and enjoy, and make comparison of size, weight, utility, beauty, of single or divided things, of captured animals or human beings, of land or tools, this quality is essential. From general comparison the special formal activities of measuring, weighing, and calculating develop, which all have to do with the definition of quantities and their relations.

The same function is performed by causal thinking insofar as it compares a preceding event with a following one with respect to its objective, or, as we may say, with regard to the quantity of the energy in each case. All scientific procedure is based upon this; it is, in its rudiments, also contained in all practical acts and performances, although for direct observation and feeling for what is correct, intuitive more than discursive recognition and consciousness of relations and rules is required. The popular assumption, however, is that the latter is always the original datum, while the former originates from it through the growth of interrelated associations. This theory can be accepted only in a considerably modified form, as is evident from our previous arguments. For such knowledge is different if accepted by a predisposed mind with original talent than it is when merely appropriated and used without such qualities. In the first case it is like a lyre played by an artist, in the second case like a hand organ which can be put into motion by anyone. This holds true also for the knowledge of justice; it is either, according to its nature, an understanding through inner conviction and vivid belief, or it is and remains a dead conception which is adopted and applied. The first is the way of a noble person; the second, anybody's way.

34. *Artistic and Sophisticated People*

In connection with the previous sections the following observation returns to our attention. If the privilege of cleverness is attributed to the man, it must be kept in mind that cleverness is by no means the same as general intellectual power. On the contrary, to the extent that intellectual power is productive or synthetic, the female mind excels. In the constitution of the male the muscular system prevails; in the female constitution, the nervous system. In accordance with their more passive, constant, limited activity, women are generally more receptive and sensitive to the impressions which come accidentally and unexpectedly from the outside: they rather enjoy present, constant happiness instead of striving for remote, future, rare happiness. The more this is true the stronger and more passionate their will reacts, therefore, to pleasant or unpleasant changes of their condition. Thus, sensuality as intermediary of affirmative and negative feelings and also as the capacity to distinguish between good and evil, beauty and ugliness, develops and becomes refined to a degree which in no way corresponds with the recognition of objects and processes (objective knowledge). This latter capacity is gained (as is the ability to perceive) primarily through intensive activity of the eye, secondarily of the ear, with the aid of the sense of touch; the other capacity belongs (in addition to general feeling) to the special organs of smell and taste, and requires only passive apperception. It is characteristic of woman and natural will. Moreover, all activity which expresses itself in a direct manner, either originally or from habit or memory, as consequence and expression of life itself, belongs to the realm of the woman. Thus, all expressions and outbursts of emotions and sentiments, conscience, and inspired thoughts are the specific truthfulness, naïvete, directness, and passionateness of the woman, who is in every respect the more natural being. And upon these qualities is based the creativeness of mind and imagination which develops into artistic creativeness through a feeling for and delicacy of choice, or of "taste."

Although the performance of great works has usually required masculine strength and cleverness and often also the egotistic motives which spur the man on, the best part, the core of genius, nevertheless, is usually a maternal heritage. And the most general artistic mind of the common people, which expresses itself in trinket, song, and story, is carried by the girlish mind, mother love, female memory, superstition, and premonition. Thus the man of genius is of a feminine nature in many respects: naïve and frank, soft, sensitive, lively, changeable in emotions and moods, gay or melancholy, dreamy and enthusiastic, as if living in constant intoxication with a trustful belief in and surrender to objects and persons, thus planless, often blind and foolish in important or unimportant things. Therefore, an inspired person may appear unintelligent, stupid or silly, foolish or insane among the "real" men of a dry, businesslike mentality, resembling an inebriated person in a sober company. These men, if they judge without prejudice, interpret the conduct and nature of a real woman in the same light: they do not understand it; it is absurd to them.

In reality, the genius has all the qualities—fully developed—of which there are only traces in other people. He resembles the type of the perfect human being, as we conceive this. Masculine force and courage differentiate animals among animals; mental force and genius are reserved as the privilege of the human species and are its potentiality. The genius is the artist; he is the perfected form (the "flower") of the natural (simple, true) human being. All intentional and conscious doing and acting which surpass him constitutes the artificial man—the natural man's opposite. The genius appears to have made of himself another man, whom he carries before him because it seems useful and right to do so. If the woman is the natural human being and the man is the artificial one, any man in whom natural will prevails remains closer to the female mind. Through rational will he frees himself from it and appears in his pure masculinity. On the other hand, the woman in whom rational will prevails is in this sequence the last phenomenon in which the free masculine spirit has, actually or approximately, reproduced itself.

Poets and thinkers are inclined to praise the natural behavior, the secret depth of woman's being and mind, the devout simplicity of her soul; we sometimes feel that we have lost by becoming cold and calculating, superficial, and enlightened. Here the old truth holds that nature destroys only to let elements of vitality rise to new life. Thus, when science becomes philosophy, the human being regains, through the highest and purest knowledge, the joy of contemplation and love which had been destroyed through reflection and ambition.

If we desire to present the contrasting dichotomies previously outlined in connection with our theory, they receive their dominant form and expression as:

the temperament

| of the woman | of the man |
| through sentiment | through intention |

the character

| of the woman | of the man |
| through mind | through calculation |

intellectual attitude

| of the woman | of the man |
| through conscience | through conscious behavior |

Concerning the total expressions of natural will which do not enter these dichotomies, it may be said that passion and courage can be conceived in the same analogical manner as genius is related to feminine and to masculine nature. Passion, because it belongs to vegetative life and the force of reproduction, prevails more in feminine nature; courage, which belongs to animal life and irritability, is stronger in the man. Passion, conceived as passive will, is more active in the man than in woman; courage, conceived as active will, in the woman may take a more passive form, as in patience and endurance. Genius, as mental will, has an equal part in both characters: based upon feminine nature but perfected in the man, it is as much inner, dark, and passive as outer, bright, and active life and thinking.

35. *Youth and Old Age*

In most of these respects we find between youth and old age the same relation as between feminine and masculine beings. The youthful woman is the real woman; the old woman becomes more like a man. And the young man has still many feminine elements in his nature; the mature, older man is the real man. Women and children belong together as they have the same mentality and understand each other. Children are naïve, harmless; they live in the present, their way of living and simple faculties being determined by nature, home, and the will of those who love and educate them. The growth or development of their slumbering abilities, inclinations, and talents forms the real content of their life. Thus, they appear as really innocent creatures in the sense that what evil they do originates from an alien spirit, active in them. Only through thinking and knowledge or learning what is right and dutiful, through memory and conscience, does the human being come to feel himself responsible, that is, to know what he does. This comes to its perfect development when his acts as an intelligent being are, so to speak, committed in cold blood, deliberated and calculated to redound to his own advantage. Thus, law and rule are no longer superior to and a part of him, but they are inferior and outside of him. He does not follow them if and when he thinks himself able to arrive at his goal better in another manner. He accepts the consequences of his violation either as probable or as certain. He can calculate wrongly and may be called foolish because he prefers one kind of evil to another, inferior goods to better ones; perhaps he may see himself in this light and repent after he reaches his goal.

But as he planned and decided, he could (according to the supposition) dispose of and control with his own power of thought only things of which he was conscious and which were at his disposal. The judgment concerning things was his real activity; he might judge them differently not because he desired to judge them differently, but only if and when his knowledge was larger and more extensive. Therefore, the correction and improvement of understanding remains the most desirable attainment for the furtherance of any individual's development of the cleverer and better way of behaving. Through unconstrained, calculating thinking the human being becomes free from impulses, feelings, passions, and prejudices which otherwise seem to rule him. With progressing age the passion of love and friendship diminishes, as do also hatred, anger, and animosity. But, on the other hand, to a considerable degree those same emotions had first to come into existence as the individual was growing older, as is the case with sexual love and its correlate, jealousy. In addition, through the passing of time, habit, along with the permanent, growing feeling of their value, becomes a strong power which links human beings together. This becomes even more true if intellectual development and maturity are taken into consideration. Therefore, a passionate individual, insofar as his passions are desires which necessarily require fulfillment and satisfaction, will apply the endowments which are at his disposal at the time more easily and with less consideration of other motives which are still weak and less restricting on his cunning, planful thought. This is truer of a young person than of an older one. He will also more readily endanger his body and life to attain his ends because youthful courage, which in and of itself is careless, aids him. However, the main condition for a purely rational procedure always continues to be the independence of the thinking mind and its wealth of assembled experience and assimilated scientific knowledge.

In this way an individual becomes clever and recognizes what is good for life and body and, finally, for his soul. This is the quality which is characteristic of old people, especially if their interests and thoughts are centered upon certain simple aims which can be reached by cleverness, as, especially, the accumulation of property or the attainment of a higher rank, or more influence and honor. These are natural aims which as objects and pleasures are welcome to all human beings under all conditions but gain their specific value and desirability (1) if they have already been enjoyed and are known, and (2) if other, less mature and sensible hobbies, which are familiar to young people as expressions of original, effervescent stimulation and vitality, have lost their attractiveness. Thus, the statement which was chosen as a motto by Goethe, who frequently contemplated this phenomenon, that "what one has been wanting in youth, one possesses in age in abundance" should be understood in terms of the means and methods of happiness. The real enjoyment of happiness, on the contrary, and its inner condition, are youth itself, and what belongs to youth no art can regain.

36. *The Common People and Educated Classes*

The contrast between the sexes is lasting and inflexible, therefore is rarely found in complete development, whereas the contrast of age is more definite but nevertheless always in a state of flux and observable only in development. The first contrast is based upon vegetative life, the influence of which is much more dominant in the woman; the second contrast refers mainly to animalistic life, which is more important in the man and designates the declining part of a normal life as compared with the progressing part, and thus designates especially the life of a man. In the first case, the antinomy of sentiment and intention prevails; in the second case, the antinomy of mind and calculation.

The third distinction which is of importance here belongs to the mental realm and is concerned with the intellectual attitude, with knowledge. It is the contrast between the common people and educated classes. It is as inflexible a distinction as the first one because it distinguishes entire classes, but at the same time it is in a state of flux insofar as these classes can only be defined artificially. Constant changes from one into the other take place, and several intermediate gradations can be observed. Its validity is also obvious to the superficial observer but is nevertheless difficult to understand in its abstract and real meaning; we must say, however, that conscience is really active only among the common people. It is a common good and organ possessed by the individual in a special manner. It depends upon the general will and mind, the traditional intellectual attitude, and is inherited as a potentiality. It grows with the general development of thinking and as essential content of memory in relation to individual instincts and habits. Therefore, it manifests itself as affirmation and sanctification of matured affection for others, as feeling for that which is one's own good or evil, and as taste in relation to good and evil in alien things. On the one hand, it is feeling for what is natural, familiar, approved; on the other hand, it is taste for what is unnatural, strange, hostile. Conscience, on the whole, for a group of human beings to which it refers, is a feeling that friendliness and kindness are good, but that hostility, anger, and mischief are evil. It requires obedience and complete acquiescence, especially toward the older, stronger, ruling individuals; disobedience is felt to be stubbornness and deception. All these feelings are increased by example and doctrine through arousing fear and hope, and teaching respect, trust, and belief. They are extended and refined in application and, as the commands of tradition which they represent, they have reference to higher, more general authorities and powers, the dignitaries and nobles of the community, and are especially important in the sanctification of the invisible, holy deities and demons. In the child this devout will of the mind can decay instead of grow, or be repressed instead of developing, if all the manifold required favorable conditions are denied. This is especially true if the basis of and conditions for development of the original disposition are weak or defective. The weaker the devout will becomes, the more easily it will succumb to hostile influences in the struggle of life. It will be eliminated by the rational individual as an obstacle because it is recognized as a complex of prejudices to be dissolved into elements.

Only the educated, knowing, enlightened individual, insofar as he is a noble, erudite, and thinking individual in whom it reaches its highest perfection and most subtle expression, can destroy conscience in himself in a complete and radical manner by abandoning the belief of his ancestors and his people because he understands their underlying principles. On a scientific foundation he may try to establish better opinions concerning what is right and permissible or false and forbidden for him, and perhaps also for every other intelligent person. He has made up his mind and feels entitled to act not according to blind and stupid feelings but according to clearly understood reasons. Such a rational, individual view of life we call consciousness. Consciousness is the freedom of rational will in its highest expression.

37. *Morality*

Conscience, on the other hand, appears in its simplest and deepest form as shame. Shame manifests itself as a reluctance to do or say certain things or, after a deed of wickedness, as displeasure toward oneself or possibly toward other individuals, the conduct of whom one identifies with one's own. As repugnance or shyness, shame is related to fear; and as displeasure or indignation, it is related to anger; it is always a mixture of these two emotions in whatever sequence they may follow each other. Shame is, in the first place, covering, hiding, evasion, shyness from nakedness, disclosure, being known; therefore, it is closely related to sexual, marital, and family life. It is a quality of women and girls, also of children and young men. For them it is deemed a virtue because it is usual for them to live in small groups in dependent, devoted, modest relationships with their husbands or fathers or mothers or teachers.

He who, as a master of men, enters the street and the market as well as public life and the greater world, must, to a certain extent, overcome this shame or change it into a new form. Shame is always a form of natural will which retards and restrains other drives. Shame is the recognized master with unconditionally valid authority which is always right and always remains right. One dare not show and say and do to everybody what may be revealed only to some people; one dare not suffer from everybody what is with pleasure tolerated from some, accepted as habit or even desired as that which is becoming. The influence of shame extends from what is repulsive by nature, displeasing in general, to what is strictly forbidden, or to what is felt, thought, or known as passing the limits of one's own freedom and rights, as violation and injustice, or to all immodest, intemperate, excessive acts or speech. In this connection it is, therefore, not a foreign will which reacts negatively against attack on or violation of its sphere; neither is it simply a common will which grants a proper share to everybody and limits his rights, which can neither give nor take but prevents all transgressions insofar as they are against its rules; but it is at least a form of natural will which corresponds to the will of the Gemeinschaft and stands opposed to any form of natural will or any rational will which strives in another direction. Shame in this case is either painfully felt self-disapproval or painfully felt disapproval from friends or the fear of such a disapproval which, like every form of fear, is a pain felt beforehand. This pain is attended with a decrease in one's strength, a feeling of impotence, smallness. Therefore, one who is shamed is humiliated, hurt, sullied; the integrity and beauty of his mentality and his honor are no longer intact. Shame has these effects because honor is conceived as a reality since it is natural will itself insofar as it partakes in the "good" which is believed in and justified in a Gemeinschaft. Consequently, he who does something disgraceful hurts himself. This is the original and perfected idea of morality up until the time when the human being is conceived as an individual and mere subject of his rational will.

Such a natural basis can also be described as follows: nobody likes to stand in ill fame, because it makes him feel repulsive and bad. The physical meaning of the word shame reveals the functions to which the feeling of shame originally were and still are related. The reversal of this meaning applies in the Gesellschaft, where moral concepts become conventional and crystallized. Here in the Gesellschaft, in that which is useful to you and essential for your ends and purposes, you must limit your freedom in such a manner as to respect the freedom of others, because only thus can you maintain your own sphere or enlarge it. You must keep yourself in the esteem of others; they must fear and have a good opinion of your strength. Therefore, it is helpful to appear morally good and noble, fair and just, if and for so long as the appearance of these qualities has value for you. Only the appearance can be of value under conditions in which every individual thinks of himself and esteems such qualities in terms of their general or personal returns. Here the real causes do not matter since the same effects can result from entirely different motivation (from natural will or from rational will)—therefore the usual and accustomed causes are, at first, presupposed. For, if on the market everyone would act according to the principle that honesty is the best policy, it would be immaterial whether or not he has an honest sentiment. In society if one behaves in a pleasant, modest, and polite manner he will get by. Only inexperienced people refuse to accept such "paper money," which, by convention, has the same value as gold or silver.

38. *Market and Society*

In the same way as the rules of market-exchange only establish formal barriers to intention, which is by nature boundless, society or conventional sociableness restrains one from going beyond certain limits in the pursuit of the shameless mania for making oneself important. The nature of such rules becomes more evident as Gesellschaft-like circles develop in accordance with inner conditions and become alienated from their original Gemeinschaft-like character, as in the case of the royal courts in history. The subject of rational will, which appears in these courts, has in reality no qualities beyond a certain knowledge about ends and purposes and the best way to reach them. Knowledge of objects is the necessary condition for attainment of ends, and a knowledge of the available or obtainable means is required for the application of means. Thus, increase in knowledge means increase and multiplication of desires. The clearer and more certain the knowledge concerning whether or not a given means leads to a given goal, the easier it becomes to overcome a resistance or hesitancy which might exist. For the person who knows what he is doing, who weighs his actions and measures their value in terms of certain or probable results, shame is nothing but silliness. If he expects to be blamed by others, he will try to ascertain how great a disadvantage his contemplated action will be for him and whether or not the resulting pain and the shame will be more than compensated for by the advantage gained by acting. For this intellectual attitude no absolute evil exists except the abstraction, pain. Also, no absolute good exists except the abstraction, pleasure. Shame, however, is defiant and forbids some things absolutely, disapproves absolutely of some tendencies. This explains why this feeling is not characteristic of the educated, scheming classes. One should remember that shame finds its deepest influence as shame of sin and sinfulness, and that conscience finds its expression and support in religious belief. This explains why the attitude here described, which belittles shame, refers mainly to the intellectual attitude and apparently has merely a theoretical significance, and why lack of conscience does not necessarily follow from unbelief. But the destruction of belief as the objective conscience weakens the resistance of the subjective conscience. One can still stumble over the roots of a fallen tree but one cannot ram one's head against it.

Belief is a characteristic of the common folks; disbelief, of the scientific and educated classes. When a poet and thinker has indicated as the real subject of world history the struggle between belief and disbelief, the truth in this thought also indicates a struggle between the common and the educated people. The contrast between the sexes has the same significance: Women are believing, men, disbelieving. There also exists the same contrast between the different ages. Piety belongs to childhood and is also characteristic of the contemplative, poetic slant of the young man. In more mature age the man is more inclined toward doubt and scientific thinking; the thoughtful, philosophic old man sometimes returns to the gaiety and trustfulness of childhood just as he finds his youth renewed in his grandchildren. As the old man appears venerable and important to the young, men have importance for and are honored by women in organized social life, and the knowing and wise have importance for and are honored by the common people provided the one group is not alienated from the other. Wisdom is the quality of the old as compared with the young, of the men as compared with the women, and the popular teachers and scholars walk as old and wise people in the midst of rural simplicity and piety. All these antitheses must be understood as possible contrasts which are leveled out by life but are brought forth by decay and approaching death. Sooner or later, however, in the development from Gemeinschaft toward Gesellschaft, the tragic conflict necessarily evolves.

39. *Relations to Gemeinschaft and Gesellschaft*

From all this discussion the manner in which natural will carries the conditions for Gemeinschaft and rational will develops Gesellschaft becomes evident. Consequently, the realm of life and work in Gemeinschaft is particularly befitting to women; indeed, it is even necessary for them. For women, the home and not the market, their own or friend's dwelling and not the street, is the natural seat of their activity. In the village the household is independent and strong, also in the town the household is preserved and has a certain beauty; only in the city does the household become sterile, narrow, empty, and debased to fit the conception of a mere living place which can be obtained everywhere in equal form for money. As such it is nothing but shelter for those on a journey through the world.

Staying at home is as natural for the women as traveling, according to the traditional attitudes of the people, is unbecoming to them. "Anartisan who has not traveled is as good as a traveling virgin" was an old proverb of the Middle Ages. "No reason to go out can ever be as good as the reason to stay in." This statement of a mystic is an essentially feminine thought. All the women's activity is more inward than outward. The end of this activity lies in itself and not in some outside aim. Therefore, personal services belong by nature to the realm of the woman because they reach their perfection in their very existence and do not even show a good or product as a result. Also, many tasks in agriculture befit the woman and in the soundest cultures have been put on her shoulders, often however, to the point of excess; for farming is labor unconscious of itself, drawing strength from the heavenly breezes. Farming can be conceived as a service to nature, close to the household and immediately bearing fruit.

Among the arts those connected with speech belong more to the realm of the woman than do the plastic arts. Also the musical arts are her field because music, above all singing, is a gift of woman; her high, clear, soft and smooth voice is the organ of defense and attack. Yelling and screaming, jubilation and bemoaning, like laughing and weeping in words, are the expression of the feminine soul. Music is the audible expression of emotion, whereas mimicry is its inaudible expression. The sacred muses are women, and memory is their mother. The dance stands between music and mimicry. In the dance the passionate, graceful, and purposeless movements, which if subjected to conscious attention would tire one to death, are developed naturally in the feminine nurture of the daughters. They also easily learn meaningless gentle things as well as meaningful strange things. They have a good memory for forms, ritual, old melodies, proverbs, for conundrums and magic, for tragic and comic stories. They have inclinations to imitate, delight in make-believe, a fondness for play, the charming, and the simple. Also they lean toward the moods of melancholy sincerity, pious fear, and prayer, and, as has already been said, toward dreaming, pondering, and poetry.

Song and poetry are originally one and the same thing; also, song and speech were only gradually differentiated and developed. Speech in its proper form always retains a great deal of singing in its intervals and cadences. (That speech is itself the natural understanding of the contents of words originated from maternal love, we have already dared to conjecture. Perhaps it would be more correct to say that this has been its main stimulus. Sexual love also plays a great role in its development, even beginning back in the animal world, and in the musical and pathetic part of song and speech it has had an even greater influence. Everything which stirs the soul urges toward expression in pleasure and sorrow, makes one talkative and communicative, becomes art when the formless feelings find form or shape. The woman's heart expresses itself more directly in joy and sorrow and love, which are her most sacred concerns and fill her thoughts with passion, move her to artfulness and intrigue, which are always the weapons of the weaker sex. However, in this manner the direct [naïve] activity changes into a premeditated one, and this causes a more conscious use of means, a sharper differentiation from ends, and, finally, ends are set off against means.)

Among the plastic arts, using the term in the most general sense, the textile arts are, as is known, most appropriate for feminine nature because of their domestic application. Textiles are an art or work which demands, on the one hand, close sight, carefulness, correct reproduction of a pattern, faithful, patient devotion to a traditional style, and, on the other, taking liberty for the sake of creativeness and the exhibition of graceful forms and meaningless decorations. They also require the intensity of taste in warmth, gentleness, comfort, all virtues and qualities of the feminine soul. Also, the pictorial presentation of the real, the pleasant and the wonderful in lovely bodies and beautiful forms and the preservation of memories, is a real work of love as expressed in the fine Hellenic legend concerning the invention of portrait painting. Feminine genius reaches its utmost height in the projection of forms on a flat surface, an art from which writing originated. Plastics and tectonics demand a more conscious imagination and a more forceful control over the resistance of the substances used.

40. *Qualities of Man and Woman*

These, and similar arts where the substance which has to be changed or mastered is foreign or even hostile, are man's work. Nevertheless, all work belongs to the realm of natural will as long as it is not done with aversion and not desired solely on account of the end for which it is done. Thus, all work according to its nature is expression of Gemeinschaft. However, some types of work are apt to be understood as mere means to an end. This is less true of other types of work. Those which will be understood as means to an end are those in which pain and suffering is involved, therefore, those in which masculine and hard labor rather than feminine and light labor is involved. The elements of this dialectic are therefore partly contained in the object, partly in the human mind.

All art belongs, according to its nature, just as in the case of all rural and domestic pursuits, to the realm of the warm and soft labor. It belongs to organic-living, feminine-natural labor and Gemeinschaft-like labor. The Gemeinschaft, to the extent that it is capable of doing so, transforms all repulsive labor into a kind of art, giving it style, dignity, and charm, and a rank in its order, denoted as a calling and an honor. However, through remuneration in money, just as through the holding of finished products for sale, there tends to be a reversal of this process, which makes the individual, along with this mental construct, into its sole personality. In Gesellschaft, as previously stated, such a personality is by nature and conscience the businessman or merchant. The opposition and mutual exclusiveness of means and ends become the more evident because the means are not labor, even though labor in this case requires speed and is barren and monotonous activity. But, what is worse, the risk of having one's wealth decreased, even though only an imaginary possibility, is as unpleasant in its nature as a profit might be pleasing.

From this one understands how averse trade must be to the feminine mind and nature. The tradeswoman, not an infrequent phenomenon in early town life, left her natural sphere to become the first emancipated woman. Of course, trade, like every other occupation, can be conducted in an honest and conscientious manner. However, the more planfully and the larger the scale on which it is carried out, the more tricks and lies are introduced as effective means to gain high profits or cover losses. The will to enrich himself makes the merchant unscrupulous and the type of egotistic, self-willed individual to whom all human beings except his nearest friends are only means and tools to his ends or purposes; he is the embodiment of Gesellschaft. In his speech rational will is expressed most directly. The words which he chooses are calculated in terms of their effect; therefore, truthful words, when not profitable, change easily into lies as a better method. Such a lie is permitted in trade because it does not count as deception. Its purpose is to stimulate the desire to buy without selling beyond the real value. But in trade many premeditated words, although not actual lies, are nevertheless untrue in reality because the words have lost their qualities and are degraded into a mere quantity of applied means. Thus, in a more general sense, the lie becomes a characteristic element of Gesellschaft.

Woman's place in all unfree and free labor and service which is not in accordance with her liking and habit and does not originate from her sense of duty is comparable to her place in trade. This applies to factory labor and all purchasable and purchased labor which derives no trust from its own products and is not applied to human beings or nature but to lifeless tools of an uncanny, domineering power. The masters of capitalistic production find female labor especially fit for running machinery since it corresponds most closely to the concept of simple and average human labor. It stands between the versatility and adaptiveness of child labor and the strength and trustworthiness of masculine labor.

Some of this common factory labor is easy enough to be performed by children because of its mechanical nature, requiring repeated application of small quantities of muscular energy. Some of it is heavy labor, requiring men with attentiveness, strength, and calmness for the manipulation of cyclopean machinery. Everything which cannot be performed by children and does not require men falls to the lot of women. Other things being equal, women are preferred to children on account of superior reliability and to men on account of the cheaper wages for which they may be hired. As wages represent the average upkeep of a family, women as well as the available children must compete on the labor market with their "breadwinner." (The family from a commercial point of view is nothing but a co-operative society for the consumption of consumption goods and reproduction of labor.)

As the woman enters into the struggle of earning a living, it is evident that trading and the freedom and independence of the female factory worker as contracting party and possessor of money will develop her rational will, enabling her to think in a calculating way, even though, in the case of factory work, the tasks themselves may not lead in this direction. The woman becomes enlightened, coldhearted, conscious. Nothing is more foreign and terrible to her original inborn nature, in spite of all later modifications. Possibly nothing is more characteristic and important in the process of formation of the Gesellschaft and destruction of Gemeinschaft. Through this development the "individualism" which is the prerequisite of Gesellschaft comes to its own. However, the possibility of overcoming this individualism and arriving at a reconstruction of Gemeinschaft exists. The analogy of the fate of women with the fate of the proletariat has been recognized and outlined long ago. Their growing group consciousness, like that of the isolated thinker, can develop and rise to a moral-humane consciousness.

41. *Child Labor*

It would also be possible to produce a corresponding series of deductions from the contrast between youth and old age and from the contrast between the common and the educated people. That children need home and family is evident. It is also evident that they thrive naturally in village and town, but that in the city and in the great world of Gesellschaft they are exposed to every form of destructive influence. Playful and gamelike work and practice are adapted to or even necessary for increasing the strength of the body and the intellect of the youth. Trading, making profits, becoming a capitalist are not good things for youth, who resemble women in their lack of understanding of these activities. Thus, a youth also will not easily come to understand that his working force or energy is an economic good lying in his hand and that labor is only the form in which it must be traded.

From the point of view of capitalistic production—in contrast to youthful will to become something, to acquire skill by gradual growth of brain and brawn—youthful hands are evaluated only according to what they are at a given moment: employable or not employable. "In so far as machinery dispenses with muscular power, it becomes a means of employing laborers of slight muscular strength, and those whose bodily development is incomplete, but whose limbs are all the more supple. The labour of women and children was, therefore, the first thing sought for by capitalists who used machinery. That mighty substitute for labour and labourers was forthwith changed into a means for increasing the number of wage-labourers by enrolling, under the direct sway of capital, every member of the workman's family, without distinction of age or sex. Compulsory work for the capitalist usurped the place, not only of the children's play, but also of free labour at home within moderate limits for the support of the family." (*Capital,* by Karl Marx, Chapter XV, Section 3, p. 431, edited by Frederick Engels, revised and amplified by Ernest Untermann, New York, 1936.) How the childish, youthful mind reacts to science does not need to be clarified. Science requires a certain dry imagination which, however, can be aided by the energetic use of existing forces and the understanding of mathematical schemata and formulas. Mathematics remains the prototype of all real science, which is in its inner nature arbitrary and artificial and therefore offers the most perfect of thinking.

The future persons of capitalistic Gesellschaft must be educated to methodical, correct thinking. This could be combined with the stimulation of a spirit of Gemeinschaft, the creation of a social sentiment, the ennoblement of the mind, and the education of the conscience. Development would naturally go in this direction if the social forces did not work against it. These social forces are more interested in maintaining the conflict between moral forces and philosophies which belong to a culture of Gemeinschaft which is continually decaying. These forces are consequently doomed to become ineffective, whereas scientific knowledge becomes more esteemed and important. Further, the same social forces seek and desire a satisfying solution to those contradictions and conflicts in a planfully created, partly individualistic, partly Gesellschaft-like conventional hypocrisy. In all these respects the power of resistance in the will and talents of the mature man has grown weaker or has diminished. This weakening has gone further if they were originally weak and have been broken in the course of life. In every regard the capable man of Gesellschaft, whether he considers himself free master of his wealth or master only of his labor power and other capabilities, is always ambitious and calculating, accepting opinions critically and using them to his advantage. Thus, so far as possible he conducts himself toward others as a merchant and toward himself as a hedonist, but dislikes to go about unmasked.

42. *Culture and Trade*

The common people are similar to women and children in that to them family life, along with neighboring and friendship, both of which are closely related to family life, is life in and of itself. Among the educated classes, insofar as they separate themselves from the common people and arrange their institutions quite independently (which process can hardly be carried out in every respect and is hidden through the conventional maintenance and the renewal of antiquated ideas), these relations disappear more and more as the rational freedom of the individual comes to the fore. The family becomes an accidental form for the satisfaction of natural needs, neighborhood and friendship are supplanted by special-interest groups and conventional society life. The life of the common people finds its fulfillment in home, village, and town; the educated classes are urban, national, international. With reference to these contrasts, only one point needs more emphasis. Trade is for all original forms of a sedentary homeculture a foreign and much disliked phenomenon. The merchant is at the same time the typical member of the educated class. He is without home, a traveler, a connoisseur of foreign customs and arts without love or piety for those of any one country, a linguist speaking several languages, flippant and double-tongued, adroit, adaptable, and one who always keeps his eye on the end or purpose he plans to attain. He moves about quickly and smoothly, changes his character and intellectual attitude (beliefs or opinions) as if they were fashions of dress, one to be worn here, another there. He is a mixer and smooth fellow who uses either the old or the new, whichever is to his advantage. In all these respects he is the absolute opposite of the peasant who lives and clings close to the soil; he is also the opposite of the commoner who plies his handicraft. In comparison, these latter are provincial, immature, uneducated. We are taught: "If a people is mature enough to need trade but not sufficiently mature to produce a national class of merchants, it is in its own interest that a foreign, more civilized people fills this lack temporarily through an active commerce." (Roscher *N. Oe.* Ill, p. 134.) But in reality such an arrangement never establishes a relation of people to people. The relationship is one between single, scattered foreigners (although they may individually belong to a real people's Gemeinschaft of their own) and a real people. For a real people cannot be conceived without an inhabited (if not cultivated) country of its own.

Even where the merchant is not really a stranger, he is regarded as one. "... the Grain-dealer is never a hereditary trader incorporated with the village group, nor is he a member of the municipality in towns which have grown out of one or more villages. The trades thus remaining outside the organic group are those which bring their goods from distant markets." (H. Maine, *Village-Communities in the East and West*, p. 126.) To the extent that the common people, with its labor, is subjected to trade or capitalism, it discontinues being a people. It adapts itself to foreign forces and conditions and becomes educated or civilized. Science, which in reality distinguishes the educated classes, is offered to them in many forms and shapes as a medicine for their rudeness. Thus, the common people become a "proletariat"; and much against the will of the educated class, when this latter group is to be identified with capitalistic Gesellschaft, they learn to think and become conscious of the conditions under which they are chained to the labor market. From such knowledge, decisions and attempts to break these chains originate. They unite into labor unions and parties for social and political action. These unions are extended to become of metropolitan, national, and finally of international constituency, as was true in the case of the organizations of the educated classes of the capitalists of real Gesellschaft which preceded them. Thus, the common people also become active members of Gesellschaft insofar as this requires the same attitude of mind and action. Their goal is to share in the ownership of (national or international) capital as the substance and means of their labor. Since this would stop the production of goods for sale and foreign trade, it would mean the end of Gesellschaft (understood in its economic meaning).

Note 1. Since this book starts from individual psychology, there is lacking the complementary but opposing view which describes how Gemeinschaft develops and fosters natural will, on the one hand, and, on the other, binds and hinders rational will. The approach does not describe how Gesellschaft not only frees rational will but also requires and furthers it, even makes its unscrupulous use in competition into a condition of the maintenance of the individual, thus destroying the flowers and fruits of natural will. Thus, adjusting to the conditions of Gesellschaft and imitating such actions of others as lead to gain and profits are not only the results of a natural drive, but such action becomes imperative and failure to conform is punishable under pain of destruction.

Gemeinschaft requires and cultivates in the rulers, who are always models, an art of ruling and of living together. The only danger confronting Gemeinschaft is the destruction of natural relations, because everything hostile creates hostility; the greater the superiority of force and power of one side to damage another, the stronger the impulse for the oppressed to develop their intellects into rational will and aggressive tricks. One opponent always invites the other opponent to forge the same weapons or to invent better ones. This explains why in all conditions of social disorganization the women use cunning against the men, the young against the old, and the lower classes against the higher. Rational will (like violence) against enemies has always been permitted, has even been considered praiseworthy.

But only Gesellschaft makes such a condition general and necessary. This is because in its elementary relationships, ends are postulated by at least one party in a relationship, who regards their attainment as justifying all means as being right means. Because of this condition, these relationships become not only a possible source of hostility but a source in which hostility is natural and only veiled (and consequently highly probable, requiring slight provocation to cause an outbreak).

Note 2. The relationship between (social) forms of life and forms of will leads toward their unity in the form of law. Law does not originate from thoughts and opinions concerning justice. Life creates both of these two expressions of its reality, which stand related to each other in mutual causality.

PART THREE

The Sociological Basis of Natural Law

SECTION ONE: Definitions and Theses

1. *Whole and Parts*

The self or the ego of human natural will is a unity like the form of the natural will, i.e., a unity within a unity as well as a unity which encompasses other unities. Like an organism and its components, it is, however, a unity because of its intrinsic distinctness, *unum per se*, or because of the relation of its parts to itself as a living entity. As such it maintains itself in and through their changes, eliminating decayed parts, creating new ones or assimilating them from the inorganic matter. Nothing is unity that is only a part, and everything is unity that is a whole. As such it is not only part of another whole but also an example of its kind, of its species, or of its real concept. For all organic entities are ultimately included in the idea of the organism. This, then, can be conceived of only as a mode of the infinite energy or the general will from which it has developed under given conditions.

Scientific research has shown that all organic individuals are also a conglomerate of such elementary organisms (the cells). These are each determined by their origin and interrelationship. They represent and constitute in their permanent relations the form and unity of the whole to which they belong. The whole, in its various transitory manifestations, may, therefore, appear to be their product, although it is conceived as a lasting material or metaphysical existence, i.e., as the unity of these permanent relations. In this sense, the whole creates these elementary organisms; they are, so to speak, accidental and capable of being destroyed. Such contradiction is the adequate expression of real interdependence and interplay among the related wholes which grow and decay within their encompassing whole and as parts are

subordinated to it, while only through their co-operation as separate entities is created a whole of higher order, the idea of which is represented
by their common will. This is the specific characteristic of an organic
entity the ultimate components of which are themselves organisms.
These ideas can be applied to the very important concept of purpose or
ends. Every whole is in itself an end: This is only another expression
of its unity, i.e., of its evidence as something permanent which is supported from moment to moment by its strength even if there are other
forces which, through a conjunction of favorable conditions, further it.
Life is the continuous assimilating of such beneficial energies and the
constant struggle against inimical ones, mastering or adapting them,
eliminating internal and conquering external obstacles. In living, the
organism proves its fitness for life, i.e., the appropriate (correct, good)
condition, organization, and order of its forces or parts. But life per se
and the ability to live must be distinguished from the fitness for living
in a special form and consequently under special favorable or unfavorable conditions. Where conditions are favorable, therefore, the weaker
organism can live or live longer than it could otherwise; where they are
unfavorable, even the strong one is not able to survive.

And when given characteristics serve no purpose, a change in these,
i.e., adaptations to conditions, may insure survival. This applies not
only to the individual but also to every group of common origin, if it
represents a unity. An individual and his special qualities may be more
or less fitted to represent, conserve, and continue the group to which
he belongs. Barring differences in conditions and assuming average,
equally favorable conditions, there is no other criterion but duration for
the fitness which characterizes a living being in relation to itself as well
as to another entity. But it is the form, not the matter, which endures.
In this respect, the forms of organic structure and those of the natural
will belong to the same category; neither can be perceived by the senses,
neither can be conceived in material categories.

The form, as a whole, is constituted of its elements, which, in relation to it, are of a material character and maintain and propagate themselves through this very relationship. For the whole as a lasting form,
each of its parts will always represent a more transitory modification
of itself which expresses its nature in a more or less complete manner.
The parts are equal insofar as they participate in the whole, different
and manifold insofar as each one expresses itself and has its specific
function. Each part could be regarded as a mere means to the life and
end of the whole, if it were not for the fact that it is itself, during its
existence, this life and this end. The parts are similar in that they are
segments of a whole; they are different to the extent that they have

their own particularities. The same relation exists between classificatory concepts, that is, the genus and the groups and individuals which belong to it. This is also true of the relation between the individuals and every actual group encompassing them, which may still be developing or already decaying or in transition to a higher form, but which must always be conceived as active, living, and changeable. Consequently, the starting point for these reasonings is the essence of the human being, not an abstraction but the concrete concept of mankind as the most general reality of this kind. The next step leads to the essentials of the race, the people, the tribe, and smaller groups, and from there finally to the individual, who is, so to speak, the center of these many concentric circles. The more narrowing the circles which bridge the gap to him, the better the individual is understood. The intuitive and purely intellectual understanding of such a whole can be made easier and more readily grasped through classification by types, each of which is conceived as comprising the characteristic of all examples of the respective groups before their differentiation was made. Thus, the types are more nearly perfect than the individuals because they embody also those forces and latent capacities which have withered away through lack of use. But they are also more imperfect, in that they lack the qualities which have been developed to a higher degree in reality. For the theory, the sensual, but nevertheless constructed, image of such a typical example and its description is substituted for the intellectual idea of the real essence of this empirical whole. In real life, however, the fullness of the spirit and of the force of such a whole can impart itself to its parts only through the natural gathering of the real living bodies in their totality. However, in addition, it may be conceived as being in a chosen group of leading minds or even in one single individual who embodies in himself the will and being of the rest of the community.

2. *The Person*

The person or the ego of rational will is, as a structure of rational will, a unity by external determination, *unum per accidens*, mechanical unity. That is to say, in the same way as a formation of rational will has reality and unity only for the person possessing it, and through its relation to possible results, the concept of the person is a figment, a product of scientific thought. It is intended to express the unity of the origin of such formations, i.e., the disposition of a complex of force, power, means. This unity is only a creation of thought, based on a multitude of single possible acts, whatever the unity of these may be. Therefore, its purely imaginary existence is dependent upon the existence of these single acts, outside and above it. It is, therefore, supposed that this complex of single acts contains elements for which the unity represents their real model and counterpart, as direction and purpose are the same for both. Thus, they tend to reach beyond and above reality, for we are given to imagine that pure thought is, so to speak, floating above the real things. On the other hand, the unity of organic existence is not only embodied in the complex of single acts but also underlying it, without being distinguished and apart from it. In the same way, if a number of such empirical, imaginary unities are abstracted (or condensed) into an intellectual concept, this common denominator has the same relationship to the quasi-material multiplicity as the unity of the single object has to their multiplicity. The *universale* is *post rem* and *extra res*. Hence their conceptual or generic unity is only nominal, imaginary, and fictitious.

In a system of thought, the person who forms part of it is conceived as the thinking agent of real acts of rational will, i.e., as pursuing real ends and disposing of real means. Consequently, if it is to be a human person, a real human being (or a number of them) must think, plan, and act in its place, pursue its ends, and dispose of its means. This may be a single individual or a number of individuals, for the many can think and formulate their rational will together just as can an individual. (1) They can deliberate, any one expressing his thoughts as to what he himself wishes and what he thinks all the others should wish. Also, this stimulates the other to react. They advise the same or something similar or they speak against it. (2) They decide, all or at least as many as desire to do so, announce by certain words or signs that they will or will not do something, that they approve or disapprove of some action; the rest being indifferent thus make themselves and their own power ineffective. As every voice or every rational will is conceived as of equal weight, the result may be a state of equilibrium, in which case no decision can be made. If there is a majority on one or the other side, a definite decision will be made, either adopting or rejecting the proposal in question. The single human being must be conceived as always capable of making a decision. It is always possible that he, if asked or advised, can give an affirmative or a negative answer. If he wants and tries to decide, i.e., begins the process of deliberating, he must also be able to come to a decision. It is not only possible, but even quite easy, when considered as a task. Of course, one often says that he cannot decide or "it is very difficult for me to decide," but, in such cases circumstances are not strong enough to prompt the action of deciding. The question is not, so to speak, put with enough urgency. If anybody realizes that he has to decide (for example, to escape starvation), it is almost certain that he will overcome this inner resistance. The result, with regard to some proposed action, will thus never be zero or a dead center, but either acceptance or rejection. In contradistinction, a multitude is, in this sense, constantly capable of decision only if its number is uneven. Such unevenness of numbers constitutes, therefore, an essential requirement of the concept of the multitude in this context. It is, of course, possible, by tacit or open agreement, to accept a drawn vote as a decision in the negative. This means that preference is given to the negative wills. Or the decision can be left to balloting. A multitude willing to decide and capable of deciding as a unity is called an assembly. It may have a continuous existence, like an individual human being, (1) if theoretically the assembly remains permanently in session, but actually convenes for deliberations according to definite and known rules, and (2) if its members are recruited as soon as there is a need for it.

Every individual is the natural representative of his own person. The concept of the person cannot be derived from any other empirical egos than the individual human beings. For insofar as every individual is endowed with thought and will, he is perceivable. Consequently, there are real and natural persons insofar as there exist human beings who conceive themselves as such, accept and play this "role," each one assuming the "character" of a person like a mask held before his face. And, as natural persons, all human beings are equal. Everyone is endowed with unlimited freedom to define his own ends and to apply, in their pursuit, whatever means he chooses. Each person is his own master. No one is anybody else's master. They are independent of each other.

3. *The Assembly*

An assembly also represents its own person. But its existence is by no means an empirical one in the same sense as that of the persons of actually perceptible human beings. The reality of the assembly presupposes the reality of the person which it represents, whereas the concept of the person is derived from the reality of the human being. An assembly, insofar as it represents itself, is an artificial person. The assembly can act as a homogeneous ego of rational will only because the human beings who, as natural persons, constitute it, postulate the affirmative or negative consensus of their majority as the rational will of a homogeneous personal being which is imagined apart from and above the rational wills of the majority or the aggregate of the assembly. By this act the assembly is co-ordinated with the natural persons; it exists for the individual persons as these exist for one another, i.e., through mutual recognition and perception of their quality as persons.

Theory can create for many reasons other personifications which are represented by natural or assumed artificial persons. But every person exists for the others and their system only by dint of such recognition of his quality as a person and thereby of equality of persons. The very fact of postulating a person necessarily implies recognition as a secondary element. On the other hand, general recognition involves the special recognition of the validity of a given representative where such is not self-evident (like that of an intelligent human being and of an appointed assembly) but such representation is conceived as being based on sufficient grounds. Wherever a real person is represented by another real person, the underlying basis for the validity of such representation is the delegation of power (authority) from the former to the latter. This delegation presents such a formally valid type of sufficient basis, because the fact itself is identical with the effect which results from this normal and evident cause.

It is not conceivable where a fictitious person is represented, for such a person would not be capable of delegating power without representation. From a system of real individual persons, a fictitious person (represented by an individual or an assembly) can be conceived as emanating only by virtue of the rational will of one or several of its members who combine parts of their freedom and their means and thus constitute a separate person with given or construed representation. Such constituting act must imply the nomination of a representing person. In the case of an assembly, agreement of its "members" on the valid expression of their will is assumed. But such a fictitious person will be created by intelligent individuals only as a means to a definite end, which must be common in order to unite the majority. The fictitious person is the end (or a complex of ends) conceived as homogeneous and existing by itself. The existence of the person is in reality the existence of the means combined with regard to these connected ends or purposes. But through the transformation (in the mind of its authors) into the existence and concept of a person, these means become an end in itself, personal but not different from it. For the person as such does not think and has no end or purpose of its own, and, according to the hypothesis assumed, it has no end or purpose other than the one which is embodied in its meaning and concept.

But as the concept of the person is itself an artificial product or a figment, a fictitious ego of rational will corresponds to it more adequately than an ego of natural will. No human being can be thought of as so completely pursuing nothing but his own advantage as to be interested in nothing but his own profit and to confine his actions strictly to his own supposed ends, as is the case with a thinking and acting thing which as such merely exists in the imagination. Therefore, any individual as well as any assembly is better able to act in this way "in the name" of such figment of thought than it would in his or its own name.

4. *Family and Obligation*

Every relationship of the character of Gemeinschaft is, either potentially or intrinsically, a higher and more general self similar to the type or idea from which the different selves (whom we may more loosely call the "heads") derive themselves and their freedom. In contradistinction, every relationship of the character of Gesellschaft constitutes the beginning and the potentiality of a superimposed artificial person which disposes of a certain amount of forces and means; consequently, Gesellschaft as such is conceived as an effective whole (or entity). In a more general way, Gemeinschaft is thus the personality of united natural wills, Gesellschaft that of united rational wills. But in order to be conceived as an independent unity (or unit) and as being in possible relation to its parts as such unities, Gemeinschaft must have passed the stage where it cannot be distinguished from the majority of wills which, united in it, logically constitute its being. That is, it must be represented either by a special continuous will of its unanimous total or of several of its parts. This is a process of development which, in its completion, must be discerned by the observer. In contrast, the separate existence of an artificial person must be willed and postulated for a particular preconceived purpose by a special act of contracting rational wills. The simplest example of such purpose is guaranteeing other existing contracts whereby their fulfillment, hitherto dependent on the will of the interested parties, is now made the will of this homogeneous artificial person. That person is thus given the task of pursuing this end with the means furnished to it therefor. If objective law is the volitional meeting of any association of wills with regard to the associated parts, Gesellschaft per se has its own law in which it upholds the rights and obligations of its constituents. But such law must derive from and be composed of their original complete freedom, as the substance of their rational wills. In contrast, the Gemeinschaft, which is understood best as a metaphysical union of bodies or blood, possesses by nature a will and force of life of its own. Consequently, it has its own law with regard to the wills of its members. This may become apparent only as modifications and emanations of this organic all-composing substance take place.

In accordance with this distinction, then, are two diametrically opposed systems of law: one in which human beings are related to each other as natural members (or parts) of a whole, and another where they come into relation with each other as independent individuals, merely by virtue of their own rational wills. In empirical jurisprudence, especially of the Roman-modern school, which is a science of binding statute law within and for a Gesellschaft, the Gemeinschaft type of law persists under the name of family law, but the relationships regulated thereby are lacking in complete legal exactness. It is in this point that it differs most from the law of contracts. For the law of contracts permits a real mathematics, a rational mechanics of law, which can be reduced to identical statements because they are concerned only with modified acts of barter and the resulting claims of one person to certain consequent actions of his partner. Actions and claims change hands like goods or coins, so that there is subtraction on one side and addition of the same amount on the other, just as in simple equations. These two bodies of law, however, develop fully only in that middle region, the law of property, where they necessarily meet.

5. *The Spheres of Will*

The sphere of natural will is, in my definition, the essence of all forces that a human being or a group of human beings embody and encompass, insofar as these forces represent a unity the ego of which brings all their outer and inner conditions and changes into relation with itself through its memory and conscience.

To me the sphere of rational will encompasses the whole being and the entire possessions of a human being insofar as he determines the conditions and changes of this being and possessions by his thinking and is conscious of their dependence on it.

The sphere of the natural will, or the sphere of will per se, is identical with the material substance of natural will insofar as this is conceived as extending to (or comprising) external beings and things. If the general concept of will is freedom, this special aspect or concept of it can be defined as property. The same relationship exists between the sphere and the material substance of rational will. Property within the sphere of natural will is possessions; within the sphere of rational will, wealth. The relationship of possession to the forms of natural will is the same as that of wealth to the forms of rational will. External objects are taken into consideration only insofar as the will of an individual is embodied in and related to them. As the forms of will as such are determined forces and potentialities of action, possession and wealth are determined forces and potentialities of enjoyment or use of things.

The dual category of organ and instrument can be applied for better understanding of this dichotomy. Possession can be understood as organic and interior (or internal) property, wealth as external and mechanical property. From a purely psychological point of view, possession is an extension of one's own real being and therefore is itself a reality. In its most perfect form, the possession is represented by something that is itself living or consists of living things. In contrast, the psychological value of wealth lies in the extension of and increase in the objects of one's thought as so many potentialities of action. Wealth as such being an immaterial concept, it finds its most perfect real manifestation in things which represent only the subjective potentiality of realization. This is the use and satisfaction (or pleasure) which characterize wealth.

Possession, in accordance with its idea and normal concept, is absolutely one with and a part of its individual self and his life, but it has, nevertheless, a life of its own and possesses qualities which express this in many ways. It is a natural and indivisible unity, inalienable and not to be separated from its individual self except in a reluctant and painful manner in which force must be applied.

In contradistinction, wealth is conceived as a quantity and sum of individual things, each of which is to represent a certain amount of power to transform itself into and realize satisfaction. These quantities can be divided and combined in any manner, and, moreover, they are not only transferable, but are in fact intended to be alienated.

6. *Body and Soul*

Apart from the concept of freedom as the possession of one's own body and its organs or as the wealth of one's own possible actions, the idea of possession is most clearly expressed in the relationship to body and life of another human being, that of wealth in the relation to possible actions of other human beings. The concept of property is delimited by these two extreme cases. Possession is related to family law, whereas wealth belongs in the categories of the law of contracts. Thus, family law is only a manifestation of the natural right of the Gemeinschaft to its members, i.e., of its freedom. The law of contracts is the adequate expression of a relationship characteristic of the Gesellschaft per se. The latter type of relationship exists in the transfer of such a part of freedom from one sphere of rational will to another. In both concepts, real property, as a right to things or objects, means extension of freedom. That is, freedom is extended to other freedom as well as to things; it is also a right to human beings or persons. For this reason, the right of the Gemeinschaft to the bodies of its members necessarily extends also over all things which belong to these members and, therefore, to the Gemeinschaft. It is, for this reason, irrelevant whether the partial surrender of someone's freedom to the Gemeinschaft means acts as services or the transfer of a certain object. The importance or value of the services can be measured like the value of goods, which is more readily understandable. Of all things which form the organic property of a Gemeinschaft, the living animals are nearest to the heart of man. They must be raised and cared for as helpers. In the daily work they belong to the house, and the house is really the body of the

Gemeinschaft itself. The primordial thing, however, which is owned by human Gemeinschaften, is the land. Parts and shares of the land belong to every free family insofar as it derives from a higher Gemeinschaft as the natural sphere of its natural will and all its activities. With the people developing and differentiating, the land is divided and cultivated, but it remains a unity and common property. However much labor is spent on it, it can only improve the conditions for the unimpeded growth of the plants; it merely conserves and furthers the productive forces of the soil itself and prepares the fruits of the soil for human consumption.

It is a different thing, however, when labor produces new things or goods in which the form is as important for their use, or even more so, as the material itself. They receive their forms from the mind and hands of the individual, of the artist or the artisan. But through him the whole house or family of which he is a member—father, son, or servant—works and produces. The same holds for the community of which he is a member or the guild of which he is a fellow and a master. The Gemeinschaft retains ultimate equity in his work, even when the use of it is granted to him exclusively, as a natural right resulting from his authorship. Actual use is, in the natural and regular course of events, use either by the Gemeinschaft or by the individual. Natural use of the object as such means either direct use or conservation for future use or further production. In each case it means a more complete possession (or appropriation), an assimilation, even where a precious metal is buried as a treasure in the earth, if the land is the organic property of the Gemeinschaft. Diametrically opposed to this is the use through sale (alienation), which in reality is nonuse. This distinction has been made in a famous passage of a classical author: "The real use of a shoe is in the wearing, the other possible use is its sale. For whoever exchanges it for money or goods with the one who is in need of shoes uses the shoe as a shoe, but not in the real sense, for the shoe has not been made for barter."

Barter, on the other hand, constitutes the only completely arbitrary use. It is the adequate expression of a simple act of rational will, of premeditated action. It therefore presupposes an individual comparing and calculating. But it presupposes this individual alone, not with another person but opposed to him. Where several individuals constitute one of the parties in the barter they must be conceived as an assembly capable of decisions and thus equal to a natural person. As alienable objects or exchange values, goods become commodities. A commodity is for its owner nothing but a means to acquire other commodities. This essential quality makes all commodities as such equal and reduces their differences to a quantitative level. Money is the expression of this equality. All commodities are potential money, power to earn money. Money, in turn, may be considered as potential commodities, power to buy any commodities. Therefore, money is the sphere of rational will in a material sense. The single act which can leave the realm of freedom and become the object of a contract, i.e., an obligation, possesses as such exchange value and is equal to a certain amount of money. "Only those acts are suited for obligation which can acquire such a material character and therefore are capable of being subjected to an alien will like commodities. But this presupposes that these acts possess some property value or can be evaluated in money." (Savigny, *Das Obligationrecht,* I, p. 9.) Vice versa, a promise of goods with exchange value, especially a promise of money, i.e., an obligation, can serve and circulate as money. The promise as expression of a form of rational will, of a decision, is itself power to obtain goods or money insofar as it is accepted. It is wealth. General acceptance must be thought of as the object of a (tacit) agreement, a Gesellschaft-like convention. The basis for giving such credit to a person is, however, the degree of probability that the promise will be kept, the obligation fulfilled, the draft honored. Such tokens of credit are, therefore, like money and function the more perfectly as such the nearer probability approaches actuality. Money as obligation and obligations as money are the perfect abstract expressions of Gesellschaft-like wealth. Wealth thus represents well-founded power over alien rational wills which, although free by nature, are bound.

7. *Status and Contract*

From the preceding chapters we obtain the following table of corresponding and opposite concepts:

Gemeinschaft	*Gesellschaft*
Natural Will	Rational Will
Self	Person
Possession	Wealth
Land	Money
Family Law	Law of Contracts

With these opposites belongs also the one which is contained in all given concepts, namely, the distinction which has recently been treated as the opposing poles in legal forms: status and contract. The statement of the learned and penetrating English author whose theory has attracted widespread attention deserves to be quoted. Henry Maine states in a summary (*Ancient Law,* 7th edition, p. 168):

The movement of the progressive societies has been uniform in one respect. Through all its course it has been distinguished by the gradual dissolution of family dependency and the growth of individual obligation in its place. The individual is steadily substituted for the Family, as the unit of which civil laws take account. The advance has been accomplished at varying rates of celerity, and there are societies not absolutely stationary in which the collapse of the ancient organisation can only be perceived by careful study of the phenomena they present. ... Nor is it difficult to see what is the tie between man and man which replaces by degrees those forms of reciprocity in rights and duties which have their origin in the Family. It is Contract. Starting, as from one terminus of history, from a condition of society in which all the relations of Persons are summed up in the relations of Family, we seem to have steadily moved towards a phase of social order in which all these relations arise from the free agreement of individuals. In Western Europe the progress achieved in this direction has been considerable. Thus the status of the Slave has disappeared—it has been superseded by the contractual relation of the servant to his master. The status of the Female under Tutelage, if the tutelage be understood of persons other than her husband, has also ceased to exist; from her coming of age to her marriage all the relations she may form are relations of contract. So too the status of the Son under Power has no true place in the law of modern European societies. If any civil obligation binds together the Parent and the child of full age, it is one to which only contract gives its legal validity. The apparent exceptions are exceptions of that stamp which illustrate the rule. ... The great majority of jurists are constant to the principle that the classes of persons just mentioned are subject to extrinsic control on the single ground that they do not possess the faculty of forming a judgment on their own interests; in other words, that they are wanting in the first essential of an engagement by Contract.

The word Status may be usefully employed to construct a formula expressing the law of progress thus indicated, which, whatever be its value, seems to me to be sufficiently ascertained. All the forms of Status taken notice of in the Law of Persons were derived from, and to some extent are still coloured by, the powers and privileges anciently residing in the Family. If then we employ Status, agreeably with the usage of the best writers, to signify these personal conditions only, and avoid applying the term to such conditions as are the immediate or remote result of agreement, we may say that the movement of the progressive societies has hitherto been a movement from Status to Contract.

This clear insight will serve as the theme for the following discussion and its application will be elaborated and explained.

8. *Control and Property*

Control of human beings over human beings is here distinguished from, but studied in closest connection with, the concept of wealth. Control under the family law is essentially control of a whole over its parts. It is control of parts over other parts, as, for example, control of the father and master of the house over sons and servants, only insofar as one part is itself a manifestation of the invisible whole in its entirety. The same holds true of all wealth of the Gemeinschaft, especially landed property. In contradistinction, control characteristic of the Gesellschaft, as well as property, belongs a priori to the individual. Insofar as the obligation presupposes the participation of another person, this person is co-subject to his own act of concession as long as this act is still within the sphere of freedom. The participating person has co-ownership of the object or the money value constituting the obligation until fulfillment cancels the obligation or the continued ownership becomes illegal on maturity, i.e., is no longer existent as wealth in the legal sense. It is possible that even then such co-ownership may legally continue as possession or actual ownership, subject to special rules. Correspondingly, the act, activity, or labor, when and as directed, is also, from its very start, legally an act, activity, or labor of the recipient. The theory of natural law assumes, rightly, that a person cannot sell himself, because the receipt of a seeming equivalent, and thus the persistence of a sphere of rational will into which it will be received, are conditions precedent to every barter. It is, however, conceivable that a human being may sell his labor for the duration of his life but otherwise remain free and competent to hold wealth. Furthermore, one can conceive of a person being property like a commodity and used as a consumption good. For absolute affirmation and absolute negation of the autonomous person are reciprocal. Therefore, slavery is by no means legally incompatible with the system of the Gesellschaft, although it is a thoroughly artificial institution, because the premise that all adult human beings are equal through their rational wills is offered by nature itself and is therefore the simplest and first scientific assumption.

The individuals of all values and evaluations can by agreement be made objects of wealth and thus become marketable just as is the case of things of no intrinsic value (for example, pieces of paper). Indeed, human bodies are more naturally commodities than human labor, if only the labor can be offered for sale by its natural owner. Complete slavery, just as complete freedom, is, however, not compatible with the essence of Gemeinschaft. Servitude in Gemeinschaft implies first of all belonging in some way to its whole, for example, to the house, although this relationship is more of a passive nature, like that of a natural possession, than active relationship, like those of the agents of the Gesellschaft. It takes an intermediate position between the two, in fact, but it includes at least the possibility of participating in the place and rights of the Gemeinschaft and attaining special right by force of habit and by watchful faithfulness. All this conveys the concrete concept of a culture which is dominated by agriculture and labor instead of by commerce and usury. All forms of dependence and servitude are modified after, and thought of in the terms of, the pattern of domestic relations. And a kind of patriarchal dignity and power corresponds to all of them.

The function of the ruler has a twofold character. He is mainly entrusted with the care of his subjects: protection, guidance, instruction. In this relationship the ruled are the inferior *(Inferiores)*. Although their well-being is just as much their own wish and will, more befitting is the form of command by which he guides their will seemingly to his own bent, for they are thought of only as part and parcel of himself. Or it is first and foremost his own cause to which the ruler devotes himself. He is the originator and leader of an enterprise for which he is in need of help. In this case, he takes, if possible, equals to himself, although at the same time he puts them in his custody and care. It is the request as summons, demand, or orders of the superior as well as the equal and the subordinate which in its form corresponds most closely to such mutual interdependence. Domination of the first type is found in its purest form on a completely Gemeinschaft-like basis, for example, in the domination of a father over his children *(potestas);* domination of the second type is exemplified by the marital relationship *(manus)*. All relations between dignity or authority and service, which are less deeply rooted and have a less emotional basis than these, can nevertheless be reduced to one of these forms or to a mixture of them both. Servitude can be like the status of a son or it can be similar to that of a helper, vassal, follower or friend. In both forms it can approach complete dependence to a greater or lesser degree. But the dependence itself varies with these types, especially where it develops into a recognized membership in the family. It then becomes similar to the status of a child or even to marital companionship. The twofold character of domination becomes again apparent in the relationship of the master (of a craft or art) to his apprentices and disciples, on the one hand, and to the "freed" journeymen helping in his work and carrying out his ideas, on the other.

9. *Wage and Barter*

A recent treatise on the purpose in law (R. v. Jhering, *Der Zweck im Recht,* Vol. I) defines the relationship of the Gesellschaft as "egotistical" and attempts to define the cardinal point of all these relations and of all social intercourse as wages. The concept itself is not open to criticism, but the terminology is misleading. This is because anyone, whoever he may be, who strives to reveal the deeper meaning of words, will discover that it is unsuitable to define a commodity offered for sale as the wage for the payment of money or the price as wage for the transfer of a commodity. Nevertheless, in an age where nobody hesitates to consider labor a commodity and the labor contract a barter, it has remained common usage to adorn the sum of money involved in such barter with the name of wage. But wage really means a favor which is granted voluntarily and regularly, i.e., in this case by the natural will, in consideration of services well rendered and of qualities of being and character highly esteemed, viz., carefulness, industry, faithfulness. But such favor is always based on one-sided discretion, liking, and esteem and may, therefore, be considered as a gift, a kindness, or an act of grace. In short, it behooves the superior to extend such favors according to deserts; this implies that they reward good deeds and assistance rendered. It is, of course, possible that the servant, in expectation of such wage, makes special efforts and does all he can in order, so to speak, to buy such high remuneration, just as in a race, where everybody tries to surpass the others, or in commercial competition or, in fact, wherever men compete for the prize of ambition. But here we begin to confuse what must remain quite separate. Where prizes are awarded, the competitors might well be considered buyers or sellers, but that never applies to the person who gives the rewards. His promise is, as a rule, not that of the party to a contract; he is morally obliged to keep his promise only if the conditions are fulfilled. But he himself is judge of the achievements, like a feudal lord (thus he can also confer, i.e., delegate the office of the judge), and whatever he gives is awarded after and on the strength of a good deed. In contrast, barter is essentially a dual and simultaneous act. It does not know of any "before" or "after," nor of any "high" or "low" (viz., of rank). There is an act of distributive justice, here of commutative justice. This important distinction is, at root, identical with our dichotomy of Gemeinschaft and Gesellschaft and opens up new and significant perspectives.

But to go back to our discussion: competition in trade and elsewhere (where anyone runs along with another and strives to become rich, powerful, and respected) is only metaphorical; it is faced not with another individual, either selling or giving, but with the calculable circumstances of fate, with fortune which, for known or unknown reasons, rewards the industry and daring of one and brings them to naught for another. Furthermore, the promise of a prize is identical with its imaginary transfer only if the action or achievement required is of a wholly objective character and can, therefore, like a thing or commodity, be detached from the sphere of the rational will of the acting person. For in this way the barter is completed as soon as the commodity has been transferred to the other party, resulting in a claim to the prize or an obligation.

10. *Service and Contract*

In this way every service-relationship can develop into a pure contract-relationship, as is known from experience. But we also know that no effort and arbitrary endeavor will bring forth what only nature itself and, in harmony with it, human natural will can create. In this category belong the intrinsic qualities of natural will as well as its peculiar achievements. Everything of this kind can be rewarded, but never paid for. Qualities can be paid for only in so far as they are materialized in certain acts, i.e., acts of which every human being, even without these qualities, can be conceived as capable if he is only willing, that is, if the attraction of an imagined end or purpose is strong enough to induce him to action. This is, of course, fictitious reasoning, for there are in nature no such extraneous psycho-physical forces. But the general human capabilities, of which everybody possesses a quantitatively measurable share insofar as the stimulation of the brain is followed by a contraction of the muscles, are in this respect similar to external things. In regard to them, all human beings who can handle and apply them to their proper use are equal. Such use is for all things the same and is most easily made if they are given the character of commodities, i.e., if use is only apparent and changes into nonuse. But this is the same insofar as they require only the exertion of human muscular force. The concrete-general element, which potentially contains all specific ones, touches here the abstract-general element in which, through the act of individual or Gesellschaft-like thinking, all specific differentiations have been artificially effaced; the general principle of the idea and the general principle of the concept meet at this point.

In reality, however, the offer and sale of an activity does not necessarily imply that every human being is qualified for it. It is only the individual person who makes such activity an extraneous function for himself, and it thereby takes on the form of something within the potentialities of any human being as such. Whether and to what degree performing such tasks actually involves only labor of a general average quality is another matter. It is true that a process is set in motion whereby the labor employed in one productive process, i.e., within the workshop, is divided and the separated functions are simplified, the machines become more and more automatic, and all the work they require is merely that of tending. The methods of production follow the same trend: they too, tend at first to make skill and craftsmanship more nearly perfect, but, in the end, they make them superfluous. The more work requires only simple, so to speak, abstract labor, the more clearly this fact determines the price of labor, which is reduced to a value derived from the use and exploitation of an object which the entrepreneur buys in the market. The average price, which represents at first only the fictitious mean between high and low prices, gradually approximates the level of the low prices, because these outweigh the high prices which correspond to qualified skilled labor. This process takes place within the system of production characteristic of Gesellschaft, which is based on the separation of the worker from his materials and tools.

From this it may be judged how inappropriate the term of wage-laborer is for the proletarian of the system of Gesellschaft. It is as inadequate as the term of master (or bread-giver) for the entrepreneur, the manufacturer, or the still less patriarchic corporation, and especially for the fiscal authorities which are supposed to represent the common interest of all groups but which interpret these to mean solely the interests of capitalists.

11. *Voluntary Contribution and Payment*

The contribution as a payment of the inferior in support of the household of his superior is the counterpart of the wage as a gift of the superior to his inferior. Both develop through actual repetition into custom and, as such, acquire under favorable conditions the character of a duty, this also with regard to type and quantity. If they are on a voluntary basis, their correlates are the request (this especially of the wage) and the promised or anticipated favor (this of the contribution). If compulsory, the corresponding concepts are the demand *(postulatum)* and the title to a right. In the end, both categories change to contractual obligations or, what does not enter into the present argument, into legal imposts where they are simply stipulated and agreed equivalents for received or promised commodities or services. Since the contribution as well as the wage derives, by origin, from the recognition of a relationship characteristic of the Gemeinschaft, they are both visible tokens of gratitude for favors received. Thus, the contribution can be conceived as a wage which honors and exalts the recipient, and, vice versa, the wage as a contribution which constitutes a gracious and understanding act on the part of the donor. In one sense it is pleasant to receive a gift, apart from its value and usefulness, in the other it is a burden. For this reason contributions have been abolished, commuted, and changed into taxes, etc. This is an incident in the decay of the Gemeinschaft-like relationship that destroys the social status of the superior, which was determined by these contributions, even though, on the other hand, it is an incident which makes possible their importance in Gesellschaft, viz., the complete independence of property obtained through fixed money incomes from trade or usury. The unencumbered landed property develops into a business of this type even if not run as a business, through the form of the leases and of the resulting income from rent.

There are two aspects of this change for the landlords: a bad one for their honor, a good one for their wealth. The abolition of the wage also has a twofold meaning for the laborers, although in this case the result is reversed. After all real ties between the landlords and the masses are severed, the former are nevertheless keenly interested in opposing the full consequences of equality among all individuals of rational will insofar as these imply a negation of their superiority. In fact, this superiority not only persists but becomes more rigid and more marked as it is transformed into a phenomenon of the Gesellschaft. There, the superiority rests no longer in the individual, the person per se, but much more in the object, in the extent of his sphere of rational will, especially of his wealth. Therefore, the superiors take pleasure in the semblance and name of wage. This semblance, if not the name, is felt by the inferiors to be a sign of servitude and dishonor. But, judged purely by its economic value, the phenomenon as such is favorable for them in all those relations which can be reduced to barter and contract. For whoever refuses (thinks it incompatible with his dignity) to haggle the price of a commodity or a service foregoes his main advantage as a buyer. If a service is already rendered, i.e., if a tacit agreement is concluded, in accordance with the scheme of the Gesellschaft he can avoid the danger of being forced to do it by an additional claim of the seller only by making a generous payment which, over and above the value and price of the object, is supposed to include a voluntary gift. It is, of course, possible to consider the latter as the remuneration and real wage for qualities and activities which have not been or cannot be offered. Otherwise it acquires the character of an alms, of a voluntary contribution of the superior to the inferior, for which the only reason is supposed to be the need of the latter.

But the meaning of alms is different in Gemeinschaft than in Gesellschaft, or, to put it more clearly, it is different if originating from an individual natural will than from a general rational will. In the first case it is given out of special or general sympathy or out of a special or general sense of duty and prompted by a desire to help. It then involves the idea of a necessity (on one's own initiative) or of an obligation (resulting from a kinship or neighborhood relationship or social and professional ties, or, finally, from a religious or humanitarian feeling of brotherly love). But it makes a significant difference if the alms is given with complete detachment for an external purpose, for instance, to get rid of the unpleasant sight of a beggar, or in order to show generosity, thus sustaining a reputation of power and wealth (for the sake of one's credit strength). Finally, and that is the most frequent incidence, but closely related to the others mentioned, alms are given under the pressure of social conventions and etiquette, which have very good reasons to prescribe and enforce such rules. That is the type of charity practiced by the rich and socially prominent people, a conventional charity which by its very character is detached and void of feeling. From this point of view it is also possible to evaluate the interesting phenomenon of the gratuity, or tip. It is a strange mixture of price, wages, and alms, not suitable to maintain or further a Gemeinschaft of human beings. It signifies, so to speak, the tail end and the extreme degeneration of all these phenomena.

In contrast, the present represents their original and most general form: the present exchanged between lovers, relatives, and friends is given as much for the sake of the donor as for that of the recipient. It shares this characteristic with all perfect hospitality and all real existence: donor and recipient feel themselves as a unity. The present, too, can become conventional and arbitrary, but the semblance of a corresponding sentiment is most anxiously kept up because otherwise it would be tantamount to a rather absurd exchange of goods without comparison and evaluation. On the other hand, a gift of money can be made without violating every logical and aesthetic standard only if no requital is possible that would lead to a mutual canceling out. Money can, therefore, be offered as the friendly gift of a superior who has the power and the will to increase the abstract wealth of his inferior, especially if the recipient, in his sphere of will, is related to the donor, as, for instance, the son to his father. In contrast, a gift of money from the poor to the rich is absurd as a contradiction in terms. For the same reason the wage can retain its character if transformed into money, but not the contribution. For taxes, on a monetary basis, presuppose a common (public) fund which has been set apart by the individual persons and into which they are paid. The public fund is a concept of the Gesellschaft which is related to the concept of the state and similar associations and special-interest groups.

12. *Life and Law*

The development from status to contract in law is paralleled in life. Law is, in every respect, nothing but common will; as natural law it is the form or the spirit itself of all those relationships the substance of which is social life, or, in the most general sense, the union of spheres of will. Consequently, on one hand, this form is conceived as the necessary unity of wills and spheres of wills or as emanation from such a unity; i.e., it possesses the same reality as the substance of which it presents the subjective (psychical or metaphysical) aspect. This is true even if the substance is itself nothing but a product of social imagination or memory (in the same sense as the concept of a poetic and creative folk spirit [*Volksseele*] is used in scientific discussion). On the other hand, law is "form" added from the spheres of rational will to the substance which exists only in thought; it is nothing but the manifestation of a certain structure of this substance. In the first case, the simple underlying fact is the close relationship of bodies which is taken as continuous, for instance, in the saying: "wife and husband are one body." This close relationship is a union of natural wills and forms the basis of the natural law which encompasses marital and other relationships as an organic substance. As a product of rational will, however, law centers around the elementary phenomenon of property transfer or exchange of goods. This is a purely mechanical process which derives its significance only from the intentions and calculations of the persons involved. Their determined rational will makes such process a legal act and creates a type of law which may be called "natural" because it represents the simplest and most rational legal structure of its kind. A common rational will based on contract, and consequently the legal system centered around it, exist, however, only for the persons concerned, who acknowledge such contracts and legal system as their common thought or concept. To obtain a quasi-objective existence, therefore, such law needs recognition and confirmation by the general rational will and requires Gesellschaft itself as the thinking agency of its general rational will. That will of Gesellschaft, which is of natural and simple nature, expresses itself in convention and, in this quasi-objective sense, constitutes a natural law. But the thinking agent of such will and law does not exist, either by virtue of the special or of the general contract, as a separate unit apart from and outside the total of individuals, unless specifically stipulated. If so, these units have the same relation to each other as do the contracts. Through the general unity the special unities attain an objective reality; they require a twofold constitutive act. But the general unity, if a homogeneous person (as the state), can also institute special unities dependent on it which do not rest upon the contracts of individuals but are subjects for parts of the sphere of its rational will, permanently or temporarily belonging to it.

This leads to the theory of legal persons and institutions. In neutral terms, the two basic forms of social existence are "union" (closed unity) *(Verbindung)* and "association" (loose relationship) *(Bündnis)*. In a Gemeinschaft (as status) union is the earlier phenomenon; unity is prior to multitude, even if in reality unity and multitude may not yet have been separated. Association is a later and special phenomenon wherein the special unity is conceived as persisting, though undeveloped, just as the man as an idea is prior to the boy. For the boy can be considered as the future man as well as a boy in his undeveloped stage. In Gesellschaft, association comes first, while union is a twofold or manifold association. Gemeinschaft descends from union to association; such an association can, however, be conceived only within an objective organization, because there the wills resemble most nearly rational wills. Gesellschaft advances from association to union. For the union of individual wills association proves the more adequate form; it is the only possible one for a simple combination. But for uniting of many, which involves associations of all with all others, a union provides the more adequate form. If, as finally developed, the union becomes more similar to the Gemeinschaft and the determining rational will more similar to the natural will, the union becomes more general in its extent and its purpose. For there the underlying contracts are more difficult to trace and more complicated in their meaning.

13. *Union and Association*

Within a people's Gemeinschaft, which is in the process of development and stratified into many groups, the exchange of goods and consequently the use of contracts must be conceived as steadily expanding. But there are enormous obstacles to prevent these facts and phenomena from becoming predominant. The whole development is first of all an extension and differentiation of Gemeinschaft phenomena and of the forms of status, as natural law would term it, which adapts itself to every new construction. Every status, like every contract, results in dues and duties for the individuals or persons. The status does not presuppose the individuals, but is coexistent with them; its own idea and form, however, is presupposed, as either conceived through itself or derived from another one. The contract acquires its full meaning only if it is conceived of or made by individuals and is their intellectual creation.

Law, as a reflection of life, advances from unions of Gemeinschaft to associations of Gemeinschaft. For them are substituted associations of Gesellschaft which finally develop into unions of Gesellschaft. The

relationships of the first type come under family law and law of possession; the others belong to the law of contracts and property law. The
prototype of all unions of Gemeinschaft is the family. By birth man enters these relationships: free rational will can determine his remaining
within the family, but the very existence of the relationship itself is not
dependent on his full rational will. The three pillars of Gemeinschaft—
blood, place (land), and mind, or kinship, neighborhood, and friendship—are all encompassed in the family, but the first of them is the
constituting element of it. The associations of Gemeinschaft are most
perfectly interpreted as friendship, Gemeinschaft of spirit and mind
based on common work or calling and thus on common beliefs. But there
are federations for which the Gemeinschaft of spirit or mind represents
its main significance and which are not only maintained but also formed
voluntarily. These are especially the corporations or fellowships of the
arts and crafts, the communities, churches, and holy orders. In all
these the idea of the family persists. The prototype of the association in
Gemeinschaft remains the relationship between master and servant, or,
better, between master and disciple, especially insofar as it is actually or
conceptually embodied in a house of one of the above-mentioned unions.
Between union and association lie many important relationships, the
most important of which is marriage. On one side marriage is the basis
of a new family; on the other side it is a free union of man and wife
which, however, can be understood only in terms of the idea and the
spirit of the family. Marriage in its moral sense, that is, single marriage
(monogamy), can be defined as a perfect neighborhood—living together,
constant physical proximity. Community of daily and nightly abode, of
bed and board, is its very essence; their spheres of will adjoin but are
one, like the communal fields of the villagers. Thus, the possession of
the same land and buildings is the fullest expression of their community
property.

All these relationships of the status can, in life as well as in law,
become contracts, but not without losing their real organic character. Men enter into them on the strength of specific qualities, without
which they would be necessarily excluded. As contracts, however, these
relationships do not require such specific qualities, but only human
beings who conform to the concept of a person by virtue of quantitatively measurable capacities or wealth. Where the contracting parties
always meet on the basis of equality, their inner indifference toward
each other is no hindrance to such contracts; on the contrary, it is
an advantage and constitutes a condition precedent to the concept of
the contract. Seemingly, contracts, insofar as they are not executed
concurrently, are based on confidence and faith, as the term credit

indicates. This element of natural will can, in an undeveloped stage, be and remain really effective, but more and more calculation is substituted for it. Future compliance with the contract is, from a calculating point of view, more or less probable on objective grounds; i.e., it is to the self-interest of the contracting party because he has given a valued security or because possible future business depends on proven solvency. The debtor is then no longer a pauper or a servant, but a businessman, as, vice versa, every businessman is a debtor. There are, further, the service contracts, especially the labor contracts which connect the two large classes of Gesellschaft. Under such contracts masses of people are united for common work. From a contract between individuals, they develop to contracts between groups. With the increasing consciousness of a conflict of interests, they become free contracts, and as such the object of ever renewed struggle, from which a way out to "social peace" is painfully sought.

14. *Associations of Gesellschaft*

Associations of Gesellschaft can be formed for purposes of all kinds which are conceived as possible results attainable by united forces and means. But an artificial person cannot dispose of human forces unless they are its property or wealth and thus, through their value, are comparable to any other property. Like a natural person it can buy labor, which presupposes moneyed wealth, or its founders can, with or after the constituting act, grant it certain contributions in labor, like sums of money. These contributions can be equal or different for all the founders, whereby it is possible that equality may mean the same relation to the total personal forces for each individual. The desired success and stipulated purpose of the association is a repeated result or a continuous activity. The result may be divisible at will, like a return in money. If it is to be divided, then with equal shares (in personal and money contributions) there will take place a division into equal parts of the return, with unequal shares a division into proportionate parts. If it is indivisible, the possible and anticipated utility of the return to the members must be either equal or proportionate. The same holds true of the utility of a continuous activity. But in all these cases it is assumed that the means spent will be at least balanced by the results, so that the quantity of force is not wasted. The associates intend only a transfer and conservation of their energies such as is produced by every act of their natural wills. For this reason, an association of the nature of Gesellschaft is not as such bound to activities of rational will (in substance, not only in form), and this does not distinguish it from associations of Gemeinschaft which, through their leaders, can also represent their will as rational will. But in a system of Gesellschaft, which presupposes every individual person with separate spheres of rational will, the association is the only possible type of interrelationship.

The difference lies in the fact that all its activities are restricted to a definite end and definite means of attaining it, if it is to be valid, i.e., to conform to the will of its members. (In contrast, it is the essential characteristic of the associations of Gemeinschaft to be as universal as life itself and to derive their forces not from the outside, but from within.) There are, however, quite a number of such societies formed for a definite purpose where an underlying contract to this effect is no longer discernible because there is no resulting legal obligation. To this category belong also those associations which take the form of a straight contract but without, so to speak, any tangible obligation which can be expressed in inventory terms. "It is possible to imagine an agreement on the part of several people to meet regularly for instruction in science and art. Such agreement may take the outward form of a contract, but no obligation with regard to the activities agreed upon can ensue." (Savigny, *op. cit.*) Thus, a special-interest group *(Verein)* can be founded which for its members has the full reality of a person, without existing at all in the legal system (non-legal, artificial person). But the associations with definite legal character, which are also the most important within the Gesellschaft, are those whose basis is wealth. Their purpose is an increase in wealth through a pooling of means. To this category belong the associations of capital for the purpose of usury, trade, and production. Such an association wants to make profit, just as does a single individual. To this end it acquires houses or ships or machines and raw materials. All its property belongs to its members, not individually but as an integral person. As such, they are, therefore, interested in the maintenance, production, and multiplication of these things. Distinct from this is the interest in the income to be distributed. This is the ultimate end, to which the collective interest is subservient and for the sake of which the association has been formed. With a real individual person this division can be made only in the abstract. For this reason, the association brings out more clearly the essential interrelationship of motives of individual actions under rational will.

The actions of an association are partly directed outward, partly toward itself and its members. The association, i.e., its representative, is responsible to them for those actions directed outwardly. For the purpose of control, the members can institute a special representative body of their own, the simplest way being a shareholders' meeting, which, in turn, is responsible to the individuals and under obligation to proceed according to the established rules of a mandatory contract. But the internal activity of the association, i.e., the distribution (at regular intervals) of available profits (as the result of its actions) between itself and its members, is also subject to the same special or general legal rules and has, therefore, as far as the individuals are concerned, the semblance of an external action. But as such it is not the fulfillment of an obligation which the association has incurred; it is only the result of its general obligation to manage the wealth of the association in an appropriate manner and to the greatest possible advantage of its partners. The share of each member is thus in reality only a part of his own property, delegated to and managed by the association of which he is a partner. In the same way everybody can treat his own business as a strange person, although of his own making, and consider only his private property his very own. But while such fictitious persons may acquire legal existence under the commercial law, they cannot publicly take action against their own actual individuals or against each other, because they are one and the same person in every important relationship. Property or wealth associations, however, are different in this respect, that is, as far as their legal status is concerned. Such a company may be identical with the association of its members, although such association was formed for a definite purpose, because as a real partnership or open company it exists only for its members and is not an independent agency. It does not, therefore, represent a homogeneous legal person *(no universitas),* just as a business enterprise, separated from its owner, does not (although the "firm" may perpetuate his person); it is only the representative of the majority of the partners, who are considered a unity in certain cases. In contradistinction, a property or wealth association is a free and independent agency if it is conceived as a subject which requires representation. Such an association cannot be imagined without obligations toward its shareholders, but it owns the wealth brought together by them and, like any other person, is liable for its obligations up to the amount of such wealth.

Other forms of wealth associations, such as the registered fellowship or partnership, the partners of which carry an unlimited or higher liability than their shares, are derived from special contracts, but to be effective and workable they must be based, like the open company, on a relationship of Gemeinschaft among their members. Experience proves that such associations are, because of this characteristic, not amenable to the laws of Gesellschaft. They either retain their character as free persons, and this becomes unbearable for their members, or they lose it and are reduced to mere partnerships, the characteristics of which have already been discussed. The corporation or stock company, on the other hand, which is liable only for itself, represents, in its exclusive concentration on profit making, the perfect type of all legal forms for an association based on rational will. This is because it is from its very origin a relationship of Gesellschaft, without any admixture of elements of Gemeinschaft, and thus does not allow, as in other cases, any misconception as to its real character.

Addition (1912). During the last decade, associations composed for the most part of the poorer people, first for the collective purchase of goods, later for the production of commodities for their own use, have obtained considerable power and importance. In Germany these associations are called co-operatives. Many small associations or special-interest groups form co-operatives for wholesale purchasing or mass production. The legal form of these co-operatives is based on the principle of limited liability and thus follows the pattern of the stock company. But it is evident that, under a form adapted to conditions of Gesellschaft, there has been revived a principle of Gemeinschaft economy which is capable of further significant development. This antipodal movement (as it is called by Staudinger) is also important for the pure theory of social organization. It may become the focus for a resuscitation of family life and other forms of Gemeinschaft through better understanding of their significance and their essential qualities. The moral necessity for such resuscitation has, since this book was written, been recognized more and more by all those who have proved themselves capable of judging the tendencies of modern Gesellschaft clearly and without bias.

Addition (1922). After the terrible disruption which the capitalistic system of Gesellschaft has undergone, it has still more ruthlessly used its destructive forces. In view of these phenomena, the cry for "Gemeinschaft" has become more and more vocal, very often with explicit (or, as in the case of British Guild socialism, tacit) reference to this book. This cry deserves the more credit, the less it voices a Messianic hope in the "spirit" alone. For the spirit as a separate entity is real only in "ghost" magic. To attain reality, it must incarnate itself in a living principle capable of development. Such principle is found in the idea of co-operative production, if and when it is able to protect itself against relapsing into mere business.

SECTION TWO: The Natural Element of Law

15. *The Essence of Law*

Classical philosophy of law was concerned with the problem of whether law is a natural product *(physei)* or an artifice *(thesei* or *nomô)*. Modern theory holds that everything originating from or formed by human will is natural as well as artificial. But in the course of its development the artificial element prevails over the natural the more the specifically human, and especially the mental, power of will gains in importance, until, in the end, it attains (relative) freedom from its natural basis and may even come into conflict with it. All law of the nature of Gemeinschaft is a product of the human mind. It is a system of thoughts, rules, and maxims and as such is comparable to an organ or product which has been created through corresponding activity, i.e., through practice as a modification of an already existing similar substance, with progress of development from the general to the specific. Thus, it is an end in itself, although necessarily related to the whole to which it belongs, from which it derives, and in which it embodies itself. This presupposes a solidarity of mankind and, furthermore, a protoplasm or essence of law as the original and necessary product of their collective living and thinking, the further development of which has in the main been due to its own activity, so to speak, that is, to the reasonable use made of it by its authors. Such reasoning led to the theory of law which nature has taught to all its creations and which, as such, is common also to mankind. Although law, in this context, has only a rather vague meaning, its more specific implications can be readily deduced therefrom. Thus, the instinct which unites man and wife is the nucleus of their common and binding will which creates the family. An analysis of every type of positive customary law in the light of this idea leads to the basis of all those norms, which, within the family, rule the relationships between man and wife, parents and children, master and servant. These do not, on the whole, depend on the idea of property, which acquires deeper significance only with the development of agriculture. Property as the visible sphere of will forms the nucleus of a law of its own which is more concerned with the relationship between the families than with that between the individual family members. The relations between representative members, especially the masters, belong to an intermediate category insofar as they together belong to a higher group, the explicit or tacit will and idea of which governs them. With the expansion of this field of law, the individuals become more and more distinct and separate persons; in the end, son and father, wife and man, servant and master confront each other as individuals of equal right. And those selling goods, however remote from and indifferent to each other and hostile in their natural wills, will barter and conclude contracts with feigned amiability. This freedom in getting together, this ease in doing business, and the equality of reasonable human beings will then seem to them quite natural.

16. *Natural Reason*

Natural law, in this sense, superseded the civil law of the Romans and of all political communities of the classical culture. It was defined, as is well known, as the law common to all mankind, as the rules of natural reason among all human beings, which, therefore, are observed by all people in the same way and called common law *(jus gentium)*. From the correct assumption that the development from general to specific rules was a progress in time, the conclusion was reached that this common law was prior to the specific law of the cities. But in reality the common law conformed to the requirements of intercourse not between cities and cities, i.e., between the citizens of each as such, but between all kind and manner of people, i.e., between the individuals per se, after they dropped the burgess attire. It acted as a reagent in the melting pot which dissolved all the various substances into similar elements. Therefore, it followed upon the specific law; it was not its basis or precedent, but its follower and negation. For common law is nothing but an impediment to specific law; it is as natural and simple as if it had existed since the beginning of time and as if it were not bound by any conditions precedent but had only been obscured by artificial inventions and regulations, the deletion of which, therefore, means the restitution of the original status. This gives a solution to the contradiction, for here confusion is almost inevitable. The originality or priority of common law does not exist in time, but is an eternal truth *(aeterna veritas)*, a product of thought or an ideal which could belong to a remote future as well as to the distant past. That common law actually existed at any time is not an historical thesis but a convenient hypothesis which will further a future realization of the concept. Such an hypothesis is made more convincing by the idea that a general human element is the nucleus of all quaint customs and forms, and that a rational interpretation of this nucleus is identical with the findings of reason apart from all experience.

Jus Gentium was, in fact, the sum of the common ingredients in the customs of the old Italian tribes, for they were all the nations whom the Romans had the means of observing, and who sent successive swarms of immigrants to Roman soil. Whenever a particular usage was seen to be practised by a large number of separate races in common it was set down as part of the Law Common to all Nations, or Jus Gentium. Thus, although the conveyance of property was certainly accompanied by very different forms in the different commonwealths surrounding Rome, the actual transfer, tradition, or delivery of the article intended to be conveyed was a part of the ceremonial in all of them. ... It was set down as an institution Juris Gentium, or rule of the Law common to all Nations. (H. Maine, *Ancient Law*, p. 49.)

When the more highly developed Greek systems of law were included in such study, the constituent elements of the various contracts such as purchase, rent, deposit, mandate, as well as the institutions of marriage, guardianship, etc., were discovered in all of them, although in manifold guises. Thus, the elements of corresponding legal concepts were recognized as general and necessary.

17. Conclusions

From the premises the following conclusion was drawn: the essential element of common law is the ability of all human beings to trade and form relationships together, if they so desire. Furthermore, it is also an essential fact that everybody is absolutely free except for obligations voluntarily incurred, contracts concluded, and relationships established. But with such freedom not only an institution like servitude was incompatible, but also paternal authority (except over children and insane persons) as well as all laws which in a city, for example, Rome, privileged the native citizen and his property against the foreigner. Insofar as the conceptual sequence was transformed into a temporal one, it seemed as if the arbitrary discretion of lawmakers had erected these barriers against nature. But over this doctrine of the inborn reasonableness, liberty, and equality of men there prevailed in the end the historically better founded theory of Ulpian and other jurists.

This theory distinguishes between natural and common law and asserts that these categories are diametrically opposed and essentially different. Although in this theory common law represents an intermediate stage between natural and civil (statute) law, the latter is nevertheless considered only an appendix to and a special development of the earlier common law. Here natural law is the complex of those arrangements which are also found among the animals; common law, of those peculiar to men. The former are, therefore, not based on natural reason, but have been created by a much more general necessity of collective living. It seemed obvious to infer that such a necessity was also present in the specific human institutions of common and civil law. The objection that only the general element constitutes a necessity and as such has to be preserved and restored, could first be countered by the question as to what this general element really is. The answer is: there are actually in existence separate peoples and countries, slavery, property, business transactions, and contracts. To civil law is to be ascribed only a few elaborations and changes in these institutions.

It is evident that this conception is based on an entirely different definition of the general element. Thus, entirely different conclusions result. Certain types of union and close relationship are implied in the animal idea of man. They are not prompted by any will, let alone a human will. It does not follow, therefore, that they exist also among animals or that man could or should have such relation to an animal. Neither can it be inferred that, because they are common to all men, every human being, if only he so desired, could establish such relations with every other human being. Nor are similar conclusions as to specifically human institutions valid. The relation between the idea of man and that of the animal is like that between the idea of the Hellenic and that of man in general. Thus, human beings mate with human beings, although mating is also the way of animals; the Greek must wed the Greek if the union is to be valid, although marriage is general among human beings and a man may mate with or have sexual intercourse with any woman, or, physiologically, even *(turpe dictu)* with animals.

18. *Marriage*

The generality of marriage among human beings has a twofold meaning: in the first place, that such a sexual living together between men and women is possible at all; secondly, that every people, or even every town, expresses this general idea in a special manner and relates the possibility of a marriage to certain conditions in such a way that it will be valid according to its will and law. Every human being as such is thus subject to a definite law—the Roman as Roman to a more definite law. There is no reason in this instance why the general law should be better or more reasonable. The more general form in its previous meaning presupposes a legal order which rules human beings as Roman law rules Roman citizens.

But also, in the latter meaning, common law can be understood as an order which is not known in an objective way but felt as a necessity, as an aversion against evil, that is, as law of conscience. "This law is not written but inborn; it has not been learned, accepted, read, but was received from nature itself; it was created, not taught, given, not constructed," according to the rhetorical expression of Cicero (p. Mil. c. X). Animal as well as human being has the instinct of maternal love; the human being has besides the instinct its development into a sense of duty; thus maternal law is common law. The illegal child belongs to the mother and follows her position. This order is more dignified and important in commandments and orders; it has a greater moral importance.

Incest is forbidden according to common law as a monstrosity; illegal relations of another kind are mainly forbidden in holy law on account of their faulty consequences. Law of nature is at the same time holy and divine law and is interpreted by the priesthood. It is something different if the analogy of civil law is extended to an unlimited realm as world law after its connection with the law of nature has been severed. In this case, civil law is only an accidental limitation which has been postulated by the remaining empirical-real freedom of the human being. This limitation can be postulated again and again and it can be discontinued just as two contracting parties can discontinue their contract.

Every special order is accidental; but it is necessary that there exist order of a general nature, a world order, even if this order does not exist as reality but only as a means for reasonable living which the thinking person postulates and affirms. The more the human beings, as such, unite, or the more human beings of different kinds come together and recognize each other as intelligent beings or equals, the more probable and, in the end, necessary becomes the erection of a universal society and order. This mixture takes place in reality through trade and communication; and rule of Rome over the *Orbis Terrarum,* which has its material foundation in commerce, brings all towns closer to the one town, assembles all conscious, trading, rich individuals, the entire group of the lords of this immense empire, together on the forum. It extinguishes differences and inequalities, gives all the same behavior, the same way of speech and expression, the same money, the same culture, the same cupidity, and the same curiosity. It forms the abstract human being, the most artificial, regular, and unscrupulous type of machinery, which appears as a ghost in broad daylight.

19. *Order of Gesellschaft*

In this new, revolutionary, disintegrating, and leveling sense, general and natural law is entirely an order characteristic of Gesellschaft, manifested in its purest form in commercial law. In its beginning it seems quite innocent, it means nothing but progress, refinement, improvement, and facilitations; it stands for fairness, reason and enlightenment. This form persisted even in the moral decay of the (Roman) empire. Both trends, the elaboration, universalizing, and finally systematizing and codification of the law, on the one hand, and, on the other hand, the decay of life and mores along with brilliant political successes, capable administration, and an efficient and liberal jurisprudence, have often been described. But only few seem to have realized the necessary connection between, and the unity and interdependence of, these two trends. Even the learned writers are seldom able to free themselves from prejudices and to arrive at an unbiased, strictly objective view of the physiology and pathology of social life. They admire the Roman Empire and the Roman law; they abhor the decay of the family and of mores. But they are unable to discuss the causal relationship between the two phenomena.

In the real and organic world there is no dichotomy of cause and effect as between the pushing and the pushed ball. But a rational scientific and independent law was made possible only through the emancipation of the individuals from all the ties which bound them to the family, the land, and the city and which held them to superstition, faith, traditions, habit, and duty. Such liberation meant the fall of the communal household in village and town, of the agricultural community, and of the art of the town as a fellowship, religious, patriotic craft. It meant the victory of egoism, impudence, falsehood, and cunning, the ascendancy of greed for money, ambition and lust for pleasure. But it brought also the victory of the contemplative, clear and sober consciousness in which scholars and cultured men now dare to approach things human and divine. And this process can never be considered completed. It finds its final expression in the empirical declaration which elevated all free men in the Empire to Roman citizens, granted them access to court, and freed them from taxes. That this was not followed by a constitution which also declared all serfs free men was due to a final honesty or final stupidity of the emperors and jurists. They should have known that this would not have changed the existing peaceful social conditions. The old household servitude had disappeared or was disrupted. Formal slavery was rather an inconsequential matter, as would have been the formal liberty in civil law. Arbitrary freedom (of the individual) and arbitrary despotism (of the Caesar or the State) are not mutually exclusive. They are only a dual phenomenon of the same situation. They may struggle with each other more or less, but by nature they are allies.

20. *Analogy with Modern Times*

Within the Christian culture an analogous process is repeated: life and law disintegrate, which, however, allows law to attain its perfection as a system; the social phenomena tend to become intermingled, generalized, leveled, and less and less stationary, and this on an increasingly large scale, as the regions affected are larger than in former times, trade across the oceans is more diversified than the trade of the Mediterranean, industrial techniques are more complex, and science attains greater importance. The whole culture, in its command of external resources, seems a continuation of the classical cultural system; with this heritage, it may reach higher and higher in its endeavors, although it must sacrifice for that the harmonious development of its structure. The assimilation of Roman law has served and still serves to further the development of Gesellschaft in a large part of the Christian-German world. As a scientific system of great clarity, simplicity, and logical stringency, it seemed to be "written reason" itself. Such reason favored all people of wealth, enabling them to make their wealth and power absolute. It was equally necessary for the merchants as for the feudal lords who tried to transform their rents received in kind or in services into cash revenues, and for the princes who attempted, by new financial methods, to defray the expenses of larger standing armies and a constantly expanding court. But it is incorrect to consider the Roman law the ultimate cause, or the one cause, of this whole development. It was nothing but a ready and useful tool, and it was used not so much deliberately as with the honest belief in its justness and suitability. In England the same development has taken place without the influence, or at least with only a comparatively slight influence, of Roman law. Common law, i.e., law of Gemeinschaft, was gradually superseded by the statute law of Gesellschaft; the principle of personal wealth won over the principle of real property.

The general civil law of contracts is the corollary of general contractual trade and grows with it until it finds its most adequate expression in a codified commercial and maritime law, the national character of which is obviously not more than an accidental and provisional aspect of it. In this form it is also independent of Roman law inasmuch as its underlying facts and conditions have left behind the foundations of the latter. For the greater part, it has developed from the conventional customs of its people. But Roman law has been definitely instrumental in the disintegration of all Gemeinschaften contrary to the basic concept of civil law, i.e., contrary to the concept of the legally responsible individual. Property held by a Gemeinschaft or in entail is, for a rational theory of law, an anomaly and an absurdity. The maxim that nobody can be kept in a Gemeinschaft against his will *(Nemo in communione potest invitus detineri)* aims at the root of all law of Gemeinschaft. Family law is preserved only insofar as the family is conceived as consisting of legal minors, whereby the wife falls into the same category as children, and children into the same category as servants. The concept of the servant as a slave in unrestricted wealth (he was not that in Rome so long as the *res mancipi* formed a distinct group) is an elementary concept of Gesellschaft. With the women attaining that characteristic of Gesellschaft-like independence and consequently civic emancipation, marriage and marital community of wealth degenerate into civil contract. If not concluded for a definite period, such contract may be ended any time by mutual consent, and its monogamic limitations become purely accidental. These are some of the most important trends in a process of rapidly advancing disintegration.

Side by side with the Roman law there exists, as its legitimate kin, the philosophical and rational natural law of modern times. From its beginning it found itself barred from the most important fields for its application by the assimilated Roman law and by causal legislation. It was relegated to the maxims of public law as its proper sphere. There it has maintained its place, although somewhat surreptitiously, in spite of the mortal blow which the historical interpretation of Roman jurisprudence was thought to have dealt it. Through the influence of public on private law, or of the state on the Gesellschaft, natural law has, however, been used before for purposes of codification and planned legislation, and this role has not yet come to an end. After serving the evolution of the ruling class, natural law is revived as the program of the oppressed classes. This is evident in the demand for the product of one's own labor, which denies the right to income not earned by labor or that obtained solely by cleverness and luck. In this demand the Catholic Church's old interdiction of usury is revived. This fight is immediately directed against the unrestricted and absolute private wealth in land because its misuse, resulting in land speculation and rack rents, is most obvious; moreover, the primordial memory of a right of Gemeinschaft that "is born with us" has persisted in the folk soul, slumbering like the wheat-grain in a mummy, but capable of new growth. For if understood as the idea of justice, natural law is an eternal and inalienable possession of mankind.

SECTION THREE: Forms of Concerted Will,
Commonwealth, and State

21. *Interrelationships*

If modern theory wants to retain the twofold meaning of the concept of natural law, it implies the proposition that law can be conceived as common natural will as well as common rational will. The roots of individual natural will lie in vegetative life; individual rational will, on the other hand, derives from the possibility of uniting two thoughts of similar or opposite value of satisfaction. Similarly, will of Gemeinschaft, too, is rooted in vegetative life, for a process of mating and family life are vegetative in a sociological sense, as they form the basis of human collective existence. Will of Gesellschaft is at root a meeting of individual rational wills which intersect each other at a point of barter reasonable or correct for both. Every understanding is derived from a more general form of understanding which we above termed concord. For the same reason it is evident that the single socialized rational will requires for its consummation or generalization the concept of social rational will. In the case of natural will a real or individual objective mind develops from the substance of the general objective mind as its expression and modification. In the other case there develops an atom of the fictitious objective substance which must adapt itself to an entity of the same nature to be able to be conceived independently from the individual persons in objective existence.

We proceed now to describe and define the forms of the will of Gemeinschaft and the will of Gesellschaft. It must be remembered that these forms can be studied only insofar as they possess binding force within or determine the individual wills. In this sense, understanding is analogous to liking or sympathy, concord to sentiment, and they can be mutually explained from each other. The analogy of habit is custom of heart or mind, folkways and mores. Custom and mores are, therefore, the animal will of human Gemeinschaft. They presuppose an often-repeated common activity which, whatever its original meaning, has become easy and natural through practice and tradition and is therefore considered necessary under given conditions. The most important folk customs are connected with the events of family life, birth, marriage, death, which occur regularly and in which, although they concern the individual families most, the neighbors also are concerned. Where clan and community coincide, the community itself is one large family. Later, it looks upon the individual families as its members. The more important, noble, or exalted a member is, the more genuine and stronger is his or its general participation (if there exist no motives for hostility). This always remains the inner meaning of custom. Its original meaning, however, which is partly a simple natural action, partly the symbol or outward token of a thought, can become an empty form or sink into oblivion (like everything that relates to memory). The underlying thought is either proof, confirmation, or preservation of a Gemeinschaft; consequently, it implies the intention to foster and venerate such feelings as those of love, respect, and piety, which evolve from it. Or else the thought means an attempt to do a good deed and to ward off evil and is related to the prevailing belief in the interdependence of cause and effect. With primitive people it usually takes the form of a communication with good or evil spirits.

22. *Mores and Home*

For a settled people, the real substance of the will of Gemeinschaft which is the basis for numerous individual customs is its folkways and mores. We have seen that to the blood Gemeinschaft is added the Gemeinschaft of the land, of the home country (*Heimat*), which brings a new influence to bear on the minds and hearts of men and therefore represents partly a substitute for, partly a complement of, the earlier allegiance. The land has its own will, which tames the roving spirit of nomadic families. It signifies the close interrelationship of a group of human beings living at the same time who have to obey the rules embodied, so to speak, in the land itself.

The people see themselves surrounded by the inhabited earth. It seems as if, in the beginning of time, the earth itself had brought forth from its womb the human beings who look upon her as their mother. The land supports their tents and houses, and the more durable the houses become the more men become attached to their own ground, however limited. The relationship grows stronger and deeper when the land is cultivated. With the plow furrowing the soil, nature is tamed just as the animals of the woods are domesticated. But this is only the result of the ever-renewed efforts of countless generations, where every step in progress is handed down from father to son. The area settled and occupied is therefore a common heritage, the land of the ancestors toward which all feel and act as descendants and blood brothers. In this sense, it can be regarded as a living substance which, with its spiritual or psychological values, persists in the everlasting flux of its elements, viz., the human beings. It represents a common sphere of will and not only upholds the unity of contemporaneous generations but also links together past and future ones. Habit, next to the ties of blood, forms the strongest bond among contemporaries, and, likewise, memory links the living to the dead. The homeland, as the embodiment of dear memories, holds the heart of man, who parts from it with sorrow and looks back to it with homesickness and longing from abroad. As the place where ancestors lived and died, where their spirits will dwell and command the thoughts of the living, it acquires for simple and pious minds and hearts enhanced and sublime significance. Even in the times of nomadic wanderings, family and home are the source of such sentiment, but it grows stronger the more permanent the dwelling place becomes and the more closely it is tied to the land which, in its cultivation, embodies the toil and trouble of past generations. The metaphysical character of the clan, the tribe, the village and town community is, so to speak, wedded to the land in a lasting union. The mores have the same function in this relationship as custom in marriage.

23. *Customary Law*

In ancient myths the husband is likened to the plowing and sowing farmer; his children are thus compared to the fruits of the planted field, while illegitimate children are like the weeds growing in the swamps. Hence mores, folkways, and the customary law based thereon are chiefly concerned with the regulation, consolidation, and sanctification of true marriage (especially where it develops into pure monogamy), as well as with the allocation, protection, and utilization of the fields. Customary law also rules where these two spheres meet, i.e., it regulates possession and rights of the individual families and their members, dowry, and succession by inheritance.

Folkways and mores of our ancestors, of the country, of the people, are all one and the same. Folkways and mores manifest themselves more in action than they do in sentiment and opinion. They portray sentiment only as grief and indignation. When they are violated there follows a reaction in judgment and deed. The attitude of the older people, as opposed to the younger ones, supports them the more strongly the more changes become evident.

Folkways, mores, and customary law also rule the village community and the surrounding countryside. They represent the valid common will to which the people there, masters and servants alike, conform in their daily rounds and common tasks, because, in their belief, they are bound to do so. For their fathers did so before them, and everybody does so. And it seems to them the right thing, because it has always been that way.

Concord, folkways, and mores depend upon and further each other, but they may also come into conflict, and their boundaries may undergo changes. Both concord and mores are necessarily identical with and require peace, i.e., they must counteract the numerous causes for struggle within the community and mediate existing strife. To concord, as the incorporation of the family spirit, belongs the first task; to folkways and mores, the latter. For within the family, friction and quarrel are more likely to occur, due to continuous close contact, but, with changing moods, they also more easily pass off and more readily submit to the natural authority of the family head.

With family ties being replaced by merely neighborly relationships, strife will become less frequent, but also more embittered. And here the power of traditional norms, in which experience and precedent are accumulated, must come into play to heal the breach which arises out of the violations or conflicts resulting from thirst for power, greediness, and wantonness. But concord, folkways, and mores also have a positive task; they affirm and nurture individual relationships based on habit or on natural ties and make friendly action and aid a duty. They give symbolic expression to an original or imaginary unity of spirit—family spirit—thereby renewing it and recalling it to memory. That is the significance and value of festivals and ceremonials wherein participation in joy and sorrow and common devotion to a divine exalted spirit manifest themselves in measured harmonious forms.

24. *The Commonwealth*

The meaning and form of collective living which derive from concord and exist a priori in it are a natural order in which every member does his part harmoniously in order to enjoy his share. Such an order exists by virtue of the organic nature of man before all human culture and history. For its development it needs only unimpeded growth, which requires nothing but favorable external conditions, as may exist in historic circumstances. In contradistinction, folkways and mores, in their very essence, presuppose the fully developed mental faculties and the conscious efforts of man. They can develop only with and through such labor, especially as manifested in agriculture and later in other pursuits. In the community all this derives from a general natural will having equal validity to all, but developing only through individual effort and capacity. In so far as the community collectively produces such labor, this will becomes the mores and (positive) law. Thereby the community assumes the same relation to its members as an organism to its tissues and organs. This leads to the concepts of office and social estates (*Stände*). By acquiring permanency and becoming hereditary in families, office and estate strengthen and consolidate their connection with the whole as well as their own freedom, if the one is not achieved at the expense of the other. There is always, however, the likelihood and danger that the development of this close organic relationship among the servant and subordinate members will work toward increasing the freedom of the controlling functions.

All these relationships and their institutions, whatever form they may take, are positive law of the nature of customary law; i.e., they belong to the will of the community in so far as it expresses itself in custom, folkways, and mores. The people of a country, as subject and agent of such positive law, may be called a commonwealth. A commonwealth is the people organized as an individual self or personality which may enter into manifold relations with its members or organs. In its essence, a commonwealth represents an institution of natural law, which, however, by the very act of its creation, passes into the sphere of positive law. The original organic interrelationship among men, which is based on concord, is at a certain stage of development and under certain conditions transformed into the idea of a commonwealth. Insofar as folkways and mores presuppose a commonwealth, it cannot be brought into existence by them. In the constitution of a commonwealth the essential and therefore necessary and natural elements must be distinguished from the accidental and therefore changeable ones. This leads to the following classification: (1) patriarchal commonwealth, in which common possession of land already exists but is not yet essential,

(2) regional commonwealth, where this element is essential, (3) urban commonwealth, where it is still in existence but no longer essential. These represent an attempt to cope with the fluctuating and many-sided character of the objects in question. House, village, and city, which can each constitute a commonwealth, are also the types of large units within which they may persist and grow. The single house has least of all the character of an independent commonwealth, while the city possesses it in full degree. It is, therefore, conceivable that a far-flung social grouping is constituted a patriarchal commonwealth within which many smaller ones exist as regional, neighborly commonwealths, and these, in turn, are composed of still smaller urban commonwealths.

25. *The Idea of the Social Body*

Commonwealth is relative to Gemeinschaft in the same way as is animal *(zoon)* to plant *(phyton)*. The general idea of the living being is represented more purely by the plant, more completely by the animal. The idea of the social body is, likewise, embodied more purely in the Gemeinschaft, more fully in the commonwealth. Like the plant, the life of which is fulfilled by existing, feeding, and propagating, the house Gemeinschaft is entirely self-centered in all its activities. The commonwealth, like the animal and his special organs, turns to the outside, defending, searching, conquering, that is, fighting, but in a way which preserves the vegetative functions, for they are essential and the others only serve their purposes. The nervous system provides the animal with the faculty of synchronized sensations. In the commonwealth, the army serves the same end. Within the army some of its elements assume leadership and communicate their impulses to the rest. Thus, the authority of the leader is acknowledged in every unit. The highest authority thus established is that of the king, more or less clearly distinguished from the others. Commonwealth and army remain at a low stage of their development as long as a people or a tribe is still nomadic and always ready for fighting and robbing. Only the men are fit to be warriors, and of men a real army is composed. It must be replenished from the ranks of the boys left behind, and its strength, therefore, depends also on the ability of the women to bear and raise strong boys. Commonwealth itself is not the army but a system of families, clans, and communities; however, the army, as an embodiment of united will and power, represents the commonwealth to the outside world.

The organized assembly of the men, distinguished as a leading group from the mass of the adults (which represent a natural unity as opposed to children and old people, aliens and servants) has rights and privileges only as an assembly of the army and can as such oust and supersede the leading group. Each of its groups is centered round its leader and chief, and all groups together are united under their common chief, be it prince or king. He may be elected or designated by tradition or creed. As the leader is also a kinsman, and this tie of kinship is quite consciously felt, his selection must unequivocally conform to the rules and norms of traditions; election is only confirmation of tradition, or a substitute for tradition which is lacking. The less arbitrary the selection, the more it seems to depend on divine aid and inspiration for its success. In this sense, the drawing of lots entrusts fate or the invisible power with the choice. These conceptions live as long as the objective unity strives to prevent their destruction by the rational attitude of its subjects. This unity is most perfectly represented by the concord and unanimity of the mass. But it can also be embodied in the common resolutions of the leaders and, finally, in the decisive will of a single prince. All these forces must be co-ordinated in order to effect concerted action. This is unlikely or difficult if their binding norms are no longer hallowed by custom or creed and are, therefore, independent of their decisions. All these organs, though united, cannot, therefore, make the right decisions; they can only discover them. They are under, not above, the law.

26. *Warrior Caste—Nobility*

An army destined to defend or conquer land must consist of men who have a share in the ownership of the land, for only they can have the strong will to fight for it and feel in duty bound to do so. Agriculture gives value to the land, but a warlike community, whether engaged in a serious struggle, practicing warlike games, or given to the age-old pursuit of hunting, is hardly suited to devote itself to the painstaking task of working the soil. As long as fighting is either a necessity or a habit, work in the fields and stock raising are left to women and servants. But if the commonwealth of a whole people rules a large region in undisturbed peace so that only its frontiers have to be protected, a special warrior caste comes into existence, drawn from the ranks of those who formerly were the leaders of the individual groups. This is especially true if, in such times of peace, the heavily armored and mounted warrior represents the regular fighting unit. Insofar as the lords of oldest lineage and the direct descendants of the clan's fathers are connected with this body, the warrior caste is identical with the nobility and is called the nobility. The nobility is free in a special sense, i.e., with regard to the whole commonwealth or the land which it is called upon to protect and to increase. Compared to that, the freedom of the common people is more restricted, except where they continue capable and ready to fight in the army themselves or send their men to do it. The same holds where

they belong to a smaller commonwealth which is only under obligation
to pay tribute in kind to the greater commonwealth (or empire). The
nobility may manage its landed property, which makes its members the
equal of the villagers or only to a small degree their superiors, with the
help of servants (or serfs) who are entirely dependent on it. Such a class
(or estate) of serfs may have its origin in a once conquered population
or in the immigration of foreigners or may construct itself from the
offspring, especially the illegitimate ones, of the free people. If the
nobility cannot live, or at least live adequately, on its own estate, it re-
lies for its support and maintenance on the contributions and services
of the neighboring peasants. As long as the village communities are
considered, by tradition, the lawful owners of their common land, such
contributions can only be voluntary, although obligatory by custom,
folkways and mores. The baron or knight is the superior of the peasants
in a political sense, i.e., as far as the commonwealth is concerned, but
economically, i.e., in the sense of patriarchal Gemeinschaft which is at
the root of every commonwealth, he is their inferior; he is dependent
on their good will and is supported by the community as an organ in its
service.

27. *Citizens and Community*

Every commonwealth, as a regional unity, is composed of a number
of estates, villages, and towns, or represents a confederation of such
regional units. Each of these constituents which is capable of self-pro-
tection tends to develop itself into a commonwealth. If it succeeds and
is not composed of potential commonwealths, it will represent the most
perfect and comprehensive expression of this type of social organization.
For the close proximity of its members and the lessened probability of
friction among independent militant bodies give it opportunity to act
as an effective army assembly and consequently also as a competent
judicial body. In this sense the city which dominates a certain region
is the perfect incarnation of the idea of commonwealth. Like the *polis*
of Hellenic culture, it may even represent the only real commonwealth,
which itself, as a member of a confederacy, creates its superior, more
inclusive commonwealth. The latter can only by virtue of religious fiction (myth) be conceived of as the original, creative element. The city
commonwealth can, also, like the free city of Germanic culture, form
part and parcel of a country or empire within which it is distinguished
by its wealth and power. Its relation to the confederation to which it,
with the other cities, belongs, is then analogous to that of the Greek
polis. In this case, however, the confederation is in reality a priori and
of a sacred character so that it is not liable to become merely a purely

fictitious and conceptual unity. The same relationship exists between the burgher as a free man, who is capable of bearing arms, and his city. The burghers as a whole look upon the civic commonwealth as their idea, a product of their craft and skill. Thanks to it, they have their freedom, their property, and their honor. Nevertheless, the commonwealth can exist only through their united rational wills, even though it may be a necessary and unintentional product of these wills. It is founded not only on their accidental present unity but on the essential one which outlasts the generations.

The will of a commonwealth is usually represented in its assembly either by one man (the prince), several (the nobles or aldermen), or many (the masses, the people). In a patriarchal commonwealth a monarch is most frequently the representative of the common will; in a rural commonwealth it is the nobility; in the city it is the people. The people will finally represent the common will most perfectly because their close contact with each other confronts them with more difficult problems, while, at the same time, frequent practice and manifold experience qualify them for their task.

In the end, the masses become the intellectual center, the brains of the social system; as such this center can function much more perfectly than its predecessors in that role, for, although confronted with more difficult problems through the close contacts of its members (or elements), its faculties are heightened by constant practice and experience. It is, therefore, much more likely to produce the highest and noblest intelligence in the political field. But the commonwealth derives its full dignity only from the consensus and co-operation of those three organs, even though, in reality, one may become predominant while the others wither away. The community of the people as a specific phenomenon of co-ordination may, however, retain its older and more general significance in representing the totality and substance of the commonwealth from which those bodies of political power originate. And this factor will, in turn, influence and determine the character of such community. In this sense the people ultimately consists of all those united in Gemeinschaft and, therefore, comprises women, children, old men, vassals, and servants as its integral parts. It is the changing phenomenon of their lasting Gemeinschaft.

28. *Fellowship and Association or Special-Interest Group*

It follows from the foregoing that every organized body of human beings can be considered a kind of organism, an artificially constructed but organic implement, as well as an instrument or a tool. For, in reality, the essential character of such organizations is an existing common natural will or a constituted common rational will, both of which are conceived of as unities. A fellowship is an organization of Gemeinschaft; a special-interest group is a phenomenon of Gesellschaft. Consequently, a fellowship is, so to speak, a product of nature and can be comprehended only from its origin and the conditions of its development. This holds also for the concept of commonwealth. In contradistinction, a special-interest group is a fictitious being which serves its authors, expressing their common rational will in certain relationships. It is, therefore, of prime importance to find out the end for which it is intended. This reasoning also applies to the concept of the state as the general association or special-interest group characteristic of Gesellschaft.

The psychological or metaphysical essence of a fellowship and consequently of a commonwealth is being a will, i.e., having a life of its own and existing in the endless community of life of its members. Therefore it always goes back to the original unity of natural wills which I have defined as understanding. In whatever way the fellowship may have developed therefrom, its significance will always be equal to the power of its existence. This significance, embodied in laws, folkways, and mores, has, therefore, absolute and eternal validity for its members. They derive from it their own law, which regulates their relations among themselves and with the fellowship, considered as a separate identity or self insofar as it cannot arbitrarily change its will. But the sphere of will of the whole is conceived as prior to all individual spheres of will and as involving all of them. Thus, freedom and property of men exist only as modifications of the freedom and property of the commonwealth. In a general interrelationship of Gemeinschaft the sphere of the fellowship would be conditioned and determined by earlier and higher fellowships of which it is a member and of which the highest one would represent a commonwealth encompassing all mankind. This is the idea of the church and of the universal empire which is ecclesiastical and temporal as well. That idea is eternal; it can and perhaps will be resuscitated by virtue of a consciousness strengthened and purified by knowledge.

In contrast, every association or special-interest group is based on a complex of contracts among its members. These contracts are agreed upon as a statute by which the fictitious person of the association or special-interest group is brought into existence. The statute, through the appointment of a definite representative body, gives to the group a will, and it also gives it an end or a purpose, upon which all of the contracting parties have agreed. The statute further provides it with the means to achieve this end; these means consist of the contributions of the members, i.e., represent a pooling of their means. In part, these means represent rights to certain actions of the individual persons of which the association or special-interest group may legally dispose, just as any individual encompasses his actions in the sphere of his rational will and is free to dispose of them at will. Consequently, these rights are elements of freedom. They are compulsory rights. We have already studied how such rights result from every obligation, but an association or special-interest group is no more able to carry out such coercion than is the single individual. It can act only through the representative, i.e., through an individual or an assembly. An individual as representative is in the same situation as any individual attempting to exert coercion in his own name.

An assembly can adopt resolutions as a whole, but in carrying them out it dissolves into numerous individuals whom its will would induce to or coerce into action because it is itself not capable of it. It is, however, by no means certain that even a majority as the sum total of individuals is capable of concerted action according to the will of the group. To be able to enforce its will, the association or special-interest group, like any other person, must, therefore, have at its disposal superior power obtained by means other than coercion. In a system based on Gesellschaft this is feasible only by acquiring such power through contract. The group must, therefore, have a sufficient amount of money, the general medium of purchase. But even then the effectiveness of coercion rests on one important condition. This is the co-operation, at least in a negative sense, of the whole Gesellschaft. Coercion can be carried out safely and regularly only if nobody is willing and ready to lend assistance to the object of coercion or if the number of such people is irrelevant with regard to the power of the coercing parties so that such opposition can be as easily suppressed. The compulsory force of the legal provisions of a contract (or barter) depends to the same degree on the co-operation of the Gesellschaft as on the validity of its economic provisions. Gesellschaft, by its neutrality, makes any resistance impossible if the claimant has superior power. The superiority of an individual over another individual cannot be effectively demonstrated in the average case because everybody has enough power to oppose another single person. The claimant has, therefore, to secure aid and assistance. For this reason, every association or special-interest group without wealth or income (i.e., in a developed Gesellschaft, without money) would be powerless against real persons. Such money must be given or granted to it before any action is taken. It must be free to dispose of it. Thus, it will also be able to dispose of human forces. It may need these for purposes other than internal or external coercion; for instance, for running a business. Regulations or bylaws represent the form in which the association or special-interest group expresses, in general terms, its rational will to its subordinates. To carry out these regulations as binding norms is the service for which money may be expended. These regulations are not in themselves compulsory, but more like the equivalent offered in a barter.

The individual person, too, is able to clothe his will in the form of general commands and have it thus carried out. Every client is legislator to his solicitor. But the formal character of the regulations and bylaws is better suited to the association because, even if represented by an assembly, it is in need of a definite procedure, as provided by the bylaws, to form its will and announce it as a valid resolution. For this reason, a very general formulation of these regulations and bylaws is quite natural for it, as it ensures the highest efficiency in their application.

29. *The State*

The state has a dual character. First, it is a general association characteristic of Gesellschaft, existing and, so to speak, established for the purpose of protecting the freedom and property of its subjects, i.e., implicitly, of representing and enforcing the natural law based on the validity of contracts. It is, like any other especially constituted association or special-interest group, a fictitious person, and as such it is, under the law, on equal footing with all other persons. A natural law governs its relations to the individual, which are the same as those existing between a lawyer and his client. This law, as the will of Gesellschaft and conventional law of nature, is above the state. The constitution, through which the state gives valid expression to its will, is itself part of that law. Such law may, like any other law, be contentious matter. A special person or agency may, therefore, be appointed, to which the state, on one side, and the individual, i.e., society, on the other side, can appeal for a decision in such questions. This judicial body will recognize no other law, because its will should be nothing but the scientific truth in the interpretation of the law, its action nothing but the handing down of an opinion. It has, therefore, much less than in the case of any real person, the right or the power of coercion. It is social reason incarnate and, therefore, devoid of all other powers. In contradistinction, the state, especially by legal definition, is nothing but force, the holder and representative of all natural rights of coercion. The state makes the natural law an instrument and part of its own will; it interprets that law. But the state can also alter what is thus under its control. It must be able to do so not only *de facto* but also *de lege*. For it can make the regulations of its interpretation of law legally binding for its subjects. Interpreting what is law amounts, for them, to announcing what shall be law, with all the ensuing legal consequences. In this sense the state can make law at will by ordering its judges to conform to it and its officers to enforce it. Gesellschaft, which, as the sum total of individuals, by asserting its own right exists side by side with the state although seemingly under it, can resist an unlimited expansion of the legislative power or the substitution of state or political law for natural or common law. In such a case, the legal decision would rest with the above-mentioned court of arbitration.

But, secondly, the state is itself Gesellschaft or the social reason which is implied in the concept of a reasonable thinking agent of Gesellschaft. Here Gesellschaft means a unity, not a specific person apart from and side by side with the other person, but an absolute person from which the other persons derive their existence. In this sense there is no law against the law of the state; the law of legislation is the law of nature. Consequently, it is no longer possible to conceive of a judicial body arbitrating between state and Gesellschaft, for the state itself must have its origin in Gesellschaft. The whole jurisdiction becomes dependent upon the state and develops into an application of its laws. For it is deemed impossible that Gesellschaft without a state can have a common will and thus recognize the will of the state as its own. From this follows a natural order which determines the place of individuals in a positive way, not merely in the negative. The state invests some of them with its power, which they are then able to delegate further. In the end, every person should participate in the will of the state by being thus indirectly dependent on it. This idea is, within limits, realized in the system of administration. If generalized, the entire production of goods would become part of the administration and this would constitute in its concept a possible form of (seeming) socialism. Such socialism can be conceived of without the corollary of an elimination of the fundamental social class structure. The state would represent a monopolistic coalition of capitalists; production would continue to be undertaken for their benefit. In the international division of labor by which the world market is regulated, the united capitalists would still function as the producers and sellers of their total output. Even if the means of production were the property of the state, the capitalists, as the managers of production, would retain all the surplus value which was not required for the necessary replacement of machinery and so on. But as soon as Gesellschaft had expanded beyond all frontiers and the world state had been established, the capitalistic production of goods might come to an end and with it the real cause of entrepreneurial profits and all other forms of surplus value. Goods produced as heretofore by the lower classes would be appropriated by the upper classes only because and insofar as they represent the state, i.e., in the name of the state. They would, also in the name of the state, distribute among themselves that part of the total product which would not be required for the support of the workers. The arbitrary basis of the law becomes more evident when the state law has absorbed all law of Gesellschaft and contract. It is always in existence, but it is not fully comprehended until the subject of natural law, too, appears as a person capable of continuous rational will although wholly fictitious in character (legal person). Even according to the first concept, which makes the state a mere agent of Gesellschaft, it is apparently only the rational will of all sellers of commodities that establishes the conventional natural law, which is only secondarily political law. This is the same line of reasoning as applies when labor appears to be only a commodity. In reality, labor is the rational will of all sellers of real commodities, i.e., of labor embodied in products.

The state is a capitalist institution and remains so if it declares itself identical with society. It ceases, therefore, to exist when the working class makes itself the controlling agent of the state's will in order to destroy capitalistic production. It follows therefrom that the political intentions of this class lie outside the framework of Gesellschaft which comprises the state and legislation as necessary expressions and forms of its will.

But the deepest social and historical difference exists between the two above-mentioned concepts of the state. There is the system of the sovereignty of the people and the sovereignty of the state, just as there is the sovereignty of Gesellschaft and sovereignty of the ruler, but both systems nevertheless intermingle and are interrelated in manifold ways.

30. *The Religious Element*

The third phenomenon of a common uniting will must be conceived of as mental in character. For the sake of greater clarity, it can in theory be thought of as having a thinking agent. This thinking agent can be either an intellectual (ecclesiastical) union or an association or special-interest group, and if conceived as general, an intellectual (ecclesiastical) commonwealth or state. The forms of will themselves are defined as follows: (a) that of the Gemeinschaft; from the point of view of the individual, faith; from the point of view of the whole, religion; (b) that of the Gesellschaft: individually considered, theory; generally considered, public opinion. These are the powers which do not assert themselves through human (physical) forces or by the instrumentality of material things (money) but simply through imagination and thought, which are intended to influence the mental activities of man. In their most important social actions they assume the functions of an arbiter; i.e., they judge by their own principles, maxims, and rules the deeds and actions, i.e., the will, of those with whom they are concerned, and especially the will of the commonwealth, the state. Thus, religion assumes authority over commonwealth; public opinion, over the state. Religion approves folkways, mores, and customs as good and right or condemns them as false and bad. Likewise, public opinion condones policy and legislation as effective and clever or condemns it as ineffective and stupid.

Faith is essentially a characteristic of the masses and the lower classes; it is strongest among children and women. Theory can be understood only by the few, and still fewer are able to work it out. They are rational, calculative, and detached individuals. Faith and theory have the same relation to each other as poetry (i.e., its roots, as a mood for song and epic or mimic presentation) has to the perfect prose of mathematical reasoning or other conceptual combinations.

The relations of religion to morality, the folkways, and family life have already been mentioned. Religion is family life itself, for the care and assistance given by father or mother is the origin of all divine and godlike guidance and remains its innermost truth. Religion itself is, then, part of morality made real and necessary by tradition and age, and the individual human being is born into and brought up with it as he is brought up with the dialect, the way of living, the manners of dress and food of his native land, faith of the fathers, belief and custom, hereditary sentiment and duty.

Everywhere religion, even in the state of highest development, retains its hold and influence over the mind, heart, and conscience of men by hallowing the events of family life: marriage, birth, veneration of the elders, death. And in the same way religion hallows the commonwealth, increases and strengthens the might of the law. The law as the will of the elders and ancestors possesses its own dignity and importance; as the will of the Gods it becomes still more powerful and infallible. Thus, the earlier conception requires and creates the later one, which in turn reacts on the earliest conception. The religious commonwealth especially represents the original unity and equality of a whole people, the people as one family which by common ceremonies and places of worship keeps up the memory of its kinship. This is the extensive meaning of the religious commonwealth. The intensity of its force is strongest in the town commonwealth. There religious faith and the interpretation of the divine will become determining factors in amending, modifying, and adapting morality to the more complex life of the town. This is done mainly by use of the oath, wherein the presence of the divine being is invoked more as a threatening than a beloved element to exhort to faithfulness and truthfulness and to avenge deception and lies. Thus, one is not mistaken in recognizing marriage and oath as the two pillars with which religion supports the edifice of commonwealth and heightened communal life of the Gemeinschaft. They are the essential elements of morality, which is just as much a product of religion as law is the product of folkways and mores.

31. *Public Opinion*

Public opinion claims that it establishes general valid norms, not on the strength of blind faith but of clear insight into the correctness of the doctrines accepted by it. In tendency and form, it is a scientific and enlightened opinion. If formed with regard to all possible problems which may concern the human mind, it is primarily directed toward the life and relationship of Gesellschaft and state.

All conscious participants in this life and these relationships must be interested in those concepts and opinions; they must help form them and must fight the wrong and harmful ones. What is permissible in trade practice, and what is not permissible, what should be thought of the reputation of this or that firm, of the value of this or that commodity, claim, currency (or coin), or share, how values and persons in other social groups which are imagined analogous to those of trade and stock exchange should be judged—all this is condensed into general maxims and developed into a sort of moral code. Such a code of conduct is changeable with alterations and seeming progress in knowledge, and encounters much opposition. But it is nonetheless strict in its prohibitions, indictments, and punishments. As it is not concerned with sentiments and actions consequent upon them, but solely with the formal correctness of actions as such, it reacts only against infringement of its rules. Rewards for positive acts are not possible, because anything more than regularity is neither required nor expected. Admiration is not the line of public opinion, which, on the contrary, tries to bring all phenomena to the level of its own understanding. But it is concerned not only with correct actions and good deeds, but even more with correct and good opinions. For it must require a consensus of individual private opinions with itself, i.e., general public opinion. This is especially true because it presupposes reasonable, independent thinking agents who act according to their opinions. Among those opinions many are irrelevant; however, none are less irrelevant than are the political opinions. In the last analysis, the state seems to depend on them to determine what laws the state will decree or maintain, what domestic or foreign policy it will pursue. If Gesellschaft only partly agrees on such subjects and strongly disagrees on many points, each party must endeavor to make its own opinion public opinion or to give it at least a semblance of it. It must try

to present its own will as the rational general will, intent on furthering the common weal, in order to take the reins of government and to
get hold of the legislative arm of the government. On the other hand,
the state itself or the government, i.e., the party which represents
the sovereign power (person) or exerts the greatest influence on it, is
equally interested in "making" and "working upon" public opinion, in
determining and in changing it.

Whatever may come to be considered a public opinion, it confronts
the individual with an opinion which is in part an extraneous power.
Such encounter is mainly brought about through that kind of communication wherein all human relationship, faith and trust between
speaker and teacher on one side and listener and disciple on the other,
is, or at least can be, effaced: the literary communication. In this form
of communication, judgments and opinion are wrapped up like grocers'
goods and offered for consumption in their objective reality. It is prepared and offered to our generation in the most perfect manner by the
newspapers, which make possible the quickest production, multiplication, and distribution of facts and thoughts, just as the hotel kitchen
provides food and drink in every conceivable form and quantity. Thus,
the press is the real instrument ("organ") of public opinion, weapon and
tool in the hands of those who know how to use it and have to use it; it
possesses universal power as the dreaded critic of events and changes
in social conditions. It is comparable and, in some respects, superior
to the material power which the states possess through their armies,
their treasuries, and their bureaucratic civil service. Unlike those, the
press is not confined within natural borders, but, in its tendencies and
potentialities, it is definitely international, thus comparable to the
power of a permanent or temporary alliance of states. It can, therefore,
be conceived as its ultimate aim to abolish the multiplicity of states
and substitute for it a single world republic, coextensive with the world
market, which would be ruled by thinkers, scholars, and writers and
could dispense with means of coercion other than those of a psychological nature. Such tendencies and intentions will perhaps never find a
clear expression, let alone realization, but their recognition serves to
assist in the understanding of many phenomena of the real world and
to the realization of the fact that the existence of natural states is but
a temporary limitation of the boundaryless Gesellschaft. In this context it must be pointed out that the most modern and Gesellschaft-like
state, the United States of America, can or will least of all claim a truly
national character.

But the artificial, even forced, character of these abstractions must
always be kept clearly in mind, as must also the close interrelationship

between all those powers of Gesellschaft and their Gemeinschaft-like basis, i.e., the original natural and historical forms of common life and communal will. The case of the social rational will is the same as that of the individual rational will, which can be separated only in theory from the impulses of life and natural will, and which applies objectively as a product of memory.

All regulations and norms of the powers of Gesellschaft retain a certain resemblance to the commands of religion, for, like those, they originate from the intellectual or mental expression of the spirit of the totality, and the presupposed isolation and independence of this spirit is perhaps in reality never found to be perfect and general. Thus, the oath is the original guarantee of the contract; the "binding force" of contracts does not detach itself easily from trust and faithfulness in the consciousness of men, although in reality these are not required at all, because the simple consideration of self-interest should suffice to impress on the rational subject the necessity of fulfilling this basic condition of life in Gesellschaft.

It is not easy to make clear or to understand this point, but insight into and full comprehension of its meaning provide the clue for the solution of the most important problems of growth and decay of human culture. For its existence is change and, as such, development and dissolution of existing phenomena or forms. All change can be comprehended only from the continuous sequence and interrelation of fluctuating concepts.

PART FOUR

Conclusions and Outlook

1. Order—Law—Mores

There is a contrast between a social order which—being based upon consensus of wills—rests on harmony and is developed and ennobled by folkways, mores, and religion, and an order which—being based upon a union of rational wills—rests on convention and agreement, is safeguarded by political legislation, and finds its ideological justification in public opinion.

There is, further, in the first instance a common and binding system of positive law, of enforcible norms regulating the interrelation of wills. It has its roots in family life and is based on land ownership. Its forms are in the main determined by the code of the folkways and mores. Religion consecrates and glorifies these forms of the divine will, i.e., as interpreted by the will of wise and ruling men. This system of norms is in direct contrast to a similar positive law which upholds the separate identity of the individual rational wills in all their interrelations and entanglements. The latter derives from the conventional order of trade and similar relations but attains validity and binding force only through the sovereign will and power of the state. Thus, it becomes one of the most important instruments of policy; it sustains, impedes, or furthers social trends; it is defended or contested publicly by doctrines and opinions and thus is changed, becoming more strict or more lenient.

There is, further, the dual concept of morality as a purely ideal or mental system of norms for community life. In the first case, it is mainly an expression and organ of religious beliefs and forces, by necessity intertwined with the conditions and realities of family spirit and the folkways and mores. In the second case, it is entirely a product and instrument of public opinion, which encompasses all relations arising out of contractual sociableness, contacts, and political intentions.

Order is natural law, law as such = positive law, mores = ideal law. Law as the meaning of what may or ought to be, of what is ordained or permitted, constitutes an object of social will. Even the natural law, in order to attain validity and reality, has to be recognized as positive and binding. But it is positive in a more general or less definite way. It is general in comparison with special laws. It is simple compared to complex and developed law.

2. *Dissolution*

The substance of the body social and the social will consists of concord, folkways, mores, and religion, the manifold forms of which develop under favorable conditions during its lifetime. Thus, each individual receives his share from this common center, which is manifest in his own sphere, i.e., in his sentiment, in his mind and heart, and in his conscience as well as in his environment, his possessions, and his activities. This is also true of each group. It is in this center that the individual's strength is rooted, and his rights derive, in the last instance, from the one original law which, in its divine and natural character, encompasses and sustains him, just as it made him and will carry him away. But under certain conditions and in some relationships, man appears as a free agent (person) in his self-determined activities and has to be conceived of as an independent person. The substance of the common spirit has become so weak or the link connecting him with the others worn so thin that it has to be excluded from consideration. In contrast to the family and co-operative relationship, this is true of all relations among separate individuals where there is no common understanding, and no time-honored custom or belief creates a common bond. This means war and the unrestricted freedom of all to destroy and subjugate one another, or, being aware of possible greater advantage, to conclude agreements and foster new ties. To the extent that such a relationship exists between closed groups or communities or between their individuals or between members and nonmembers of a community, it does not come within the scope of this study. In this connection we see a community organization and social conditions in which the individuals remain in isolation and veiled hostility toward each other so that only fear of clever retaliation restrains them from attacking one another, and, therefore, even peaceful and neighborly relations are in reality based upon a warlike situation. This is, according to our concepts, the condition of Gesellschaft-like civilization, in which peace and commerce are maintained through conventions and the underlying mutual fear. The state protects this civilization through legislation and politics. To a certain extent science and public opinion, attempting to conceive it as necessary and eternal, glorify it as progress toward perfection.

But it is in the organization and order of the Gemeinschaft that folk life and folk culture persist. The state, which represents and embodies Gesellschaft, is opposed to these in veiled hatred and contempt, the more so the further the state has moved away from and become estranged from these forms of community life. Thus, also in the social and historical life of mankind there is partly close interrelation, partly juxtaposition and opposition of natural and rational will.

3. *The People (Volkstum) and the State (Staatstum)*

In the same way as the individual natural will evolves into pure thinking and rational will, which tends to dissolve and subjugate its predecessors, the original collective forms of Gemeinschaft have developed into Gesellschaft and the rational will of the Gesellschaft. In the course of history, folk culture has given rise to the civilization of the state.

The main features of this process can be described in the following way. The anonymous mass of the people is the original and dominating power which creates the houses, the villages, and the towns of the country. From it, too, spring the powerful and self-determined individuals of many different kinds: princes, feudal lords, knights, as well as priests, artists, scholars. As long as their economic condition is determined by the people as a whole, all their social control is conditioned by the will and power of the people. Their union on a national scale, which alone could make them dominant as a group, is dependent on economic conditions. And their real and essential control is economic control, which before them and with them and partly against them the merchants attain by harnessing the labor force of the nation. Such economic control is achieved in many forms, the highest of which is planned capitalist production or large-scale industry. It is through the merchants that the technical conditions for the national union of independent individuals and for capitalistic production are created. This merchant class is by nature, and mostly also by origin, international as well as national and urban, i.e., it belongs to Gesellschaft, not Gemeinschaft. Later all social groups and dignitaries and, at least in tendency, the whole people acquire the characteristics of the Gesellschaft.

Men change their temperaments with the place and conditions of their daily life, which becomes hasty and changeable through restless striving. Simultaneously, along with this revolution in the social order, there takes place a gradual change of the law, in meaning as well as in form. The contract as such becomes the basis of the entire system, and rational will of Gesellschaft, formed by its interests, combines with authoritative will of the state to create, maintain and change the legal system. According to this conception, the law can and may completely change the Gesellschaft in line with its own discrimination and purpose; changes which, however, will be in the interest of the Gesellschaft, making for usefulness and efficiency. The state frees itself more and more from the traditions and customs of the past and the belief in their importance. Thus, the forms of law change from a product of the folkways and mores and the law of custom into a purely legalistic law, a product of policy. The state and its departments and the individuals are the only remaining agents, instead of numerous and manifold fellowships, communities, and commonwealths which have grown up organically. The characters of the people, which were influenced and determined by these previously existing institutions, undergo new changes in adaptation to new and arbitrary legal constructions. These earlier institutions lose the firm hold which folkways, mores, and the conviction of their infallibility gave to them.

Finally, as a consequence of these changes and in turn reacting upon them, a complete reversal of intellectual life takes place. While originally rooted entirely in the imagination, it now becomes dependent upon thinking. Previously, all was centered around the belief in invisible beings, spirits and gods; now it is focalized on the insight into visible nature. Religion, which is rooted in folk life or at least closely related to it, must cede supremacy to science, which derives from and corresponds to consciousness. Such consciousness is a product of learning and culture and, therefore, remote from the people. Religion has an immediate contact and is moral in its nature because it is most deeply related to the physical-spiritual link which connects the generations of men. Science receives its moral meaning only from an observation of the laws of social life, which leads it to derive rules for an arbitrary and reasonable order of social organization. The intellectual attitude of the individual becomes gradually less and less influenced by religion and more and more influenced by science. Utilizing the research findings accumulated by the preceding industrious generation, we shall investigate the tremendous contrasts which the opposite poles of this dichotomy and these fluctuations entail. For this presentation, however, the following few remarks may suffice to outline the underlying principles.

4. *Types of Real Community Life*

The exterior forms of community life as represented by natural will and Gemeinschaft were distinguished as house, village, and town. These are the lasting types of real and historical life. In a developed Gesellschaft, as in the earlier and middle stages, people live together in these different ways. The town is the highest, viz., the most complex, form of social life. Its local character, in common with that of the village, contrasts with the family character of the house. Both village and town retain many characteristics of the family; the village retains more, the town less. Only when the town develops into the city are these characteristics almost entirely lost. Individuals or families are separate identities, and their common locale is only an accidental or deliberately chosen place in which to live. But as the town lives on within the city, elements of life in the Gemeinschaft, as the only real form of life, persist within the Gesellschaft, although lingering and decaying. On the other hand, the more general the condition of Gesellschaft becomes in the nation or a group of nations, the more this entire "country" or the entire "world" begins to resemble one large city. However, in the city and therefore where general conditions characteristic of the Gesellschaft prevail, only the upper strata, the rich and the cultured, are really active and alive. They set up the standards to which the lower strata have to conform. These lower classes conform partly to supersede the others, partly in imitation of them in order to attain for themselves social power and independence. The city consists, for both groups (just as in the case of the "nation" and the "world"), of free persons who stand in contact with each other, exchange with each other and co-operate without any Gemeinschaft or will thereto developing among them except as such might develop sporadically or as a leftover from former conditions. On the contrary, these numerous external contacts, contracts, and contractual relations only cover up as many inner hostilities and antagonistic interests. This is especially true of the antagonism between the rich or the so-called cultured class and the poor or the servant class, which try to obstruct and destroy each other. It is this contrast which, according to Plato, gives the "city" its dual character and makes it divide in itself. This itself, according to our concept, constitutes the city, but the same contrast is also manifest in every large-scale relationship between capital and labor. The common town life remains within the Gemeinschaft of family and rural life; it is devoted to some agricultural pursuits but concerns itself especially with art and handicraft which evolve from these natural needs and habits. City life, however, is sharply distinguished from that; these basis activities are used only as means and tools for the special purposes of the city.

The city is typical of Gesellschaft in general. It is essentially a commercial town and, in so far as commerce dominates its productive labor, a factory town. Its wealth is capital wealth which, in the form of trade, usury, or industrial capital, is used and multiplies. Capital is the means for the appropriation of products of labor or for the exploitation of workers. The city is also the center of science and culture, which always go hand in hand with commerce and industry. Here the arts must make a living; they are exploited in a capitalistic way. Thoughts spread and change with astonishing rapidity. Speeches and books through mass distribution become stimuli of far-reaching importance.

The city is to be distinguished from the national capital, which, as residence of the court or center of government, manifests the features of the city in many respects although its population and other conditions have not yet reached that level. In the synthesis of city and capital, the highest form of this kind is achieved: the metropolis. It is the essence not only of a national Gesellschaft, but contains representatives from a whole group of nations, i.e., of the world. In the metropolis, money and capital are unlimited and almighty. It is able to produce and supply goods and science for the entire earth as well as laws and public opinion for all nations. It represents the world market and world traffic; in it world industries are concentrated. Its newspapers are world papers, its people come from all corners of the earth, being curious and hungry for money and pleasure.

5.   Counterpart of Gemeinschaft

Family life is the general basis of life in the Gemeinschaft. It subsists in village and town life. The village community and the town themselves can be considered as large families, the various clans and houses representing the elementary organisms of its body; guilds, corporations, and offices, the tissues and organs of the town. Here original kinship and inherited status remain an essential, or at least the most important, condition of participating fully in common property and other rights. Strangers may be accepted and protected as serving members or guests either temporarily or permanently. Thus, they can belong to the Gemeinschaft as objects, but not easily as agents and representatives of the Gemeinschaft. Children are, during minority, dependent members of the family, but according to Roman custom they are called free because it is anticipated that under possible and normal conditions they will certainly be masters, their own heirs. This is true neither of guests nor of servants, either in the house or in the community. But honored guests can approach the position of children. If they are adopted or civic rights are granted to them, they fully acquire this position with the right to inherit. Servants can be esteemed or treated as guests or even, because of the value of their functions, take part as members in the activities of the group. It also happens sometimes that they become natural or appointed heirs. In reality there are many gradations, lower or higher, which are not exactly met by legal formulas. All these relationships can, under special circumstances, be transformed into merely interested and dissolvable interchange between independent contracting parties. In the city such change, at least with regard to all relations of servitude, is only natural and becomes more and more widespread with its development. The difference between natives and strangers becomes irrelevant. Everyone is what he is, through his personal freedom, through his wealth and his contracts. He is a servant only insofar as he has granted certain services to someone else, master insofar as he receives such services. Wealth is, indeed, the only effective and original differentiating characteristic; whereas in Gemeinschaften property it is considered as participation in the common ownership and as a specific legal concept is entirely the consequence and result of freedom or ingenuity, either original or acquired. Therefore, wealth, to the extent that this is possible, corresponds to the degree of freedom possessed.

In the city as well as in the capital, and especially in the metropolis, family life is decaying. The more and the longer their influence prevails, the more the residuals of family life acquire a purely accidental character. For there are only few who will confine their energies within such a narrow circle; all are attracted outside by business, interests, and pleasures, and thus separated from one another. The great and mighty, feeling free and independent, have always felt a strong inclination to break through the barriers of the folkways and mores. They know that they can do as they please. They have the power to bring about changes in their favor, and this is positive proof of individual arbitrary power. The mechanism of money, under usual conditions and if working under high pressure, is means to overcome all resistance, to obtain everything wanted and desired, to eliminate all dangers and to cure all evil. This does not hold always. Even if all controls of the Gemeinschaft are eliminated, there are nevertheless controls in the Gesellschaft to which the free and independent individuals are subject. For Gesellschaft (in the narrower sense), convention takes to a large degree the place of the folkways, mores, and religion. It forbids much as detrimental to the common interest which the folkways, mores, and religion had condemned as evil in and of itself.

The will of the state plays the same role through law courts and police, although within narrower limits. The laws of the state apply equally to everyone; only children and lunatics are not held responsible to them. Convention maintains at least the appearance of morality; it is still related to the folkways, mores, and religious and aesthetic feeling, although this feeling tends to become arbitrary and formal.

The state is hardly directly concerned with morality. It has only to suppress and punish hostile actions which are detrimental to the common weal or seemingly dangerous for itself and society. For as the state has to administer the common weal, it must be able to define this as it pleases. In the end it will probably realize that no increase in knowledge and culture alone will make people kinder, less egotistic, and more content and that dead folkways, mores, and religions cannot be revived by coercion and teaching. The state will then arrive at the conclusion that in order to create moral forces and moral beings it must prepare the ground and fulfill the necessary conditions, or at least it must eliminate counteracting forces. The state, as the reason of Gesellschaft, should decide to destroy Gesellschaft or at least to reform or renew it. The success of such attempts is highly improbable.

6. *The Real State*

Public opinion, which brings the morality of Gesellschaft into rules and formulas and can rise above the state, has nevertheless decided tendencies to urge the state to use its irresistible power to force everyone to do what is useful and to leave undone what is damaging. Extension of the penal code and the police power seems the right means to curb the evil impulses of the masses. Public opinion passes easily from the demand for freedom (for the upper classes) to that of despotism (against the lower classes). The makeshift, convention, has but little influence over the masses. In their striving for pleasure and entertainment they are limited only by the scarcity of the means which the capitalists furnish them as price for their labor, which condition is as general as it is natural in a world where the interests of the capitalists and merchants anticipate all possible needs and in mutual competition incite to the most varied expenditures of money. Only through fear of discovery and punishment, that is, through fear of the state, is a special and large group, which encompasses far more people than the professional criminals, restrained in its desire to obtain the key to all necessary and unnecessary pleasures. The state is their enemy. The state, to them, is an alien and unfriendly power; although seemingly authorized by them and embodying their own will, it is nevertheless opposed to all their needs and desires, protecting property which they do not possess, forcing them into military service for a country which offers them hearth and altar only in the form of a heated room on the upper floor or gives them, for native soil, city streets where they may stare at the glitter and luxury in lighted windows forever beyond their reach! Their own life is nothing but a constant alternative between work and leisure, which are both distorted into factory routine and the low pleasure of the saloons. City life and Gesellschaft down the common people to decay and death; in vain they struggle to attain power through their own multitude, and it seems to them that they can use their power only for a revolution if they want to free themselves from their fate. The masses become conscious of this social position through the education in schools and through newspapers. They proceed from class consciousness to class struggle. This class struggle may destroy society and the state which it is its purpose to reform. The entire culture has been transformed into a civilization of state and Gesellschaft, and this transformation means the doom of culture itself if none of its scattered seeds remain alive and again bring forth the essence and idea of Gemeinschaft, thus secretly fostering a new culture amidst the decaying one.

7. *The Periods*

To conclude our theory, two periods stand thus contrasted with each other in the history of the great systems of culture: a period of Gesellschaft follows a period of Gemeinschaft. The Gemeinschaft is characterized by the social will as concord, folkways, mores, and religion; the Gesellschaft by the social will as convention, legislation, and public opinion. The concepts correspond to the types of external social organization, which may be classed as follows:

A. Gemeinschaft

1. Family life = concord. Man participates in this with all his sentiments. Its real controlling agent is the people *(Volk)*.
2. Rural village life = folkways and mores. Into this, man enters with all his mind and heart. Its real controlling agent is the commonwealth.
3. Town life = religion. In this, the human being takes part with his entire conscience. Its real controlling agent is the church.

B. Gesellschaft

1. City life = convention. This is determined by man's intentions. Its real controlling agent is Gesellschaft per se.
2. National life = legislation. This is determined by man's calculations. Its real controlling agent is the state.
3. Cosmopolitan life = public opinion. This is evolved by man's consciousness. Its real controlling agent is the republic of scholars.

With each of these categories a predominant occupation and a dominating tendency in intellectual life are related in the following manner:

(A) 1. Home (or household) economy, based upon liking or preference, viz., the joy and delight of creating and conserving. Understanding develops the norms for such an economy.

2. Agriculture, based upon habits, i.e., regularly repeated tasks. Co-operation is guided by custom.
3. Art, based upon memories, i.e., of instruction, of rules followed, and of ideas conceived in one's own mind. Belief in the work and the task unites the artistic wills.

(B) 1. Trade based upon deliberation; namely, attention, comparison, calculation are the basis of all business. Commerce is deliberate action per se. Contracts are the custom and creed of business.
2. Industry based upon decisions; namely, of intelligent productive use of capital and sale of labor. Regulations rule the factory.
3. Science, based upon concepts, as is self-evident. Its truths and opinions then pass into literature and the press and thus become part of public opinion.

8. *Epochs of the Periods*

In the earlier period, family life and home (or household) economy strike the keynote; in the later period, commerce and city life. If, however, we investigate the period of Gemeinschaft more closely, several epochs can be distinguished. Its whole development tends toward an approach to Gesellschaft in which, on the other hand, the force of Gemeinschaft persists, although with diminishing strength, even in the period of Gesellschaft, and remains the reality of social life.

The first period is formed by the influence of the new basis of social organization which results from the cultivation of the soil: neighborhood relation is added to the old and persisting kinship relations, village to the clan. The other epoch comes into existence when villages develop into towns. The village and town have in common the principle of social organization in space, instead of the principle of time which predominates through the generations of the family, the tribe, and the people. Because it descends from common ancestors, the family has invisible metaphysical roots, as if they were hidden in the earth. The living individuals in the family are connected with each other by the sequence of past and future generations. But in village and town it is the physical, real soil, the permanent location, the visible land, which create the strongest ties and relations. During the period of Gemeinschaft this younger principle of space remains bound to the older principle of time. In the period of Gesellschaft they become disconnected, and from this disconnection results the city. It is the exaggeration of the principle of space in its urban form. In this exaggeration, the urban form becomes sharply contrasted with the rural form of the same principle, for the village remains essentially and almost necessarily bound to both principles. In this sense, the whole continual development may be considered as a process of increasing urbanization. "It may be said that the whole economic history of Gesellschaft, i.e., of the modern nations, is in essence summarized in the change in the relationship between town and country" (Karl Marx, *Das Kapital,* I, p. 364). That is, from a certain point on, the towns by their influence and importance achieve, in the nation, predominance over the rural organization. In consequence, country and village must use more of their own productive forces for the support and furtherance of the urban areas than they can spare for purposes of reproduction. Therefore, the rural organization is doomed to dissolution, which in consequence leads later on to the decay of its organs and functions. This is the general law of the relationship between organic or vegetative and animalistic or sensitive life as it is invariably represented in the normal development of animal life, as well as its development under the most favorable conditions. In the human being, if animal life and will have changed into mental life and will, this law gains a special significance. In the first place, this is true because the human being is capable of destroying himself with his intelligence, directly, by reason, or it is likewise possible that, insofar as he can follow certain aims and purposes in determining his own fate, he may shorten or lengthen the period of his life according to his will. In the second place, this is true because his decay as well as his life can become evident in his mental life itself, and as such dominate and outlast the animalistic existence. Insofar as these phenomena are concerned, the animalistic element remains between mental and vegetative life, sometimes leaning toward the one, sometimes toward the other. In a normal development, a period of growth can be ascertained in which the vegetative element prevails over the animalistic element. In a period of decay, the opposite relationship prevails. This remains valid for the human being, but it may gain a special form in which the animalistic element, as far as it expresses itself in mental life, passes through this process, and becomes identical with the vegetative element.

Thus, in the period of growth, which means dominance of the vegetative-animalistic element, three categories or grades can be distinguished: (1) in vegetative life itself; (2) in animalistic life; (3) in mental life. There is a corresponding trinity in the period of decay, which is defined by the dominance of the animalistic-mental element.

According to this idea, rural life corresponds to vegetative-animalistic life, urban life to animalistic-mental life. The first type of life, which also remains active in the town, means the highest development of the entire organism; the other form, as it separates itself to become urban life, seems to exist by itself, producing and consuming, tending to dominate the entire country more and more, to draw from it its forces, and to lead to their destruction.

9. *Socialism and Communism*

This whole development, from its primary to its subsequent manifestations, can also be conceived as a transition from an original, simple, family communism and village-town individualism based thereon, to an independent, universal, urban individualism and, determined thereby, a socialism of state and international type. The latter is inherent in the concept of Gesellschaft, although in the beginning it exists only as an actual interrelation between all capitalistic powers and the state, which maintains and promotes order in the social organization. Gradually attempts are made to impose a uniform regulation on the social organization and labor itself through the mechanism of the state, but success in this would necessarily dissolve the entire Gesellschaft and its civilization. This same tendency necessarily implies a dissolution of all those ties which bind the individual through his natural will and are apart from his rational will. For these ties restrict his personal freedom of movement, the salableness of his property, the change of his attitudes, and their adaptation to the findings of science. They are restrictions on the self-determined rational will and on the Gesellschaft insofar as trade and commerce tend to make property or property rights as mobile and divisible as possible and require unscrupulous, irreligious, easygoing people. The state, too, feels the restrictive influence of these ties, and hastens the tendency toward their dissolution, and considers enlightened, greedy, and practical people its most useful subjects. The development of these forces and contrasts and their struggle for supremacy are common to the two spheres of culture and their people of which we may believe ourselves to have definite knowledge. One is the South-European classic culture which reached its acme in Athens and came to an end in Rome, the other is the North-European modern culture which followed it and, in many respects, was influenced and furthered by it. We discover these similar developments under an enormous variety of historical facts and conditions. Within the general uniform process to which all elements contribute, each of these has its own hidden history, which is determined partly by the general development, partly by causes of its own, and which, impeding or furthering, interferes with the whole.

The concepts and findings which have been presented in this book will help us to understand the tendencies and struggles which have come down from earlier centuries to the present period and will reach out into the future. To this end, we conceive the whole development of Germanic culture, which rose upon the ruins of the Roman Empire and, as its heir, expanded under the beneficial influence of the Church, as in a state of constant progress as well as decay. The interplay of these conflicting tendencies gave rise to those very contrasts which form the basis of the theory outlined above. In contradistinction to all historical theory deducing its findings from the past, we take as our actual, even necessary, starting point that moment in history when the present spectator enjoys the inestimable advantage of observing the occurring events in the light of his own experience, and perceives, although chained to the rocks of time, the approach of Oceanus' daughters. (Aeschyl. *Prometh.* v. 115.)

PART FIVE

The Summing Up

The following is a translation of an article by Ferdinand Tönnies entitled "Gemeinschaft und Gesellschaft," in Handwörterbuch der Soziologie, Ferdinand Enke Verlag, Stuttgart, 1931. *This article, appearing five years before its author's death and almost half a century after the first appearance of the original volume, represented Tönnies' latest thinking on the subject of the fundamental concepts of sociology, and in modern times must be considered as part of his whole work.*

GEMEINSCHAFT UND GESELLSCHAFT

1. *Knowledge and Nonknowledge*

Sociology is the study of man, not of his bodily nor of his psychical, but of his social nature. His bodily and psychical being are considered only insofar as they condition his social nature. It is our purpose to study the sentiments and motives which draw people to each other, keep them together, and induce them to joint action. We wish especially to investigate the products of human thought which, resulting therefrom, make possible and sustain a common existence. They find their consummation in such important forms as community, state, and church, which are often felt to be realities or even supernatural beings.

Nosce te ipsum (know yourself); if you want to understand others, look into your own heart. Every one of us has manifold relationships, direct and indirect, with other people. Every one of us knows many people, but only few in proportion to their total number. Thus the question arises, how do I know other people?

We shall first study the distinction between all people and those we know, without regard to the question as to how we come to know people. The distinction will head a list of four dichotomies dealing with one's relation to one's fellow beings. This distinction is:

1. *Acquaintanceship and Strangeness.* It is not necessary to do more than simply indicate the great importance of this distinction. In a crowd of strangers, in a strange city, one may meet by chance an acquaintance, perhaps even a familiar acquaintance or at least an acquaintance of long standing. This is usually a pleasant experience. One is likely to strike up a conversation with him at once, something one is seldom inclined to do with a complete stranger. Often what little inclination one has to converse with strangers is impeded by a foreign language. If the individual is only a casual acquaintance, it may be the first (and possibly the last) time that one shakes hands with him. Such a casual acquaintance may be a stranger except for the fact that he is known in some special capacity such as that of being engaged in the same profession or line of work; or it may be that the two persons have met once before and exchanged a few words. A casual acquaintance of mine may be a citizen of another country and have a different mother tongue, but he is known to me and is an acquaintance even if we had and still have difficulty in understanding each other. In the German language there is a subtle distinction between an acquaintance and a person whom one only "knows." An acquaintance, my acquaintance, knows me, too; someone whom I only know does not, in all probability, know me or, at least, will not necessarily know me. An individual occupying a high position is seen and known by many whom he himself overlooks, whom he does not know and very often does not wish to know. The person whom I know may not remember me or, even if he should, may not wish to take notice of me. I may not mean anything to him, or he may not like me. In contradistinction, an acquaintance is considered by many as being among their "friends." This may often be a sign of a superficial intellectual attitude or manner of speech, al-though, of course, acquaintanceship implies a slight tendency toward mutual approval just as strangeness implies a tendency toward mutual negation. This is, to be sure, only a tendency, but tendencies are important.

2. *Sympathy and Antipathy.* The fact that one knows a person or is acquainted with him does not necessarily imply that one likes him or is fond of him or (a rarer occurrence) loves him. There is, of course, tremendous difference between those who are congenial to us, and those whom we regard with antipathy. Sympathy and antipathy are feelings; they are often defined as instincts, that is, as something subhuman. In reality, they are frequently connected with thought and knowledge and thus with higher and nobler feelings which distinguish the human being. Indeed, they often spring from such feelings and from our thoughts and knowledge. A certain relationship of some significance exists, as has already been pointed out, between acquaintance and sympathy on the

one hand and between strangeness and antipathy on the other. The more sympathy and antipathy are instinctive, the more they are related to outward appearance, especially where women are concerned. This holds true, above all, for the feelings resulting from the impression made upon them by a man. Such impression may be produced by his figure, his face and expression, his dress, his behavior, his manners, his way of speech, even the sound of his voice. Men, too, often fall in love with women at first sight. For some a beautiful figure, for others a lovely face, is the decisive factor; for some it is the expression of the eyes alone or the polished way of speaking, for still others the elegant dress or the smart hat. Immediate and instinctive sympathy or antipathy may, however, be counteracted in actual experience, by a more intimate knowledge of the hitherto strange person. One finds, for instance, that someone who gave one an unfavorable impression at first turns out to be quite a nice person, perhaps interesting or positively charming. It even happens that women and girls may develop a passionate affection for a man who, in the beginning, was as repulsive to them as was Richard the Third to the widowed queen. It is another question whether a steadfast, faithful love can spring from such a root. In many cases experience may prove the first impression to have been correct; but the reverse is also well known and practically a daily occurrence. An excellent impression may so bias one in favor of an individual that after more intimate acquaintance one may reproach oneself for having been taken in by a brilliant outward appearance.

But our souls, our feelings, are indifferent to the great mass of people, not only to those who are unknown to us, the strangers, but also even to those whom we know reasonably well. This indifference is, however, not immovably fixed; there may easily develop a tendency fluctuating between antipathy and sympathy. Sympathies and antipathies can be of many different degrees, especially if we take into consideration the above-mentioned intelligent sympathy and antipathy which are rooted in our thinking consciousness. We shall usually have a certain degree of sympathy, even though this may be small, for those who side with us, whether we have known them before or came to know them only as fellow fighters, comrades, countrymen, or even home folks, or as colleagues, or as persons of the same faith, same political party, same profession. Sympathy may also be engendered by the fact that individuals belong to the same estate, as in the case of the nobility, or the same class, as in the case of the proletariat or the propertied class. In the same way there exists, on the other hand, some antipathy toward all those who are in the opposite camp. Such antipathy often increases to the point of hatred, especially if a real conflict exists between the opposing sides. In other instances such antipathy manifests itself only in, and is reduced to, greater indifference, so that it can easily, as a result of close acquaintance or other motives, be transformed into real sympathy. However, the same or similar interests are sufficient to arouse sympathy to the extent that such similarities are in the consciousness of those involved, and by the same token contrary interests will evoke antipathy. For example, at times the masses have and are conscious of common interests as consumers. At such times they will feel a slight sympathy for one another. Their interests are opposed to those of producers and merchants, toward whom their antipathy is directed, and such antipathy is stronger than their mutual sympathy.

3. *Confidence and Mistrust.* The third difference to which I wish to draw attention is that of confidence or mistrust toward other people. An individual whom we know will inspire in us a certain confidence, however slight; a stranger, on the other hand, is likely to create in us a certain feeling, often quite strong, of mistrust. Furthermore, sympathy may easily and rather quickly lead to a feeling of confidence which is often just as quickly regretted, whereas antipathy may arouse, strengthen, and further a mistrust which sometimes proves to be unwarranted. But here again, how many gradations exist! Only in a chosen few do we have such great and abiding confidence that we rely on their absolute sincerity, affection, and faithfulness toward ourselves and our nearest, and feel we can build upon their devotion. As is well known, these chosen few are not always our "equals." When not, they have no claim to that sympathy which is characteristic of those of the same class, the same estate. The faithful servant, the faithful maid, are not only figures of sagas and fiction, although they are more frequent under simpler and more rural than under modern conditions. Confidence betrayed—this is indeed a terrible, embittering experience which often leads to despair. But even mistrust can change into confidence, just as abused confidence, apart from arousing indignation, anger, and embitterment, will immediately turn into mistrust directed toward those formerly honored with confidence. Not only one's own but also other people's experience may lead one either to confidence in or mistrust of a person, thus investing him with either a reliable or a dubious reputation.

On the other hand, confidence has become highly impersonalized through modern trade. Personality has come to be of little or no importance. Only the "wealth" of a person counts, for it is assumed, and usually on valid grounds, that self-interest will induce even the personally less reliable businessman to pay his debts as long as he is able to do so. Personal reliability fades as it is transformed into reliability as debtor. As a rule, it is the business or manufacturing firm (irrespective of the moral qualities of its owner or manager), which has financial credit and is sound, or at least is supposed to be sound. In fact, as a result of this kind of confidence in the financial standing of the firm, the moral quality of its head may still be considered intact even though there may exist good reasons for a contrary judgment. Thus, confidence in the financial credit of the person or firm, like confidence in personal qualities, is often betrayed.

Moreover, without being conscious of it, we often trust many people on the strength of very slight knowledge concerning the persons involved. Sometimes we do not even know them or anything about them except that they are at their posts. This, too, is impersonalized confidence. Personal confidence is essentially conditioned by the personalities of those who confide; that is, by their intelligence, their knowledge of human nature, and their experience, on which the latter is based. Thus, in the case of personal confidence, simple-minded and inexperienced people are in general inclined to be trustful, whereas the intelligent and experienced persons are inclined to doubt. However, this difference all but disappears where rationalized confidence is concerned. We do not know the engineer who runs our train or the captain and the pilots who direct the course of our ship; in many cases we do not know the doctor whom we ask for advice, to whom we even entrust body and life for a surgical operation. Very often we do not know the lawyer whom we request to take our case, still less do we know the judge who will decide the case for or against us, and who, we hope and expect, will restore our rights and our honor and do justice to our claims. In all these cases we rely (a) on skill (or knowledge), or (b) on volition. As far as that skill (or knowledge) is concerned, we are justified in trusting an individual because (1) skill (or knowledge) is bound up with his profession. How could he dare call himself a doctor, a lawyer, or a judge, if he were not such? The shoemaker, the locksmith, and the tailor also know their trades, their arts. The greater the importance of a matter, the more we rely on (2) examinations, (3) experience, (4) reputation, and (5) the personal advice or recommendation which opened the door for a man or woman to this activity or this office. In many cases, however, as, for instance, in that of the engineer or pilot, only the qualifications (2) and (3) are required.

As far as volition is concerned, we put our trust in (a) certain normal moral qualities and the assumption that the individual in whose care we entrust ourselves could not possibly follow this profession if he did not possess at least a modicum of such qualities. Closely connected therewith is (b) his own self-interest, either material or nonmaterial, both of which usually merge into each other.

But it can easily be seen that something else besides these reasons underlies our peace of mind, our feeling of security. Our confidence in that which is regular and safe, although we are rarely aware of it, rests upon the three great systems of social will which I define as order, law, and morality. The two functions last mentioned, the legal and the moral orders or systems, are the fully developed types of the first one.

4. *Interdependence.* And now I come to the fourth difference, which is closely related to and partly contained in the first three. This is the difference between my condition in case I am "bound" in some way to other people and my condition in case I am completely independent and free from them. The condition of being bound to others is the exact opposite of freedom, the former implying a moral obligation, a moral imperative, or a prohibition. There exist a great variety of such "ties," which involve an individual through different types of relationships. These ties may also be called types of social entities *(soziale Wesenheiten)* or forms which link him to his fellow beings. He is bound in these social entities if he is conscious of being linked to them. His consciousness of the tie is either predominantly emotional or predominantly intellectual. From this consciousness there results a feeling or a realization of moral obligation, moral imperative, or prohibition, and a righteous aversion to the consequences of incorrect, illegal, and unlawful, as well as of immoral and indecent conduct and action.

To talk of such relationships as "bonds" implies, of course, a figurative use of the term, just as no social ties or associations are to be interpreted in terms of the literal meaning of the words. That a human being is tied to another human being can indicate a state of complete dependence. This, however, is a figurative expression indicating that one of the two beings involved does not or cannot have a will of his own, but depends for whatever he may desire on the volition of the other one. Thus, the dependence of the infant, and, in a diminishing degree, of the small child, on his mother or any other person who takes care of him, is an obvious fact. Of similar character are those types of dependence in which the well-being of a person is determined less by his own will than by the will of others. Such dependence is most typically exemplified by servitude, slavery, and the like. It finds its most visible and thus most forceful expression in such physical constraint as was used with slaves and is still practiced in transporting hardened criminals. Referring to an inability to act on one's own will which may result from a completely weak will, we also speak of hypnotized persons, sexual slavery, and the like.

5. *Social Relationship or Bond; Connection.* Social relationship or bond implies interdependence, and it means that the will of the one person influences that of the other, either furthering or impeding, or both.

If the volition of the one meets and combines with the volition of the other, there results a common volition which may be interpreted as unified because it is mutual. This common volition postulates or requires, and thus controls, the volition of A in accordance with the volition of B as well as the volition of B in accordance with the volition of A. This is the simplest case of the social will of two individuals, whom I prefer to call persons when referring to volition and action of each toward the other. In the same way as a person can be linked with another person, he can be united with many persons, and these again can be connected with one another; thus, the will of each single person who belongs to a group is part of and at the same time conditioned by the group's collective will, which is to say he is dependent on it. Such collective will can take various forms, determined by the number of persons involved, its own character, and the mode of its existence, that is, the way in which it is expressed. Also, the individuals become conscious of it in many different ways. The collective will can remain the same for an indefinite period, but it can also from time to time undergo change by renewed acts. It can affect the persons involved either directly or indirectly in that a more comprehensive collective will may influence a smaller group and this, in turn, exert its influence upon the smallest unit. Every collective will can represent itself in a single natural person or in a number of those whose common will is conceived as the representative of a higher collective will.

Every collective will can be given a special name, but it can also bear the name of a thinking agent which designates the united multitude. What this name stands for is then conceived and thought of by the persons of this group as a person like themselves. That is to say, a collective person is one on whom either other collective persons or, in the simplest case, natural persons ultimately depend. They all know of their dependence on one another and thereby on the collective will which, in the simplest case, represents their own interrelationship or unity, and it is through this very knowledge that they are connected with one another. All following discussions in which such names are used must be interpreted in this sense. These names are taken from everyday language, where they were given a fixed meaning long ago, although very often without the proper insight into their real character. No clear and conscious distinction was made between a meaning that points only to the external form or significance as a group, a crowd, a band, and so on, and a meaning which is given to them by a scientific system of concepts, in which they are to be conceived as personalities and agents of a collective or social will; in other words, as social entities or phenomena.

That all these social entities have both similarities and differences in meaning and form can be easily deduced. Similarity exists insofar as they contain a social will which determines the co-operating individual wills by giving them rights as well as imposing duties on them and by defining the right of one person as the duty of another and vice versa. The difference among them lies in the fact that each finds its most perfect form as an imaginary (artificial) social person. Such a collective person consists of single persons, first individuals or, possibly, other subordinated collective persons. Even in the simplest possible case for every person concerned there is imposed a moral imperative by the collective (joint) will as well as by his own will.

2. *Barter and Exchange as Simplest Type of Social Relation or Bond*

We shall most easily understand the diverse modus operandi of social relationships or bonds if we relate all the varieties to the simplest type, which is also the most rational one. Here we are thinking of the case of simple barter or mutual promissory obligations, which may be conceived of as prolonged barter. Barter presents a typical and clear case because, in its simplest form, it involves two separate objects which are related in no other way than that each is a means with respect to the other, which is considered an end; each of them is useful and thus of value as a means to obtain the other.

If we agree to conceive all acts of mutual aid and assistance as barter or exchange, it will be evident that all living together is a continuous exchange of such aid and assistance and that the degree of its intimacy depends upon its frequency. However, the character of these relationships is determined by the underlying motives involved, which motives will manifest definite differences. In the simple case where only two persons are considered, the essential motive on the part of those involved can be characterized as follows: from one side there may be expectation of and desire for assistance, from the other there may be expectation, desire, and restraint. This condition resembles the expectation and demands of a collective entity which binds the individual; that is to say, so connects him to others and constrains him that this entity may take the place of and represent these others. In distinct contrast is the case in which one's motives to satisfy one's volition and desires take the form of satisfying those of another individual, others, or whole groups, even though one's own volition and desire may apparently be fostered by the similar volition and desires of the other or others. Such volition and desire necessarily result in a different attitude toward the other individual or individuals. It is essentially unconditional, like the love of the mother for her infant, from whom she does not expect or require anything as long as he has not reached the age of reason. Love alone does not bind. Thus, definite liking and benevolence, even though it be love, becomes atrophied when one party fails to return it. Such love may be allowed to continue its pitiful existence on the basis of the faintest hope or mere knowledge of the presence of the other loved one because one party may make the welfare of the other his own will, as is especially true in the case of sexual love. However, such love can also turn to hate (the more passionate, the earlier) which then becomes an inverted love, just as self-love frequently leads to self-destruction.

The derived and higher type of social bond always contains that element which we may designate, on the one hand, as containing mutual advantage, assistance, or amicable activity, and, on the other, as always containing an element of binding social will which works on and controls the individual will. Always the obligation and reciprocity makes itself felt and is thereby recognizable in that an inadequate and opposing action of a partner (participant or fellow member) calls forth a counteraction of one or the other and consequently of the whole if this latter continues to exist, which will be the more likely the less this whole's continuity depends upon the action of one person. Thus, for example, a friendship of two and frequently a marriage, even though this latter is conditioned by an existing social will of a higher type, is dependent upon the behavior of both partners and may be broken. On the other hand, in an association the individual cannot as a rule accomplish this, and only the action of a group strengthens or endangers its existence. The opposition between a majority and a minority makes itself felt in such a group and thus it may differ from the condition in which two individuals are involved. This difference is apparent if the majority wishes to retain or change the whole and if it is strong enough, as opposed to the minority, to make its will prevail over the whole. One must conceive as a normal case the condition in which individuals or parts, such as a minority, which act against the social will call forth the indignation of the majority, and the latter is in possession of sufficient power to react accordingly and, insofar as this is the case, will objectively represent the will of the whole even when the will of an important minority is opposed. Sociologically more important, however, is the case in which the principle prevails, perhaps having been recorded in expressed form, that the will of the majority or, at least, an especially large majority, shall prevail as the will of the whole corporation, social organization, or commission, so that after a resolution is passed the opposition is dissolved, at least for the time being.

3. *Bases of Social Relations*

1.   *Social Entities (soziale Wesenheiten).* Sociology as a special science has as its subject the "things" which result from social life, and

only from social life. They are products of human thinking and exist only for such thinking; that is, primarily for individuals themselves who are bound together and who think of their collective existence as dominating them and as a something which is represented as a person capable of volition and action, to which they give a name. The existence of such a something, a social person, can be recognized and acknowledged by outsiders, who may themselves be single or associated individuals, or by a social entity formed by such persons. Such recognition, if mutual, may create a new, essentially similar entity, in the most perfect case, a new social person, which again is existent immediately for its founders but can also be observed, recognized, and acknowledged by outsiders. The manner of existence of this social thing or person is not unlike that of the gods, which, being imagined and thought of by men who are bound together, are also created in order to be glorified, whether the form be that of an animal, a human being, or mixed being. There is, however, an obvious difference in that the gods disappear for the people to whom they belong when their existence is no longer believed in, even though they remain as subjects of the theoretical, historical, and sociological thinking. In contradistinction, social "entities," as we call them, do not require such belief or delusion. They can be thought of as subjects of common volition and operation in clear perception of their imaginary nature. Of course, it is also possible, indeed not an infrequent occurrence, that to the social entities, just as in the case of the gods, a supernatural, or, better stated, a metaphysical nature will be ascribed. The fanciful mythological thinking to which man has always been inclined constantly prevails in this sense and will, therefore, often confuse the inventions and fantasies of one or the other type; the social entities, especially the collective persons, are superior, powerful, and exalted, and so are the gods. Thus, in the social entity there exists at least some of the godlike characteristics. They stand under the special protection of the gods, especially when to such an entity a supernatural origin is ascribed, as in the case of the church.

When the god is himself represented as a powerful and feared or as a benevolent and kind ruler, he is ruler over the earthly ruler, giving the latter his consecration, confirming and befriending him, establishing his right, especially the right of hereditary succession, as a god-given right. By the grace of God the earthly ruler reigns, enjoying a godlike veneration. All kinds of veneration, as they spring from natural feeling as childish adoration or as awe of the weak for the strong, who may be hated and detested, are interwoven one with another and with the gods in whom they find their consummation and shine forth as religion. As obedient servants of the gods, powerful men are agents and interpreters of the will of God and thereby increase their own power.

Even though this mere creature of thought does not live in the clouds or on Olympus but has ascribed to it an existence such as that which is perhaps embodied in the assembly of an armed force or other meeting of the people, it will not easily avoid that condition in which its existence is brought into relationship with that of the gods. The belief in the gods can support the belief in the republic just as the belief in the church and the veneration of the priesthood are directly related. The scientific critical attitude destroys all of these illusions. It recognizes that only human thought and human will are contained in all these imaginary realms, that they are based upon human hopes and fears, requirements and needs, and that in their exalted forms they are comparable to poetical works of art on which the spirit of the ages has worked.

Thus, we return to the simple problem and thought: what, why, and how do thinking human beings will and want? The simple and most general answer is: they want to attain an end and seek the most appropriate means of attaining it. They strive toward a goal and seek the correct way leading thereto. This is the action, the behavior, which in the affairs of practical life, of daily work, of struggle, of trade, has through the ages been directed and made easier by pleasure and devotion, by hope and fear, by practice and habit, by model and precept.

2. *Human Volition.* The general human volition, which we may conceive as natural and original, is fulfilled through knowledge and ability and is also fundamentally conditioned through reciprocal interaction with them. The whole intellect, even in the plainest man, expresses itself in his knowledge and correspondingly in his volition. Not only what he has learned but also the inherited mode of thought and perception of the forefathers influences his sentiment, his mind and heart, his conscience. Consequently I name the will thought of in this latter sense natural will *(Wesenwille),* contrasting it with the type of rational will *(Kürwille),*[1] in which the thinking has gained predominance and come to be the directing agent. The rational will is to be differentiated from intellectual will. Intellectual will gets along well with subconscious motives which lie deep in man's nature and at the base of his natural will, whereas rational will eliminates such disturbing elements and is as clearly conscious as possible.

Deliberation, the thought form of ends and means, can separate the two, one from the other. From this results the inference that the means are not fundamentally connected to the end; that is to say, the means and end are not allied, interwoven, or identical. The means may rather be completely isolated and therefore possibly even stand in strong opposition to the ends. In this case the end under consideration requires that the means be as suitable to it as possible, that no means or segment thereof be used which is not conditioned by the end, but that the means most suitable for the attainment of a given end be chosen and used. This implies a definite divorce and differentiation of end and means which, therefore, permits no consideration of means other than that of their perfect suitability for the attaining of the end. The principle of the rationalization of the means develops everywhere as a necessary consequence the more thought, in accordance with the desire and intention, is intensively focused on the end or the goal. This signifies, therefore, an attitude of indifference to the means with respect to every consideration other than their greatest effectiveness in attaining the end. This indifference is frequently attained only by overcoming resistance resulting from motives other than the consideration of the end, which motives may hinder, dissuade, or frighten one from the application of this means. Thus, action which adjusts the means to the end desired may be viewed with definite reluctance, also with fear and anxiety, or, more characteristically, with aversion and, what is akin thereto, with feelings of opposition such as come with remorse. With some exaggeration, Goethe says the acting man is always "without conscience." In reality, the acting person often finds it necessary, if he "unscrupulously" follows his goal, to repress or overcome his conscientiousness. On account of this necessity, many consider themselves justified in despising or disowning such feelings, and sometimes they even find their satisfaction in bravado and arrogance, making themselves free from all such considerations.

This means, therefore, that on the one hand there is the simple emotional (impulsive) and, therefore, irrational volition and action, whereas on the other there is the simple rational volition and action in which the means are arranged, a condition which often stands in conflict with the feelings. Between these two extremes all real volition and action takes place. The consideration that most volition and action resembles or is inclined toward either one or the other makes it possible to establish the concepts of natural will and rational will, which concepts are rightly applied only in this sense. I call them normal concepts. What they represent are ideal types, and they should serve as standards by which reality may be recognized and described.

3. *Gemeinschaft and Gesellschaft.*[2] It is not a question of contrasting the rational will with the nonrational will, because intellect and reason belong to natural will as well as to rational will. Indeed, intellect in natural will attains its fruition in the creative, formative, and artistic ability and works and in the spirit of the genius. This is true even

though in its elementary forms natural will means nothing more than a direct, naïve, and therefore emotional volition and action, whereas, on the other hand, rational will is most frequently characterized by consciousness. To the latter belongs manufacturing as contrasted with creation; therefore, we speak of mechanical work (as expressed in the German and other languages) referring to forging plans, machinations, weaving intrigues, or fabrications which are directed to the objective of bringing forth the means, the exclusive determination of which is that of producing the outward effects necessary to attain our desired ends.

When these concepts are applied to associations, it should not be understood that we are thinking only of the regular motives leading to the entrance into an association, creating of a confederation, or organizing of a union or special-interest group, or even the founding of a commonwealth. It is, however, of importance to recognize what motives lie at the basis of and explain the existence of all kinds of association or cause their persistence, and while we are here interested only in positive bases, this holds also for negative motives upon which persistence may be based. In this connection it is not to be understood that the bases belong fundamentally and persistently either to the one or the other category, that is, of natural will or rational will. On the contrary a dynamic condition or process is assumed which corresponds to the changeable elements of human feeling and thinking. The motives fluctuate so that they are now of one category, then of the other. However, wherever such development takes place a certain regularity or even "law," in the sense of a tendency toward abstract rational forms, may be observed.

I call all kinds of association in which natural will predominates Gemeinschaft, all those which are formed and fundamentally conditioned by rational will, Gesellschaft. Thus, these concepts signify the model qualities of the essence and the tendencies of being bound together. Thus, both names are in the present context stripped of their connotation as designating social entities or groups, or even collective or artificial persons; the essence of both Gemeinschaft and Gesellschaft is found interwoven in all kinds of associations, as will be shown.

4. *Social Systems*

1. *Relationships, Collectives, Social Organizations.* As social entities or forms, I differentiate: (1) Social relationships *(Verhältnisse)*, (2) Collectives *(Samtschaften)*, (3) Social organizations or corporate bodies *(Körperschaften)* (leagues, fellowships, associations, or special-interest groups).

The third form is always thought of as a kind of human person capable of creating a definite unified will which, as the will of the natural or artificial persons belonging to it, binds and constrains them to act in conformity with such will, which may be directed inwardly or outwardly. In the social relationship it is not the relationship itself which is so considered, even though it be designated by a special name. However, it is essential that its subjects or bearers, who may be considered as "members" of the relationship, are conscious of it as a relationship which they will affirmatively and thus establish as an existing reality. This manner of establishing a social relationship represents in embryonic or emergent form what is evolved to perfection in the establishment of a social organization or corporation capable of willing and acting.

The collective lies between the social relationship and the social organization. It is thought of as a plurality which, like the social organization, includes a multitude of persons so held together that there result common intentions, desires, inclinations, disinclinations—in short, common feelings and ways of thinking. However, the collective is not capable of real volition. It can reach no decision as long as it does not "organize" itself into a committee, special-interest group, or council.

2.   *The Social Relationship.* The social relationship is the most general and simplest social entity or form. It also has the deepest foundation, because it rests partly upon the original, natural, and actual conditions as the causes of connections, of mutual dependence, and of attachment among men, and because it rests partly on the most fundamental, most universal, and most necessary requirements of human beings. The one basis, like the other, is raised to consciousness with different effects. If a natural relationship exists, as for example between my brother and me, on one hand, or between my brother-in-law, my stepbrother, adopted or foster brother and me, on the other, I have the feeling that we are intimate, that we affirm each other's existence, that ties exist between us, that we know each other and to a certain extent are sympathetic toward each other, trusting and wishing each other well. This is true although in the latter case, involving persons who are not blood brothers, the relationship is not so natural as in the first where I know the same mother gave birth to both my brother and me. From this it follows that we have certain values in common, whether it be that we are obliged to manage an estate together, or that we divide possessions as inheritances between us, or that the matter of intellectual goods or ideals is involved. At any rate, out of each such relationship, even between two, there results the recognition and acknowledgment of the social relationship as such on the part of each and therefore the knowledge of each that definite mutual action must regularly result therefrom. This action is expected and demanded of each by the other, and each expects and demands of himself that it be

carried out in relation to the other. In this lies the embryo of "rights" which each claims for himself but also concedes to the other, as well as "duties" to which one feels obligated but which one puts upon oneself knowing that the other party wills that he be and considers that he is so obligated.

However, when I become conscious of my most urgent needs and find that I can neither satisfy them out of my own volition nor out of a natural relation, this means that I must do something to satisfy my need; that is, engage in free activity which is bound only by the requirement or possibly conditioned by the need but not by consideration for other people. Soon I perceive that I must work on other people in order to influence them to deliver or give something to me which I need. Possibly in restricted individual cases my mere requests will be granted, as, for example, in the case of a piece of bread or a glass of water. However, as a rule when one is not receiving something in a Gemeinschaft-like relationship, such as from within the family, one must earn or buy it by labor, service, or money which has been earned previously as payment for labor or service.

I now enter or have already entered into a social relationship, but it is of a different kind. Its prototype is barter or exchange, including the more highly developed form of exchange, the sale and purchase of things or services, which are the same as things and are therefore thought of as capable of being exchanged for things or for other services. All action which is of an intellectual nature, and consequently oriented by reason, is of this type because comparison and thinking are necessary to it and furnish a basis for it. Social relationships which result from such barter or exchange are primarily momentary in that they involve a momentary common volition. However, they come to have duration partly through repetition resulting in regularity of the exchange act and partly through the lengthening of the individual act by the postponement of fulfillment on the part of one or both sides. In this latter case there results a relationship, the distinguishing characteristic of which is a one-sided or mutual "promise." It is a real social relationship of obligation or mutual dependence resulting first of all from mutual promises, even though they may be expressly stated by one side and only tacitly understood by the other as such an eventual promise.

Also, the relationships which come to us from nature are in their essence mutual, are fulfilled in mutual performance. The relations produce this mutuality and demand, require, or make it necessary. Having these characteristics, they resemble the exchange relationship. However, the natural relationship is, by its very essence, of earlier origin than its subjects or members. In such natural relationships it is self-evident that action will take place and be willed in accordance with the relationship, whether it be what is contained on the one hand in the simplest relationships resulting from desire and inclination, from love or habit, or on the other hand from reason or intellect contained in the feeling of duty. These latter types of natural will change into one another, and each can be the basis of Gemeinschaft.

On the other hand, in the purest and most abstract contract relationship the contracting parties are thought of as separate, hitherto and otherwise independent, as strangers to each other, and perhaps even as hitherto and in other respects inimical persons. *Do, ut des* (I give, so that you will give) is the only principle of such a relationship. What I do for you, I do only as a means to effect your simultaneous, previous, or later service for me. Actually and really I want and desire only this. To get something from you is my end; my service is the means thereto, which I naturally contribute unwillingly. Only the aforesaid and anticipated result is the cause which determines my volition. This is the simplest form of rational will.

Relationships of the first type are to be classified under the concept Gemeinschaft, those of the other type under the concept of Gesellschaft, thus differentiating Gemeinschaft-like and Gesellschaft-like relationships. Gemeinschaft-like relationships differ to the extent that there is assumed, on the one hand, a real, even if not complete, equality in knowledge or volition, in power and in authority on the part of the participants, and on the other hand, an essential inequality in these respects. This also holds for the relations of Gesellschaft. In accordance with this distinction we shall differentiate between the fellowship type and the authoritative type of social relationship. Let us now consider this difference.

A. In Gemeinschaft-like Relationships.

(a) The Fellowship Type. The simplest fellowship type is represented by a pair who live together in a brotherly, comradely, and friendly manner, and it is most likely to exist when those involved are of the same age, sex, and sentiment, are engaged in the same activity or have the same intentions, or when they are united by one idea.

In legend and history such pairs occur frequently. The Greeks used to honor such friendships as those of Achilles and Patroclus, Orestes and Pylades, Epaminondas and Pelopidas, to the extent that to Aristotle is ascribed the paradox: He who has friends has no friend. In the German language and literature it is customary to designate such sentiments, the nature of which the Greeks glorified as mutual happiness and sorrow, as a brotherly relationship. This characterization is based more on the thought of the ideal than on actual observation, but it is correct insofar as brothers actually make the most natural as well as the most probable pairs of friends, more because of their origin than because of a motive.

(b) Authoritative Type. The relationship of father to child, as observations in everyday life will prove, is to be found in all the strata of society in all stages of culture. The weaker the child and the more it is in need of help, the greater the extent to which the relationship is represented by protection. Protection of necessity always carries with it authority as a condition, because protection regularly can be carried out only when the protected party follows the directions and even the commands of the protector. Although all authority has a tendency to change into the use of force, in the case of the father as well as the mother relationship such a tendency is arrested by love and tenderness. These sentiments, being of animal and vegetative origin, are more likely to be regularly accorded to a child born to a parent than to any other possessed and protected person. The general character of the father relationship can be easily extended to include similar relationships involving protection, examples of which are the stepfather, foster father, the general house father, and the guardian, even though these, as representatives of the father, do not necessarily legally stand in Gemeinschaft-like relation to the ward. The authority of the father is the prototype of all Gemeinschaft-like authority. It is especially true in the case of the priesthood, even though the basis may be different. This rests primarily upon mythological conceptions which place the father in Olympus or in heaven and perhaps ascribe numberless children to the father of the gods and men. Or in a less sensual, more refined form, the father may be represented by an only son whom the struggle against polytheism tends almost to identify with the father. Little wonder that the title Pope (Papa, literally "father") in the original church of all bishops was raised to the pinnacle of spiritual dignity in the Roman Church and that in the Oriental Church the especially high priests are called fathers (*Popen*) in the language of the common people. Also, world and political authority, which is often mixed with and may not be less sanctified than the spiritual, easily takes on the character of the well-wishing father, as is most plainly expressed in the term "father" of a country. The fatherly authority, however, is the special case of authority of age, and the prestige-giving quality of age expresses itself most perfectly in the authority of the father. This easily explains the eminence which is attributed to the senator in the worldly and the presbyter in the spiritual commonwealth.

(c) Mixed Relationships. In many Gemeinschaft-like relationships the essence of authority and that of fellowship are mixed. This is the case in the most important of the relationships of Gemeinschaft, the lasting relation between man and woman which is conditioned through sexual needs and reproduction, whether or not the relationship is called marriage.

B. In Gesellschaft-like Relationships. The difference between the fellowship and authoritative types is also to be found in the Gesellschaft-like relationships. It can, however, be derived only from the fact that the authority is based upon a free contract whether between individuals, as service contracts, or by agreement of many to recognize and place a master or head over them and to obey him conditionally or unconditionally. This may be a natural person or a collective person which results directly from individuals uniting in a society, social organization, or corporate body which is capable of volition and action and can be represented through its own totality. The Gesellschaft-like authority attains its consummation in the modern state, a consummation which many predecessors strove to attain until the democratic republic came into existence and allowed for development beyond the Gesellschaft-like foundation. The actual authority results, however, in the simple Gesellschaft-like relationship, from the difference in the power of two parties, as in the labor contract. Such authority results from contracts made between the individual "employer" and individual "employee," and also from the condition out of which come "peace treaties" between victor and conquered. Apparently it is a contract, but in actuality it is coercion and abuse.

3. *The Collective.* The second concept of social entity or form is that of the collective. I make distinctions between natural, psychical, and social collectives. Our concept concerns only social collectives, but these rest partly on natural and partly on psychical collectives, partly on both. This is because the essence of a social collective is to be found in the natural and psychological relationships forming the basis of the collective and are consciously affirmed and willed. This phenomenon appears everywhere in the life of a people and in many forms of mutualities, as, for example, in forms of life and customs, superstitions and religion. It is especially in evidence in the distinguishing characteristic through which a segment of a people, that is, certain classes, are given prominence, nobility, and authority. A distinguishing characteristic which has this function is partly an objective phenomenon and partly something positive in the people's consciousness. The consciousness of belonging to a controlling estate makes its appearance in a distinct manner as pride and haughtiness—feelings which in turn are coupled with the submission and modesty of those "lower" classes over which authority is exercised so long as the controlling estates, as such, are honored, and so long as their excellence, or even their divinity, is believed in.

In the case of the collective the concepts of Gemeinschaft and Gesellschaft should also be applied. The social collective has the characteristics of Gemeinschaft insofar as the members think of such a grouping as a gift of nature or created by a supernatural will, as is expressed in the simplest and most naïve manner in the Indian caste system. Here, to be fixed to a given calling is just as necessary and natural as being born, and the professional estate or group has the same significance as a large family for which the pursuit and means of making a livelihood, even if this should be accomplished by thievery, is represented as something inherited which it is a duty to retain and nurture. In all systems of ranks or estates, traces of this condition are to be found because (and to the extent that) a complete emancipation from the social relationships established at birth seldom occurred and was often impossible. Thus, man as a rule submits to the social status in which parents and forebears, or, as it is wont to be expressed, "God," has placed him as if it were his lot to bear, even though it be felt as a burden, which, however, is habit and is lightened by the recognition that it cannot be changed. Indeed, within these limits there can exist an intellectual self-consciousness which affirms this estate (rank) even though it be recognized as one of the less significant. This intellectual basis manifests itself partly as the group extols itself for certain superiorities or virtues, the lack of which in the dominating estate is noticed and complained about. Also, the intellectual basis is to be found partly in the consciousness of special knowledge and skill of the group, as, for example, its art, craftsmanship, and skill, which are thought of as being at least the equivalent of the other honored or ruling estates.

Consciousness of a social collective has different results when directed toward the attainment of definite and important ends which it knows to be and claims are its own characteristics. This happens in a pronounced way in the political and intellectual struggle in which the social strata of a people stand against each other as classes. The more the consciousness of authority as a feeling of superiority results in putting one class in such a position of power as to force the lower class to stay in its place, the more this latter will strive toward the attainment of equality and therefore the more indignant it becomes concerning oppression and arrogance on the part of the controlling class, which it attempts to restrict and displace.

Whether this process is called class struggle (*Klassenkampf*) or struggle of estates (*Ständekampf*) is not important. The struggle among the estates usually takes place earlier, is less radical, and can be allayed. The lower estates strive only for the opportunity to participate in the satisfactions of life and fundamentals of authority, allowing the controlling estate to remain in power. This latter remains in power by proclaiming its own fitness and disparaging that of the lower estates and by exerting effort to reduce these lower strata to submission.

The class struggle is more unconditional. It recognizes no estates, no natural masters. In the foreground of the consciousness of the whole class which feels that it is propertyless and therefore oppressed, stands the ideal of the Gemeinschaft of property in field and soil and all the implements of labor. These latter have been acquired through the art of trade or as inherited property belonging by "law" to the small minority which, as the propertied class, is set off against the propertyless class. Therefore, the class struggle becomes more conscious and general than the struggle among the estates. However, even though there be no definite form of struggle there is a corresponding consciousness which makes itself felt in many ways. The great propertyless masses prefer to think of themselves as the people (*Volk*), and the narrow class which is in control of property and its use thinks of itself as society, even though each expression is all inclusive. "The" people *(Volk)*, as in the case of the estate, resembles the Gemeinschaft; "the" society, like the class, has, in the sense in which it is here used, the basic characteristic of Gesellschaft.[3]

4. *The Social Organization.* The third and most important category of pure or theoretical sociology is the social organization or corporate body, a social body or union known by many other names. It is never anything natural, neither can it be understood as a mere psychical phenomenon. It is completely and essentially a social phenomenon and must be considered as composed of several individuals. Capacity for unified volition and action, a capacity which is demonstrated most clearly as competency to pass resolutions, characterizes it. Just as the thinking individual is capable of making decisions, so is a group of several individuals when they continuously agree or agree to the extent that there prevails and is recognized a definite will as the will of all or sufficient consensus to be the will of the social organization or corporate body. Thus, the volition of such a group can be represented by the will of a natural person behind whom the will of the whole social organization or corporate body stands. Continuing our discussion of social organizations or corporate bodies, we may make the following observations:

(1) A social organization or corporate body can originate from natural relationships provided these are social relationships. In this connection, kinship, the most universal and natural bond which embraces human beings, comes to our attention. The most important social organization or corporate body which originates therefrom and which among all known peoples occurs as the original form of a common life is the

kinship group, the gens, clan, or whatever name is applied to designate this ancient union or unity.

Whether or not the totality of adult persons includes the women, whether their council ends in agreement which is sanctioned by a supposed will of God, or whether they rejoice in and willingly accept the decisions of a leader and head, it is under these conditions that there is formed the embryo of a consciousness which matures into something beyond a mere feeling of belonging together, and there is established and affirmed an enduring self or ego in the totality.

(2) A common relation to the soil tends to associate people who may be kinsfolk or believe themselves to be such. Neighborhood, the fact that they live together, is the basis of their union; it leads to counseling and through deliberations to resolutions. Here again the two principles of fellowship and authority will be involved. The outstanding example of an association of this type is the rural village community, which attains its consummation in the cultivation of the soil practiced in common and the possession of common property in village fields or land held in common by the village, and in the Mark-community which comes to represent the unity of several neighboring village communities which originally may have formed one unit.

The rural village community is frequently identical with a great family or clan but the more alien elements are taken in the more it loses its kinship characteristics. The bond of field and soil and living together first takes its place along with and later more and more supplants the bond of common ancestry. Especially when an alien tribe and its leaders become the conquerors of a territory and establish themselves in the seats of control without extirpating or driving out all the former residents and owners does this tendency manifest itself, molding a new people *(Volk)* from the two groups, even though the one was subjected to new masters. The existence of the village community as a social organization or corporate body ordinarily continues in the form of a fellowship. Such a village community, however, may be modified by the power and rights of feudal lords.

(3) In the more intimate and close living together in the town, the fellowship and co-operative quality attains a new level. Living together tends to depend less on common nature. People not related by blood tend to assemble in the towns since these originally were walled-in villages or strongholds whose inhabitants were forced to co-operate for defense and for the maintenance of peace and order among themselves and thereby to form a political community, either under the rule of a lord or as citizens of equal rights. This was the great mission and service of the town *(Stadt)* community, the *"Polis"* which grew to be that commonwealth

which later in Europe and elsewhere up to our time has bequeathed its character and name to the state *(Staat)*, the mightiest of all corporate bodies. That assembly of the sovereign people, the religious association *(Ekklesia)*, the other great commonwealth of the Roman and post-Roman period, loaned its name to the Church and spread its glory throughout the world in a similar manner.

These social bodies and communities retain their common root in that original state of belonging together, which according to our concept is the Gemeinschaft. Indeed, although the original state of common being, living, and working is changed, it retains and is able to renew its mental and political form and its co-operative functions. Thus, a people *(Volk)* which feels itself bound together by a common language, when held together within a national association or even when only striving to become a nation, will desire to be represented in a unity or *Volksgemeinschaft*, which may become intensified by national consciousness and pride, but may also thereby lose its original genuineness.

5. *Capitalistic, Middle-Class, or Bourgeois Society (bürgerliche Gesellschaft).* During this development, the original qualities of Gemeinschaft may be lost because there takes place a continued change in the original basis upon which living together rests. This change reaches its consummation in what is frequently designated as individualism. Through this development social life in and of itself is not diminished, but social life of the Gemeinschaft is impaired and a new phenomenon develops out of the needs, interests, desires and decisions of persons who previously worked co-operatively together and are acting and dealing one with another. This new phenomenon, the "capitalistic society," increases in power and gradually attains the ascendancy. Tending as it does to be cosmopolitan and unlimited in size, it is the most distinct form of the many phenomena represented by the sociological concept of the Gesellschaft.

A great transformation takes place. Whereas previously the whole of life was nurtured and arose from the profoundness of the people *(Volk)*, the capitalistic society through a long process spreads itself over the totality of this people, indeed over the whole of mankind. As a totality of individuals and families it is essentially a collective of economic character composed primarily of those who partake in that wealth which, as land and capital, represents the necessary means to the production of goods of all kinds. Within narrow or far-flung borders which are determined by actual or supposed kinship bonds, of the existence of which the language group is the most valuable sign, it constructs its state, that is to say, a kind of unity resembling a town community which is capable of willing and acting. It develops as the capitalistic middle-class republic and apparently finally attains its perfection in the social republic. It considers the state a means of attaining its ends, of which not the least important is protecting its person and property as well as the intellectual attitude which gives status and honor to its supporters.

However, since this capitalistic middle-class society cannot, without betraying itself, admit its uniqueness as a collective of Gesellschaft in contradistinction to the people *(Volk)* or, so to speak, herald this difference by raising its own flag, it can only assert its existence through claiming to be identical with, as well as representative and advocate of, the whole people to which it furnishes guidance. This process, which does not stop with conferring equal political rights on all citizens, to a certain extent closes the always widening hiatus between the wealth monopoly of the narrow and real Gesellschaft and the poverty of the people, but it cannot change the essential character of the hiatus. Indeed, it deepens it, spreading and strengthening the consciousness of the "social question."

By means of political and other intellectual organization promoted by town and, to a greater extent, by city life, the consciousness of the Gesellschaft gradually becomes the consciousness of an increasing mass of the people. The people come more and more to think of the state as a means and tool to be used in bettering their condition, destroying the monopoly of wealth of the few, winning a share in the products. Thus, the laborer would be allowed a share in proper proportion to his reasonable needs and the leaders in production their share of certain goods which are to be divided for consumption, and those things suitable for continued common utilization would be retained as common property of the Gesellschaft, which is to say of the people or their organized association, the state.

NOTES ON TÖNNIES' FUNDAMENTAL CONCEPTS

NOTES ON TÖNNIES' FUNDAMENTAL CONCEPTS

Although few would question its importance many a reader has failed to see Tönnies' system in its entirety. Even though most of the commentators on Tönnies' works recognize the importance of the dichotomy Gemeinschaft, based on natural will, and Gesellschaft, based on rational will, there are other fundamental concepts which must be understood before all aspects of the system become apparent. At the outset it should be made clear that each concept bears a definite relationship to the four main concepts which always occupy the center of the stage in Tönnies' thinking. It is hoped that the accompanying table will assist the reader in determining the role played by the various concepts, whether related to group or to individual action.

The original book, to use Stoltenberg's[1] apt characterization, resembles the beauty of an old castle with many annexes, each dating back to a different century. The purpose of these "Notes," which deal only with *Gemeinschaft und Gesellschaft,* is to indicate to the reader that, despite the lack of a perfectly logically ordered construction in the original, the various segments have meaning when considered in relation to the whole. For instance, it has been suggested that, since the foundation for the work comprises the forms of will, Part Two, in which they are developed, might have come first.[2] The reader will find that Part One contains concepts characteristic of Gemeinschaft, such as home, village, and town (I:18), which are not matched by concepts characteristic of Gesellschaft before Part Three is reached. Part One is based primarily upon the simple, vegetative forms; Part Three, upon the various animal and mental forms.

It is through the use of these concepts that a chaotic world is made to appear to have order and meaning. As Tönnies reminds his readers, "... the artificial, even forced, character of these abstractions must always be kept clearly in mind ..." (III:31). "The concepts of the forms of will [and this holds for the forms of group life] are nothing but products of thought, tools devised in order to facilitate the understanding of reality.... As free and arbitrary products of thinking, these normal concepts are mutually exclusive; rational will and natural will are strictly separate entities," as is the case with the group forms Gemeinschaft and Gesellschaft. However, "... Observation and inference will easily show that no natural will can ever occur empirically without rational will by which it finds expression, and no rational will without natural will on which it is based" (II:25). Further, "every organized body of human beings can be considered a kind of organism, an artificially constructed but organic implement, as well as an instrument or a tool" (III:28). To understand the table the following may be pertinent:

THE INDIVIDUAL APPROACH

Basic to the discussion of the forms of individual will (Part Two) is the assumption that body and mind constitute a unity. *Wesenwille*, which has been translated as *natural will*,[3] but might well have been designated as integral will, is described as "the psychological equivalent of the human body" (II:2) which contains as well as maintains the brain. *Kürwille*, translated as *rational will*,[3] is thought of in relation to the brain controlling and guiding the body (II:3). The more naturally developed organic *natural will* "which includes the thinking" (II:1) and the more artificial, made, mechanical *rational will*, which is "the thinking which encompasses the will" (II:1), have "in common the fact that they are conceived as the causes for or tendencies toward action.... *Natural will* contains the future in embryo or emergent form; *rational will* contains it as an image" (II:2).

As respective carriers of these two forms of will or *freedom* (II: 20), there is on the one hand the *self* (III:1), and on the other, the *person* (III:2), with their corresponding *motives* and *directions* (II:10). These two forms of will are each divided into three chief forms: namely, the *vegetative, animal*, and *mental (human)* wills (II:5).[4] The three chief functions which are applicable to both natural and rational will are: for the vegetative will, (1)[5] the *temperament* with its *conduct;* for the animal will, (2) the *character* and its *actions;* for mental will, (3) *intellectual attitude* and its *judgments* (II:25). These three fundamental forms of individual will are divided further into four special forms: two *simple* forms, one of which falls under natural will and one under rational will, and two *mixed* or *complex forms,* one chiefly dominated by natural will and one chiefly by rational will (II:9 and 12). The *simple forms* corresponding to the *vegetative, animal, and mental* orders are for natural will, respectively, 1.[5] liking, 2. habit, and 3. memory (II:6,7,8), and for rational will, respectively, 4. *deliberation*, 5. *discrimination*, and 6. *conception* (II:11). See the Table of Concepts, on pages 268-69.

The *mixed* or *complex* forms of natural will which find their expression in these general forms "which involve and influence the elements of rational will" (II:9) may be called *urges*, of which there are three kinds corresponding to the *vegetative, animal,* and *mental* will, called, respectively, (1) *passion*, (2) *courage*, and (3) *genius* (II:9). Corresponding respectively to these three urges are the *urge to live,* the *urge to action*, and the *urge to create.* The *mixed* or *complex* forms of rational will which contain "elements of natural will" in them are (II:12) for the *vegetative, animal,* and *mental* wills, respectively, (4) *intention*, (5) *calculation*, and (6) *consciousness*. These mixed or complex forms, *passion, courage,* and *genius,* along with the *virtues* and *excellencies* designated as *energy, valor,* and *industry,* are further characterized by *sentiment, mind and heart,* and *conscience,* and *sincerity, kindness,* and *faithfulness,* concepts used in relation to other people (II:9). The further corresponding mixed or complex forms of rational will are not designated as virtues but are characterized by *contemplativeness, cleverness,* and *enlightenedness* (II:15).

In the sphere of *rational* will, where one is "indifferent" to "the weal and woe of other people" and where "human beings" are treated "like inanimate objects and tools" (II:16), there are no special characteristics relative to action toward others such as are listed as (1) *sentiment,* (2) *mind and heart,* and (3) *conscience* under the mixed or complex forms of natural will. There are only the three forms: (1) *lust for pleasure,* in *self-interest* and *vanity;* (2) *greediness,* in *greed for money* and *greed for profits;* and (3) *thirst for power,* in *ambition* and *thirst for knowledge* (II:14). Here the first subordinate form under each of the three forms, *lust for pleasure, greediness,* and *thirst for power,* refers to "the pleasures of the lower 'parts of the soul' of the great mass of people," the second form refers more to pleasures of "the upper parts, of the few, the select, the distinguished" (II:14).

In the third section of Part Two the concepts are used in an attempt to interpret segments of existing conditions. Natural will is claimed to be characteristic of *women, youth,* and the *common people,* who are more governed by *shame* and *belief* and are by nature *softer, warmer,* and *deeper.* Rational will is found to be characteristic of *men, aged persons,* and the *educated classes,* who are more influenced by *thirst for knowledge, disbelief, clever reasoning,* and are in comparison *hard, cold,* and *superficial.*

THE GROUP APPROACH

The forms of social or group will have their basis in individual will. As previously stated, there are three functions of individual will which are influenced both by rational will and by natural will and are consequently designated as "neutral" functions. These are: (1) *temperament,* (2) *character,* and (3) *intellectual attitude.* Corresponding to these three functions of individual will are three forms based on social will: (1) *order* (natural law), (2) *law,* as such (positive law), and (3) *morality* (ideal law) (IV:1 and 3). See the Table of Concepts, on pages 268-69.

Gemeinschaft and Gesellschaft, like natural will and rational will, may each be broken into two forms: (1) the *partial forms (Teilformen)* and (2) the *whole forms (Gesamtformen),* to use Stoltenberg's terminology.[6] As may be inferred from the table and from the text, these partial forms and whole forms are closely related.

The *partial forms* of group natural will are 1. *understanding,* 2. *custom,* 3. *belief, faith* or *creed;* those of group rational will are 4. *contract,* 5. *regulations* and/or *by-laws,* 6. *doctrine.*

The *whole forms* of group natural will are (1) *concord,* (2) *folkways and mores,* and (3) *religion;* those of rational will are (4) *convention,* (5) *legislation,* and (6) *public opinion.*

Although these *partial* and *whole forms* of social or group will are no doubt generalized on a different plane than the simple and mixed or complex forms of individual will, they are related. Thus, the simple forms of individual will—1. *liking,* 2. *habit,* 3. *memory,* 4. *deliberation,* 5. *discrimination,* and 6. *conception*—are respectively related to the partial forms of social or group will—1. *understanding,* 2. *custom,* 3. *belief, faith* or *creed,* 4. *contract,* 5. *regulations* and/or *by-laws,* and 6. *doctrine.* Similar relationships for the mixed or complex forms of individual will and the whole forms of group will may be noted from the table (III:21 and IV:7).

Also, a further relationship between these forms of individual and group will may be mentioned. On the side of the individual will, *natural disposition of the self* (II:9 and 26) being characteristic of natural will, and *apparatus* (II:12 and 26) or *person* being characteristic of rational will, may be compared with the Gemeinschaft-like *culture of the people (Volkstum)* and Gesellschaft-like *civilization of the state (Staatstum)* (IV:3).

This leads us to the actual groups discussed by Tönnies. Two "neutral" groups, *union* and *association* (I: Subject of Investigation, 1; and III:12 ff.) have characteristics of both of the chief concepts of the work, *Gemeinschaft und Gesellschaft.* The former, possessing "closed unity" (III:12), has more in common with Gemeinschaft, which is based upon natural will and is "essentially united" (I:19), being analogous to a "living organism" (I: Subject of Investigation, 1); the latter, characterized by "loose relationships" (III:12) has more in common with Gesellschaft, which is based upon rational will and is "essentially separated" (I:19) and analogous to a "mechanical aggregate" (I: Subject of Investigation, 1).

On the "forms of individual natural will"—1. *liking,* 2. *habit,* and 3. *memory*—rest the various types of unions or associations (III:12) of Gemeinschaft: (a) *Gemeinschaft of blood,* or (b) *kinship,* (a) the *Gemeinschaft of place,* or (b) *neighborhood* and especially (see Table of Concepts, pages 268-69, for other forms) (e) *commonwealth* and *fellowship,* and (a) *Gemeinschaft of mind,* or (b) *friendship.* As indicated by the table, there are fewer corresponding terms specified for the unions and associations of Gesellschaft (I:6; and III:28). They are all composed of persons who stand on business or trading terms one with another much as the merchant is related to his customers (I:25). They could be called exchange associations. There are also labor associations (I:23). The more Gesellschaft-like association of the *special-interest* type is, as indicated in the table, set off against the Gemeinschaft-like type of *fellowship* (III:28). Other contrasts, as indicated by Stoltenberg, will be noted in the table just as *commonwealth* is matched with *state.* The *Handwörterbuch* article, which appeared in 1931, and is included in this translation as Part Five, "The Summing Up," on pages 237-59, refers to social relationships, collectives, and organizations or corporations. Their characteristics have been explained in the "Introduction."

The Gemeinschaft-like life in the *family, village,* and *town* are paired respectively with the Gesellschaft-like life in the *city, nation,* and cosmopolitan, national, and world *metropolis.* Along with these types of life and culture, Tönnies specifies predominant occupations and systems of human endeavor of Gemeinschaft as *home* (or *household*) *economy, agriculture,* and art, and those of Gesellschaft as *trade, industry,* and science (IV:7).

CULTURAL CHANGES

As the reader will have gathered from the "Introduction" and the text, Tönnies believed that as time passes, natural will tends to be supplanted by rational will, Gemeinschaft by Gesellschaft.

"In the same way as the individual natural will evolves into pure thinking and rational will, which tends to dissolve and subjugate its predecessors, the original collective forms of Gemeinschaft have developed into Gesellschaft and the rational will of the Gesellschaft. In the course of history, folk culture has given rise to the civilization of the state"

(IV:3). Each of the concepts in the various trilogies also represent stages of development. Thus, the vegetative is portrayed as the "original," as the "basis" (II:9), finally as the roots (III:21) and "the foundation of all other kinds of life" (II:5). This must be remembered when thinking in terms of *animal* and *mental* life. Thus, in the case of mental life, "the entire third category should be understood as retroactive modification of the second category; and this second one has the same relation toward the first" (II:5). Opponents of the social organic school, in fairness to Tönnies, should not turn away from him at this point. He was himself a stern critic of the organic theory but recognized the importance of the biological continuity of the life of groups and the consequences involved. However, this development of the vegetative, first to the animal and finally to the mental, complicates Tönnies' system.[7] Thus, the "whole development" in the "period of Gemeinschaft" may be sketched in the table for the group approach by following in a vertical direction the development from (d) *family* (or house) to (d) *village*, then to (d) *town* (IV:8) in approaching Gesellschaft, whereas the development of the individual will can be sketched in the horizontal direction from natural will to rational will, which amounts to the same thing as the development from the predominance of vegetative, to the animal and then to mental and intellectual life (II:10).

It will be noted that the highest stage of natural will—3. *memory*— and the lowest stage of rational will—4. *deliberation*—are, as in the case of (d) *town* and (d) *city*, separated by only one stage (IV:4). Thus, in both the psychical development and the group development there are six stages, one following another, as designated in the table.

TABLE OF CONCEPTS

	Individual Will			I. PSYCHICAL (Part Two)		Individual Will		
	Simple Forms	Mixed or Complex Forms — Urge	Virtue	Temperament / Character / Intellectual Attitude	Policy	Mixed or Complex Forms — Endeavor	Simple Forms	
Vegetative — 1. Motive; 2. Embryo; 3. Heart; 4. Feeling; 5. Shame; 6. Belief	1. Liking — Development and Efforts	(1) Passion — Urge to Live — Sensuality — Sentiment	Energy — Earnestness — Sincerity	**Temperament — Conduct:** Man / Woman	Contemplativeness	(4) Intention — Lust for Pleasure — Self-interest — Vanity	4. Deliberation — End or Purpose	1. Direction; 2. Model or Image; 3. Head; 4. Intellect; 5. Thirst for Knowledge; 6. Disbelief
7. Womanhood — NATURAL WILL								7. Manhood — RATIONAL WILL
Animal — 8. Self; 9. Natural Disposition; 10. Natural; 11. Organ; 12. Organic	2. Habit — Experience and Practice	(2) Courage — Urge to Action — Intelligence — Mind and Heart	Valor — Diligence — Kindness	**Character — Actions:** Old Age / Youth	Cleverness	(5) Calculation — Greediness — Greed for Money — Greed for Profits	5. Discrimination — Reasons	8. Person; 9. Apparatus; 10. Artificial; 11. Tool; 12. Mechanical
Mental (Human) — 13. Fluid; 14. Soft; 15. Warm; 16. Deep	3. Memory — Learning and Work	(3) Genius — Urge to Create — Reason — Conscience	Industry — Care — Faithfulness	**Intellectual Attitude — Judgments:** Educated Classes / Common People	Enlightenedness	(6) Consciousness — Thirst for Power — Ambition — Thirst for Knowledge	6. Conceptions — Principle	13. Solid; 14. Hard; 15. Cold; 16. Superficial

		Group Will		Predominant Occupations	II. GROUP (SOCIAL) (Parts One and Three) Associations (Unions)	Predominant Occupations	Group Will		
		Partial Forms	Whole Forms				Whole Forms	Partial Forms	
Vegetative	1. Organism 2. Family 3. People (*Volkstum*)	1. Understanding	(1) Concord Family Spirit	Home or Household Economy	⌐Order⌐ a. Gemeinschaft of Blood b. Kinship c. Mother and Child d. Family (*Volk*) e. People — d. City e. Gesellschaft or Organization	Trade	(4) Convention	4. Contract	1. Mechanism 2. Society Life 3. State (*Staatstum*) 4. Socialism 5. Civilization
Animal	4. Communism 5. Culture GEMEINSCHAFT 6. Land Field and Soil 7. Possession 8. Work and Labor	2. Custom	(2) Folkways and Mores Law of Custom Family Law	Agriculture	⌐Law⌐ a. Gemeinschaft of Place b. Neighborhood c. Husband and Wife d. Village e. Commonwealth (Fellowship) — d. Nation e. State (Special-Interest Group)	Industry	(5) Legislation Legislative Law Law of Contracts	5. Regulations and/or By-laws	GESELLSCHAFT 6. Money 7. Wealth 8. Barter and Exchange 9. Appropriation 10. Business
Mental (Human)	9. Creation 10. Calling	3. Belief, Faith or Creed	(3) Religion	Art (Poetry)	⌐Morality⌐ a. Gemeinschaft of Mind b. Friendship c. Brother and Sister d. Town e. Church — d. Metropolis e. Republic of Scholars	Science (Prose)	(6) Public Opinion	6. Doctrine	

NOTES AND SELECTED
BIBLIOGRAPHY

NOTES

To Introduction

1. Introducing an abridged and simplified version of *Gemeinschaft und Gesellschaft,* August Baltzer in 1890 wrote, "Before us lies a book so thought-provoking and so uniquely written that we wish our contemporaries had the strong wills and intellectual fortitude to master it." Baltzer also states that one must carefully and repeatedly read the book to grasp its significance (p. 44), and further that if it is understood it will become a regulator in the political sense as have Kant's categories in applied thought.

2. Hans Freyer, "Ferdinand Tönnies und seine Stellung in der deutschen Soziologie," *Weltwirtschaftliches Archiv,* July, 1936, pp. 1 ff.

3. *Ibid.* Also see the Introduction to the first, second, and third editions of *Gemeinschaft und Gesellschaft,* 1887; and Karl Dunkmann, "Die Bedeutung der Kategorien Gemeinschaft und Gesellschaft für die Geisteswissenschaften," *Kölner Vierteljahrshefte für Soziologie* 5. Jahrg. 1925, Heft ½ , pp. 35 ff.

4. Tönnies himself states that, being influenced by Spinoza and Hobbes, he was greatly concerned by the controversy between the legal historians and the exponents of natural law. He realized along with the Hegelians that the legal historians lacked philosophical balance. Also he came to the conclusion that the students of natural law failed to express rationally the difference between animal and human groups. He thought that this difference must be expressed in terms of the human volition and thought, and that communal institutions of early times with their customary laws must be based upon an entirely different type of human will and thought than the institutions of later, more individualistic times. From this sprang the "idea of an antinomy." (See also Introduction to the first, second, and third editions, *op cit.*) See Ferdinand Tönnies, "Entwicklung der Soziologie in Deutschland im 19.

Jahrhundert," in *Entwicklung der deutschen Volkswirt-schaft-slehre im* 19. *Jahrhundert,* 1908; and Albert Salomon's article, "In Memoriam, Ferdinand Tönnies (1855-1936)," *Social Research,* August, 1936, which stresses the tremendous influence which the law of nature had upon his writings.

5. This *Geist der Neuzeit,* 1935, which was begun many years before it was published, was the first volume of a proposed treatise on modern life with which Tönnies planned to supplement *Gemeinschaft und Gesellschaft.*

6. In the preface to the fourth and fifth editions of *Gemeinschaft und Gesellschaft,* Tönnies disclaims any intended pessimism, saying that he did not deny the true facts of progress and enlightenment as well as the development of freedom and civilization. He said further that he was no believer in romanticism nor in O. Spengler's *Decline of the West,* a book which appeared long after the first edition of *Gemeinschaft und Gesellschaft* and may have been influenced by it. As pointed out by Heberle, Tönnies would probably have criticized certain aspects of the feudal system of the Middle Ages just as mercilessly as he did modern individualism had he lived in the earlier period; see "The Sociology of Ferdinand Tönnies," by Rudolf Heberle, *American Sociological Review,* Vol. 2, No. I, February, 1937.

    See also "Individuum und Welt in der Neuzeit," *Weltwirtschaftliches Archiv,* Band I, 1, 1913. Here Tönnies wrote: "Modern culture is in an incessant process of decomposition. Its progress is its distinction." Citation originally quoted by Eduard Rosenbaum.

    See also August Baltzer, *op. cit.,* p. 44, who refers to Paulsen's contention that Tönnies' book, *Gemeinschaft und Gesellschaft,* contained a note of pessimistic resignation, as follows: "... I am convinced that repeated careful reading will lead to the conviction that it was we who read the pessimistic resignation into the book."

7. In the article "Mein Verhältnis zur Soziologie," in *Soziologie von heute,* Leipzig, 1932, Tönnies answers his critics, especially Leopold von Wiese and Franz Oppenheimer, and traces in detail the various influences which led to his concepts of society.

8. *Geist der Neuzeit, op. cit.,* p. 134.

9. See especially Tönnies' *Einführung in die Soziologie,* Stuttgart, 1931, p. 269; see also his *Die Entwicklung der sozialen Frage,* Leipzig, 1907; 4. Auflage "bis zum Weltkrieg," Berlin, 1926.

10. *Rudolf Heberle, op. cit.*

11. Tönnies, *Fortschritt und Soziale Entwicklung, Geschichtsphiloso-phische Ansichten,* Karlsruhe, 1926.

12. Tönnies, *Die Sitte*, Frankfurt am Main, 1909.
13. Tönnies, *Kritik der off entlichen Meinung, Berlin,* 1922.
14. Many years before Max Weber wrote about and used Ideal Types, Tönnies had begun using what he called normal concepts or types *(Normalbegriffe)*.
15. *Soziologische Studien und Kritiken,* II, Jena, 1926, p. 131; also "Philosophical Terminology" (see *Mind, A Quarterly Review of Psychology and Philosophy,* Vol. VIII, 1899, p. 292): "Conceptual matter is the iron which we, as thinkers, have to forge. Many kinds of implements must be made thereof; for digging, for plowing, for fighting, for forging itself. Scientific thought is not a matter of chance. It must be learned by hard work and practiced in persistent endurance and eager striving; its rules and methods must be known." However, it was not Tönnies' purpose merely to build concepts. These were only a means to an end. His life's objective was the understanding of reality. See Ernst Jurkat, "Die Soziologie von Ferdinand Tönnies," *Geistige Arbeit,* November 5, 1936, p. 7; also, Karl Dunkmann, *op. cit.*
16. Alfred Vierkandt, who credits Tönnies as founding German sociology with his book *Gemeinschaft und Gesellschaft,* emphasizes the fact that it combines the historical and formal approaches. "Ferdinand Tönnies' Werk und seine Weiterbildung in der Gegenwart," *Kant Studien, Philosophische Zeitschrift,* 30. Band, Berlin, Pan-Verlag Rolf Heise, 1925, pp. 299-300.
17. *Einführung in die Soziologie, op. cit.,* and "Einteilung der Soziologie," in *Zeitschrift* für *die gesamte Staatswissenschaft,* LXXIX, 1925, also published in *Atti del V. congresso internazionale di filosofia,* Napoli, 1925.
18. See notes 1 and 2 on pages 284-85. See also the Table of Concepts, on pages 268-69, for a schematic treatment of the concepts included in the translation which are related to Gemeinschaft and Gesellschaft.
19. From a translation of an article written by Tönnies on "Philosophical Terminology," the following statements relative to the subject of will are pertinent:

    "21. ... By social will in general we mean the will which is valid for a number of men, i.e., which determines their individual wills in the same sense, insofar as they themselves are thought of as subjects (originators or sustainers) of this will which is common to them and binds them together.

    "22. By individual human will we mean here every existing combination of ideas (thoughts and feelings) which, working independently, acts in such a way as to facilitate and hasten, or hinder and check, other (similar) combinations of ideas (makes them probable or improbable).

"23. In this sense human will may be thought of as the cause of human activities or conscious omissions are, from a psychological point of view, nothing but successions of ideas."—"Philosophical Terminology," by Ferdinand Tönnies, in *Mind, A Quarterly Review of Psychology and Philosophy,* New Series, Vol. VIII, No. 29, January, 1899.

20. See "Notes on Tönnies' Fundamental Concepts," on pages 263-70, for the interrelationship of various concepts used by Tönnies.

21. *Tönnies' Kritik der öffentlichen Meinung, op. cit.,* p. 18. Tönnies identifies natural will as that which is included in Max Weber's *Wertrationalen*, or emotional *(affectuellen)* and traditional behavior; *Einführung in die Soziologie, op. cit.,* p. 6.

22. The "Sermon on the Mount" has been referred to as containing examples of Gemeinschaft-like behavior, conditioned by natural will. Alfred Vierkandt, *Gesellschaftslehre,* Verlag von Ferdinand Enke, Stuttgart, 1923. Also Dale Carnegie's very popular book, *How to Win Friends and Influence People,* 1936, offers many examples of how rational will may function in a Gesellschaft-like society.

23. Tönnies is probably open to greater criticism for his use of this distinction than on any other grounds. He uses it frequently in comparing occupational groups and periods of time. For example, he described the Middle Ages as being more feminine, the modern period as being more masculine, agriculture and art being occupations relatively more suitable for women, trade and war more suitable for men. See *Geist der Neuzeit, op. cit.,* and *Fortschritt und Soziale Entwicklung, op. cit.* Many who consider men and women identical in most important respects may smile at such ideas. However, the fact remains that cultures everywhere make sex and age distinctions in dress and require different behavior from men and women, as well as from younger and older people. It is probably no coincidence that the suicide rate is higher among men than among women, and increases with age for both sexes. According to Tönnies, just as the urbanite tends to lean more in the direction of Gesellschaft than the peasant, so do people without families more than those having families, strangers more than natives, free thinkers more than those whose thoughts are conditioned by religion, people living in thickly-settled areas more than those living in more sparsely settled regions, people who live on the sea more than those living inland, people living on streams or other arteries

of communication more than those who are isolated, people living in valleys more than those in the mountains, city people more than town people, people of capital cities more than provincial people, people of metropolises more than other cities, craftsmen more than peasants, worldly rulers more than religious leaders, capitalistic leaders more than the landed nobility. "Der Begriff der Gemeinschaft," *Soziologische Studien und Kritiken, op. cit.,* Band II, pp. 274 and 275.

24. "Zweck und Mittel im sozialen Leben," by Ferdinand Tönnies, in *Hauptprobleme der Soziologie, Erinnerungsgabe für Max Weber,* 1923. Also, *"Zur Einteilung der Soziologie,"* in *Soziologische Studien und Kritiken,* Band I, pp. 73 ff. T. Parsons has written a brief but penetrating analysis of Tönnies' relation to his theory of social action and analytical realism. To determine whether or not an action or a relationship is based upon rational or natural will, one may inquire of the parties concerning their motives for entering such a relationship. If the motive is specific and limited, it is rational; for example, "Why did you and Jones form the Jones-Smith partnership?" answered by, "To pool our resources, thereby increasing our profits"; or "Why did you go into that store?" answered by, "To buy some cigarettes." Where natural will is involved, the end is not so specific and easily stated; in such cases many considerations are involved, some to our own interest, others not; for example, "Why did you marry?" or "Why are you and John friends?" See Talcott Parsons, *The Structure of Social Action,* 2nd ed., Glencoe, Illinois, 1949. Tönnies did not carry the discussion of the means-ends schema into its manifold ramifications, and his use of it was chiefly on the descriptive level.

25. For a description of the contrasting characteristics of possessions or belongings *(Besitz)* and of property or wealth *(Eigentum),* see "Eigentum," by Ferdinand Tönnies, in *Handwörterbuch der Soziologie,* 1931. In the translation the two terms in *Gemeinschaft und Gesellschaft* which are set off as opposites, *Besitz* and *Vermögen,* have been translated respectively as "possession" and "wealth." See "Notes on Tönnies' Fundamental Concepts," on pages 263-70 of this book.

26. Here religion is meant to coincide with that which is sacred as contrasted with that which is secular. As Tönnies points out, many religious leaders are impelled by rational will and some of the activities of even the Catholic Church were highly rational in the modern world. See *Fortschritt und Soziale Entwicklung, op. cit.*

27. E. Durkheim, after stating that it was regrettable that the terms Gemeinschaft and Gesellschaft were untranslatable, criticized Tönnies for his characterization of Gesellschaft as being of the nature of a mechanical aggregate. Durkheim claimed that early societies were no more organic than present-day societies, and emphasized the collective nature of the latter. He recognized Gemeinschaft as a stage in social development considered desirable by Hegel and characterized as status by Maine, as well as the subsequent stage, Gesellschaft, which resembled Spencer's industrial society, in which there prevailed conditions analyzed by Bentham, and Maine's condition of contract. Durkheim's attention was attracted to Tönnies' belief that historically the communal life of Gemeinschaft was supplanted by the socialism of Gesellschaft, and that this Gesellschaft failed to offer the paradise presaged by the Marxians. See Durkheim's review of the 1887 edition of *Gemeinschaft und Gesellschaft* in *Revue Philosophique* XXVII, 1889, pp. 416 ff. This review is interesting, occurring as it does four years before his own *De la Division du Travail Social*, published in 1893. Durkheim's dichotomy, *solidarité méchanique* and *solidarité organique,* appearing in this later volume are types which although differently conceived correspond respectively to Tönnies' Gemeinschaft and Gesellschaft. Although Durkheim's frame of reference is essentially different from that of Tönnies, some have commented upon an apparent contrast in the meaning of the two concepts employed by the two men. See P. A. Sorokin, *Contemporary Sociological Theories*, New York, p. 491. In a review of Durkheim's *Les Règles de la Méthode Sociologique,* Paris, 1895, Tönnies states that what Durkheim calls "social facts" he himself has named "social will." Tönnies further states that G. Tarde's criticism of Durkheim resulted from Tarde's misunderstanding of, and failure to recognize, the fact that social facts must have something independent of "individual consciences." Tönnies, however, further states that Tarde is right in criticizing Durkheim for constructing sociological concepts without psychological foundation. See *Archiv für systematische Philosophie,* Band IV, 1898, pp. 495 ff.

28. Tönnies has frequently been accused of establishing two mutually exclusive concepts with no intervening gradations. See a review by Tönnies in *Archiv für systematische Philosophie,* Band IV, *op. cit.,* p. 486, in which he takes both A. Vierkandt and Wundt to task for somewhat similar accusations. In this review he also states that his psychological distinctions come from the speech of the common people. For example, they speak of individuals being without heart,

scruples, or principles. In such individuals rational will predominates but does not exclude natural will entirely.

29. These are best described in *Einführung in die Soziologie, op. cit.* Tönnies calls a complex of relations of more than two persons a social circle *(sozialer Kreis).*

30. Ibid., and Tönnies, "Stände und Klassen," in *Handwörterbuch der Soziologie, op. cit.*

31. Some of Tönnies' works in this field are listed in the Selected Bibliography, on pages 287-89.

32. For a more detailed discussion of social relationships under various types of authority in *Gemeinschaft und Gesellschaft,* see Rudolf Heberle, "Zur Theorie der Herrschaftsverhältnisse bei Tönnies," in *Kolner Vierteljahrshefte für Soziologie,* 1925, Heft ½ , *zum* 70. *Geburtstage von Ferdinand Tönnies,* pp. 51 ff.

33. In *Einführung in die Soziologie, op. cit.,* Tönnies places social values before social norms. See also Parsons' brief statement of the relationship of Tönnies' norms to those of Max Weber. In Gesellschaft where contractual relations prevail the obligations are specific and positively defined. The burden of proof is on him who would require the performance of an obligation not explicitly and obviously assumed. In Gemeinschaft the opposite is true and relationships "blanket in" many obligations. If a member of one's family be sick and unable to help himself, one must aid the sick party even though he be disliked and has done nothing to merit such aid. The burden of proof is on him who would evade such an obligation. In a business relationship devoid of friendship or other Gemeinschaft characteristics, one will scarcely render such aid unless it be a part of an agreement. Also, in Gemeinschaft infraction by an individual of a given norm is judged in terms of the attitudes involved, whereas in Gesellschaft these are immaterial.

34. Tönnies was fond of these biological analogies. They play a greater role in *Gemeinschaft und Gesellschaft* than in subsequent works, but are found elsewhere. See *Einführung in die Soziologie,* p. 207, where the three social entities, social relationships, collectives, and social organizations or corporations, are respectively characterized as vegetative, animal, and human. See Tönnies, "The Present Problems of Social Structure," in *The American Journal of Sociology,* March, 1905, Vol. X, No. 5. Here he refers to these three planes of development and discusses the problems of the biological, psychological, and sociological approach to the study of social structures. Also in Tönnies' discussion of the theories of Karl Marx he refers to these three gradations of developments; see

Marx, Leben und Lehre, 1921, p. 123. Such analogies are found
in writings of the German Romanticists. See *Novalis' Schriften,*
Verlag C. Reimer, Berlin, 1838, 3. Teil, p. 240.

35. *Einführung in die Soziologie, op. cit.,* p. 204.

36. A more complete schematic treatment of the relationships of the
other concepts and these norms will be found in the Table of Concepts, on pages 268-69.

37. E. Rosenbaum, *op. cit.,* compares Tönnies' theory of natural law
with that of Hugo, Lassalle, Grotius, Kant, Hegel, A. Müller, Savigny, A. Wagner, Gierke, Jhering, Jung, Stammler, and others.

38. Tönnies, *Die Sitte, op. cit.,* p. 35.

39. The Natural Law of the Romans and Natural Law philosophers
is not the "original natural law" of Tönnies. Chronologically the
development of the Natural Law as conceived in Rome and by the
German lawyers of the 16th century followed the customary and
special laws of the many peoples involved. A general rational law
involving many peoples, whether called "natural" or not, is a Gesellschaft-like phenomenon and possible of enforcement only after individuals are emancipated from many family and provincial
bonds as well as many beliefs, inherited customs, traditions, and
superstitions of the Gemeinschaft. Merely because some universal-
ities have been found in the customs of peoples does not justify the
assumption that rational or natural law, the law to which lawyers
may resort when many peoples are involved, is natural in the sense
of being original or organically rooted in the customs of the peoples. For Tönnies such "natural law" stands opposed to customary
law, and the "original natural law" of the Gemeinschaft.

40. "Das Wesen der Soziologie," *Soziologische Studien und Kritiken,*
op. cit., Band I, p. 353. However, Tönnies wrote that sociologists
worried their readers by continually reminding them that man
is a social being; for it was just as true that man is an egotistical
unsocial being. In a sense each person is an enemy of every other,
and socially co-operative only as a means to the attaining of a livelihood. Both theses must be considered. On one is based the theory
of Gemeinschaft; on the other, the theory of Gesellschaft.

41. *Einführung in die Soziologie, op. cit.,* p. 135, and "Einteilung der
Soziologie," *op. cit.,* p. 10.

42. See E. Jurkat, "Das soziologische Wertproblem," J. Scheible's
Verlag, Kiel, 1932. See also Table of Concepts, on pages 268-69,
for the schematic treatment of related concepts.

43. "The Sociology of Ferdinand Tönnies," *op. cit.;* see also "Sozio-gra-
phie," in *Handwörterbuch der Soziologie, op. cit.,* pp. 564 ff.

44. See Von Wiese's criticism and Tönnies' reply in "Mein Verhältnis zur Soziologie," *op. cit.* Earlier in 1901 Tönnies said sociologists were interested in antagonistic relationships but only as a biologist might be interested in unorganized substances. They were not the object of investigation. "Das Wesen der Soziologie," *Soziologische Studien und Kritiken, op. cit.,* Band I, p. 355.

45. *Einführung in die Soziologie, op. cit.,* IX.

46. *Ibid.,* XI, and *Fortschritt und Soziale Entwicklung, op. cit.,* p. 142.

47. For example, he welcomed H. Spencer's later recognition of co-operatives as a possible solution of the labor problem. It, he said, let the Spencerian bars down, allowing in the evolution from status to contract another possibility than the changes to the entrepreneur-worker types of industrial organization. Spencer should, said Tönnies, when claiming that the possibility of such co-operatives depends upon the improvement of human character, admit that the existing commercial greed and competition might be mitigated through prevalence of co-operatives; this would destroy his position as rational anarchist and weaken his liberalistic philosophy which identified progress with personal freedom. See Tönnies' review of Spencer's *A System of Synthetic Philosophy*, 1896, in *Archiv für systematische Philosophie,* Band IV, 1898, pp. 498 ff.

48. Émile Durkheim, *The Division of Labor in Society* (translated from the first French edition, 1893, by George Simpson), Glencoe, Illinois, 1933. See also note 27 above.

49. Émile Durkheim, *Suicide* (translated from the 1930 French edition—first edition 1897—by John A. Spaulding and George Simpson), Glencoe, Illinois, 1951.

50. Charles H. Cooley, *Social Organization,* New York, 1909, pp. 23-31.

51. Charles H. Cooley, Robert C. Angell, and Lowell J. Carr, *Introductory Sociology*, New York, 1933, pp. 55-56.

52. Charles H. Cooley, *Social Organization, op. cit.,* p. 5.

53. For a brief and yet comprehensive statement on the study of the primary group, with particular attention to the contributions of Mayo, Lewin, and Moreno, see Edward A. Shils, "The Study of the Primary Group," in Daniel Lerner and Harold D. Lasswell, *The Policy Sciences,* Stanford, 1951, pp. 44-69.

54. Recent commentaries on the typology would include: George M. Foster, "What is Folk Culture," *American Anthropologist*, Vol. 55, April-June, 1953, pp. 159-173; Oscar Lewis, *Life in a Mexican Village: Tepoztlan Revisited*, Urbana, Illinois, 1951; Horace Miner, "The Folk-Urban Continuum," *American Sociological Review,* Vol. 17, October, 1952, pp. 529-537; Howard W. Odum, "Folk Sociology

as a Subject Field for the Historical Study of Total Human Society and the Empirical Study of Group Behavior," *Social Forces*, Vol. 31, March, 1953, pp. 193-223; and Fred W. Voget, "The Folk Society: An Anthropological Application," *Social Forces*, Vol. 33, December, 1954, pp. 105-113.

55. To cite just some of the examples of the use of the continuum see Horace Miner, *St. Denis: A French-Canadian Parish*, Chicago, 1939; Herbert Passin and John W. Bennett, "Changing Agricultural Magic in Southern Illinois: A Systematic Analysis of Folk-Urban Transitions," *Social Forces*, Vol. 22, October, 1943, pp. 98-106; Edward Spicer, *Pasqua: A Yaqui Village in Arizona*, Chicago, 1940. Some of the more significant criticisms are contained in the following: Neal Gross, "Cultural Variables in Rural Communities," *American Journal of Sociology*, Vol. 53, March, 1948, pp. 344-350; Oscar Lewis, *op. cit.;* Julian Steward, *Area Research: Concepts and Methods*, New York, 1950; Gideon Sjoberg, "The Preindustrial City," *American Journal of Sociology*, Vol. 60, March, 1955, pp. 438-445; and Howard Becker, "Sacred and Secular Societies: Considered with Reference to Folk-State and Similar Classifications," *Social Forces*, Vol. 28, May, 1950, pp. 361-376.

56. Robert Redfield, "The Folk Society," *American Journal of Sociology*, Vol. 52, January, 1947, p. 295.

57. Robert Redfield, *Tepoztlan, A Mexican Village*, Chicago, 1930.

58. Robert Redfield, "Rural Sociology and the Folk Society," *Rural Sociology*, Vol. 8, March, 1943, pp. 68-71.

59. See in particular Howard Becker, *Through Values to Social Interpretation*, Durham, N. C., 1950, pp. 248-280; and "1951 Commentary on Value-System Terminology" in Howard Becker and Harry E. Barnes, *Social Thought from Lore to Science*, second edition, Washington, D. C., 1952, pp. i-xxii.

60. Becker describes a sacrilization process in *German Youth: Bond or Free*, New York, 1946.

61. See Howard Becker, *Through Values to Social Interpretation, op. cit.*, p. 264 and p. 276 for schematic presentation of the subtypes.

62. Charles P. Loomis and J. Allan Beegle, *Rural Social Systems*, New York, 1950.

63. Pitirim A. Sorokin, *The Crisis of Our Age*, New York, 1942, Ch.5.

64. Pitirim A. Sorokin, *Social and Cultural Dynamics*, Vol. 3, p. 40. See also *Society, Culture, and Personality*, New York, 1947, pp. 93 118.

65. We define as "action" any concrete system maintained by a sequence of what Parsons calls "unit acts." "In a unit act there are

identifiable as minimum characteristics the following: (1) an end, (2) a situation, analyzable in turn into (a) means and (b) conditions, and (3) at least one selective standard in terms of which the end is related to the situation." *The Structure of Social Action,* second edition, Glencoe, Illinois, 1949, p. 77.

66. Max Weber, *The Theory of Social and Economic* Organization, translated by A. M. Henderson and Talcott Parsons, New York, 1947, p. 115. See also notes 21 and 33 above.

67. Talcott Parsons and Edward A. Shils (eds.), *Toward a General Theory of Action,* Cambridge, Mass., 1951, pp. 76-91.

68. Talcott Parsons, *The Structure of Social Action, op. cit.,* p. 694. See note 24 above.

69. For an extensive development of the pattern-variables and their relation to social structure see Talcott Parsons, *The Social System,* Glencoe, Ill., 1951, esp. Chs. 2 and 3.

70. Parsons has stated that he had been dissatisfied with the concepts Gemeinschaft and Gesellschaft in handling the professions, especially the doctor-patient relationship. However, four out of his five variables place this on the same side: namely, the Gesellschaft side. Only on the collectivity-orientation vs. self-orientation does it fall on the Gemeinschaft side. It is interesting to note, however, that the collectivity-orientation in this relationship rests on an institutional rather than a motivational base. The collectivity-orientation of the physician has become built into a set of institutionalized expectations, and hence it is to a physician's selfinterest to act contrary to his own self-interest in an immediate situation (collectivity-orientation)—but *not in the "long run."* The long-run orientation is self rather than collectivity, and hence in this sense all the variables fall on the Gesellschaft side. See Talcott Parsons, *The Social System, op. cit.,* p. 473.

71. Charles P. Loomis and John C. McKinney, "Systemic Differences Between Latin American Communities of Family Farms and Large Estates," *American Journal of Sociology,* Vol. 61, March, 1956, pp. 404-412.

72. For a description of the methodology of typing see John C. McKinney, "Constructive Typology and Social Research," in John T. Doby, *et al., Introduction to Social Research,* Harrisburg, 1954, pp. 139-198.

73. Here we follow the distinction of Talcott Parsons, *The Social System, op. cit.*

74. Various terms are used for informal leaders in Latin America who may resemble ward heelers or public-opinion leaders in the United

States. *Gamonal, caudillo, guayacan,* and *cacique* are used, depending on the area.

75. Charles P. Loomis, paper read at Founders Day Institute, Boston University, 1953.

76. Antonio M. Arce, Eduardo Arze Loureiro, Reed Powell, Charles Proctor, Manuel Alers-Montalvo, and Roy Clifford typed Atirro and San Juan Sur. Olen Leonard and Wilson Longmore used the same procedures but typed other large-estate communities and communities of family-sized Latin-American farms known intimately to them.

77. The D and C profile on the Gemeinschaft side in Figure 1 and the U. S. profile on the Gesellschaft side in the same figure represent typological descriptions of relations within national governments. The governments of the Dominican Republic and the Republic of Cuba are filled with many relatives of the respective presidents. In the Dominican Republic, for instance, one president's son was an army colonel by the age of three and a brigadier-general at ten. This situation does not exist in the United States. As a matter of fact, norms of bureaucratic action of all kinds in the United States quite generally forbid relatives working in the same governmental branch. For example, once after "unofficial advisor" Milton Eisenhower left a meeting at the White House, the President of the United States turned and said to his associates: "Gentlemen, the man who just left the room would most certainly be a member of my Cabinet except for one, just one disqualifying factor. He happens to be my brother." *Time* LXVII (June 18, 1956), 74. In typing the action of the three national governments of the United States, Dominican Republic, and the Republic of Cuba, we have followed the same procedures used in typing the farm and estate communities. The status-*role* of the president was chosen as the subject, and the role of an immediate subordinate in the cabinet as object; in each case this was the cabinet official having the most power in the military situation involved. The specific category of action is that of preparation resulting from an actual or rumored threat of invasion. The profiles are hypothetical but suggestive.

To Part One

1. The parenthetical English renditions of the words Gemeinschaft and Gesellschaft found in this section indicate the difficulty which would be encountered if one attempted their translation by any one pair of terms. Elsewhere in the text these two substantives and

their adjective forms are not translated when they are used in the ideal typological sense.

2. *Translator's note:* Dignity, the nearest English equivalent of *Würde* as used by Tönnies, does not adequately convey all the connotations. However, as is the case with other terms and concepts employed by Tönnies, the context itself will assist in explaining the meaning. Often dignity here connotes merited authority as well as authority based upon rights and privileges. It is a prestige-giving quality. In the following sections *Würde* is usually translated by the English word "authority." This is justified by the context and by the fact that Tönnies used *Würde* and *Autorität* as synonymous in the first sentence of this paragraph.

3. Verständnis is translated "understanding." The concept as here used should also carry the meaning of mutual understanding and possession of similar sentiments, hopes, aspirations, desires, attitudes, emotions, and beliefs.

To Part Five

1. "Natural will" does not adequately portray Tönnies' concept of *Wesenwille*, which might also have been translated "integral will." Neither does "rational will" convey the entire meaning of *Kürwille*, as used by Tönnies. Only the use of the terms in the context of this part and in Part Two will portray to the reader what the author has in mind. However, Tönnies' usage of the two terms *Kürwille* and *Wesenwille* does not preclude the use of the terms rational will and natural will as the following passages will indicate: "Ich habe diesen Typus den Kür-Willen gennant. Er ist der am meisten ausgebildete rationale Wille und alles menschliche Wollen ist durch vernünftiges Denken charakterisiert und, so angesehen, immer rational. . . . Der Wesenwille—wie ich den anderen Typus benenne—, ist die ältere einfachere und in einem leicht zu verstehenden Sinne, die natürlichere Gestalt des denkenden menschlichen Willens." Tönnies, *Einführung in die Soziologie*, Stuttgart, 1931, pp. 154 and 155. See also Tönnies' discussion of the general subject of will which was made earlier: "Das Wesen der Soziologie," in *Neue Zeit- und Streitfragen*, IV. Band, 1907, p.12.

2. *Translator's note:* The two German words Gemeinschaft and Gesellschaft have frequently been translated, respectively as "community" and "society." However, since the English words do not carry the connotations peculiar to the German concepts as used by Tönnies, and since sociologists are familiar with Tönnies' use of them, it has been deemed advisable to retain the German words

in most places in the text. This procedure is in accordance with Pareto's contention that such concepts might be represented by any two different symbols. As the reader will note, the English substantives "community" and "society" and the English adjectives "communal" and "social" appear frequently in the text. In most cases "community" and "society" are respectively the translation of such German terms as *Gemeinde* and *Sozietat*. When the substantive or adjective forms of *Gemeinschaft* and *Gesellschaft* are translated into English words, they were used in the original in an empirical sense; however, when they were used as ideal types, the German forms are retained. The various meanings of *Gemeinschaft* and *Gesellschaft* as developed in German sociology are explained by Theodor Geiger in *Handwörterbuch der Soziologie,* published by Ferdinand Enke Verlag, Stuttgart, 1931; *Gemeinschaft* on pp. 173-180, and *Gesellschaft* on pp. 201-211.

3.   See Tönnies' article "Stände und Klassen," in *Handwörterbuch der Soziologie,* Ferdinand Enke Verlag, Stuttgart, 1931.

To Tönnies' Fundamental Concepts

1.   See H. L. Stotenberg's *Wegweiser durch* F. Tönnies: *Gemeinschaft und Gesellschaft,* Carl Curtius, Berlin, 1919, a little monograph which has furnished the chief basis for the following statement. Although it oversystematizes, in some instances, the translator has found it useful, and Tönnies himself cited it as one of the most important commentaries. In these "Notes" the Roman numerals refer to the Part number, and the Arabic numbers which follow these, to the numbered subdivisions in the translation. (For example, 1:18 means Part One, heading number 18, which is on pages 62-64.) Numbers and letters preceding the names of concepts are those used in the Table of Concepts, on pages 268-69.

For a longer exposition which relates these terms one to another, see August Baltzer, *Ferdinand Tönnies: Gemeinschaft und Gesellschaft,* Berlin, 1890.

2.   Tönnies himself in the introduction to the first edition (Leipzig, O. R. Reisland, 1887), wrote that, from the point of view of systematic treatment, Part Two should have preceded Part One but that the two parts mutually explained and supplemented each other.

SELECTED BIBLIOGRAPHY

Baltzer, A., *Ferdinand Tönnies: Gemeinschaft und Gesellschaft*, Berlin, 1890.

Becker, Howard, *Systematic Sociology on the Basis of the Beziehungslehre and Gebildelehre of Leopold von Wiese*, New York, John Wiley & Sons, 1932, Chapters II, III, XV, XXV, XXXIII, XLVI, XLIX, and L.

Becker, Howard and Barnes, H. E., *Social Thought from Lore to Science*, New York, D. C. Heath, 1938, Vols. I and II, Chapters XV, XIX, XX, XXII, XXIII, XXVI, XXVII, and XXIX.

Brunner, E. deS., "Gemeinschaft and Gesellschaft in Rural Communities," *Rural Sociology*, Vol. 7, No. 1, March, 1942, pp. 75 ff.

Freyer, Hans, "Ferdinand Tönnies und seine Stellung in der deutschen Soziologie," *Weltwirtschaftliches Archiv*, 1936; and *Soziologie als Wirklichkeitswissenschaft*, Leipzig and Berlin, 1930, pp. 185 ff. and 233 ff.

Heberle, Rudolf, "Ferdinand Tönnies' Contribution to the Sociology of Political Parties," *American Journal of Sociology*, Vol. LXI, No. 3, November, 1955, pp. 213 ff.

------------, "Fundamental Concepts in Rural Community Studies," *Rural Sociology*, Vol. 6, No. 3, September, 1941, pp. 203 ff.

------------, "Rejoinder to Edmund deS. Brunner," *Rural Sociology*, Vol. 7, No. 1, March, 1942, pp. 77 ff.

------------, "The Sociological System of Ferdinand Tönnies: 'Community' and 'Society,'" in H. E. Barnes (ed.), *An Introduction to the History of Sociology*, Chicago, University of Chicago Press, 1948, Chapter 10.

------------, "The Sociology of Ferdinand Tönnies," *American Sociological Review*, Vol. 2, No. 1, February, 1937.

Jahn, G., *Ferdinand Tönnies*, Leipzig, 1935.

Jurkat, E., "Die Soziologie von Ferdinand Tönnies," *Geistige Arbeit*, November, 1936.

Kölner Vierteljahrshefte für Soziologie, 1925, Heft ½ zum 70, *Ge-burts-tage von Ferdinand Tönnies*.

Leemans, V., *Ferdinand Tönnies en de deutsche sociologie*. Brugge, 1932. Translated into French.

Leif, J., *Communauté et societé*, Paris, 1944.

------------, *La Sociologie de Tönnies*, Paris, 1946.

Loomis, C. P., "The Nature of Rural Social Systems: A Typological Analysis," *Rural Sociology*, Vol. 15, No. 2, June, 1950, pp. 156 ff.; also published in *Studies of Applied and Theoretical Social Science*, East Lansing, Michigan State College Press, 1950, Chapter 1.

Loomis, C. P. and Beegle, J. A., *Rural Social Systems*, New York, Prentice-Hall, 1950.

------------, *Rural Sociology—The Strategy of Change*, Englewood Cliffs, N. J., Prentice-Hall, 1957.

------------, "The Spread of German Nazism in Rural Areas," *American Sociological Review*, Vol. XI, No. 6, December, 1946, pp. 724 ff.

Loomis, C. P. and McKinney, J. C., "Systemic Differences Between Latin-American Communities of Family Farms and Large Estates," *American Journal of Sociology*, Vol. LXI, No. 5, March, 1956, pp. 404 ff.

Park, R. E. and Burgess, E. W., *Introduction to the Science of Society*, University of Chicago Press, 1933, pp. 103-105.

Parsons, Talcott, *The Structure of Social Action*, 2nd ed., Glencoe, Illinois, The Free Press, 1949, pp. 686 ff.

Redfield, Robert, "Rural Sociology and the Folk Society," *Rural Sociology*, Vol. 8, No. 1, March, 1943, pp. 68 ff.

Rosenbaum, E., "Ferdinand Tönnies' Werk," *Schmollers Jahrbuch*, 1914.

Sorokin, P. A., *Contemporary Sociological Theories*, New York, Harper & Bros., 1928, pp. 491 ff.

Stoltenberg, H. L., *Wegweiser durch F. Tönnies "Gemeinschaft und Gesellschaft,"* Berlin, 1919.

Timasheff, N. S., *Sociological Theory: Its Nature and Growth*, Garden City, N. Y., Doubleday & Company, 1955, pp. 97 ff.

Tönnies, Ferdinand, *Gemeinschaft und Gesellschaft*, 1887; 8. Auflage, Leipzig, 1935.

------------, *Hobbes, Leben und Lehre*, 3. Auflage, Stuttgart, 1925.

------------, *Thomas Hobbes, The Elements of Law, Natural and Political*. Edited by Tönnies, with a preface and critical notes. To which are subjoined selected extracts from unprinted Mss. of Thomas Hobbes, London, 1889, XVI, 226. Repr. Cambridge, 1928 (1889).

------------, *Belemoth or the Long Parliament.* Edited by Tönnies for the first time from the original Ms., London, 1889, XIII, 204 S.

------------, *Die Enwicklung der sozialen Frage,* Leipzig, 1907; 4. Auflage "bis zum Weltkreig," Berlin, 1926.

------------, "Das Wesen der Soziologie": (Vortrag in der Gehe-Stiftung), in *Neue Zeit und Streitfragen,* IV. Band, 1907.

------------, "Entwicklung der Soziologie in Deutschland im 19. Jahrhundert," in *Entwicklung der deutschen Volkswirtschaftslehre im 19. Jahrhundert. Festgabe für Gustav Schmoller,* 1908.

------------, *Die Sitte,* Frankfurt am Main, 1909.

------------, *Der englische Staat und der deutsche Staat. Eine Studie,* Berlin, 1917.

------------, *Marx, Leben und Lehre,* Berlin, 1921.

------------, *Kritik der öffentlichen Meinung,* Berlin, 1922.

------------, "Zweck und Mittel im sozialen Leben," in *Hauptprobleme der Soziologie, Erinnerungsgabe für Max Weber,* München und Leipzig, 1923.

------------, "Einteilung der Soziologie," *Zeitschrift für die gesamte Staatswissenschaft,* LXXIX, 1925; also published in *Atti del V congresso internazionale di filosofia,* Napoli, 1925.

------------, *Fortschritt und Soziale Entwicklung, Geschichtsphilosophische Ansichten,* Karlsruhe, 1926.

------------, *Soziologische Studien und Kritiken,* Jena, I, 1925; II, 1926; III, 1929.

------------, *Einführung in die Soziologie,* Stuttgart, 1931. Norwegian edition by E. Bosse, Oslo, 1932.

------------, "Eigentum," "Moderne Familie," "Gemeinschaft und Gesellschaft," "Stände und Klassen," articles in *Handwörterbuch der Soziologie,* Stuttgart, 1931.

------------, *Geist der Neuzeit,* Leipzig, 1935. Hans Buske Verlag.

------------, "The Present Problems of Social Structure," *American Journal of Sociology,* X, 1905, pp. 569 ff.

------------, "Political Parties in Germany," *The Independent Review,* III, S. 1904.

------------, "Philosophical Terminology," *Mind, A Quarterly Review of Psychology and Philosophy,* New Series, Vol. VIII, 1889; Vol. IX, 1900.

------------, "Gemeinschaft (Community) and Gesellschaft (Society)," in *Readings in Sociology,* A. M. Lee (ed.), New York, Barnes and Noble, 1951, pp. 81 ff.

------------, "Estates and Classes" (Stände und Klassen), trans, by R. Bendix in Bendix and Lipset, *Class, Status, and Power: A Reader in Social Stratification*, Glencoe, Ill., The Free Press, 1953.

NOTE: The most complete printed list of Tönnies' writings was made by Else Brenke and appeared in *Reine und angewandte Soziologie, eine Festgabe für Ferdinand Tönnies, zu seinem 80. Geburstage,* Leipzig, 1936.

Wirth, Louis, "The Sociology of Ferdinand Tönnies," *American Journal of Sociology*, Vol. XXXII, No. 3, November, 1926, pp. 412 ff.

www.ingramcontent.com/pod-product-compliance
Lightning Source LLC
Chambersburg PA
CBHW022045020426
42335CB00012B/556